The Intercorporeal Unconscious

Stefan Kristensen

The Intercorporeal Unconscious

palgrave
macmillan

Stefan Kristensen
Faculty of arts
University of Strasbourg
Strasbourg, France

The research presented in this book was funded through a grant by the Fritz Thyssen Foundation (Germany), on “The Intercorporeal Unconscious. Resonance and corporeality in the psychoanalytic tradition” (Az. 10.17.2.031PH).

ISBN 978-3-032-22595-5 ISBN 978-3-032-22596-2 (eBook)
https://doi.org/10.1007/978-3-032-22596-2

This Palgrave Macmillan imprint is published by the registered company Springer Nature Switzerland AG.
The registered company address is: Gewerbestrasse 11, 6330 Cham, Switzerland

I don't think, as some have said, that the notion of the unconscious is purely and simply contradictory. But that is not what seems essential to me in psychoanalysis. What seems essential is the relationship with others as psychoanalysis describes it.[1]

[1] M. Merleau-Ponty, Conversation with Georges Charbonnier (unpublished); quoted by E. de Saint Aubert 2013, p. 280.

Expressions of Gratitude and Elements of Context

This is a philosophical book about the unconscious, a notion that makes and unmakes sense in real life, in clinical experience, in the political turmoil, and many other circumstances. It is not a book by a clinician trying to conceptualize his practice; it is an attempt at describing a complex problem, by reading and understanding what practitioners had to say about their clinical experience. It is based on the conviction that the truth about a notion itself is most clearly manifested by what crosses and circulates through membranes. Between disciplines, between subjects, between bodies, between organs and cells, between institutions.

Having always myself been caught between different countries and cultures, I have come to play the role of a go-between more often than not, and thereby to feel unseen and to lose the sense of my own identity. Maybe this is relevant in order to understand the reason why I have come to write about the unconscious, that most intimate and hidden part of ourselves, as an *inter*corporeal dynamic, while at the same time making sure that the individual subject is not dissolved into a common substance. The chapters navigate troubled waters, commenting and reflecting on the idea that what constitutes us as human subjects is something that always, to a certain extent, eludes us, and that it is illusory or even dangerous to hope to control it.

The project arose from the observation that the dialogue between phenomenology and psychoanalysis has a much bigger potential than what has happened in the field in the last decade. The relative absence of such literature (Jagna Brudzinska, Dorothée Legrand, Delia Popa, among others) here should not be interpreted as voluntary neglect—it is just that the project ended up exploring some little-known psychoanalytical literature from a phenomenological point of view, and that most literature on phenomenology and psychoanalysis focuses on Husserl, Freud, and Lacan. And since my point of departure is Merleau-Ponty's take on the psychoanalytic unconscious and his idea that the unconscious is first and foremost the body's unconscious, I have focused on psychoanalysts who in my view actually pursued the philosopher's intuitions, instead of summoning the forefathers yet again.

The origin of this book is a research project on "The intercorporeal unconscious" funded by the Fritz Thyssen Foundation and hosted by Thomas Fuchs and his chair for phenomenological psychiatry at the University of Heidelberg, between 2017 and 2019. Before this project was awarded, I was an Alexander von Humboldt fellow in Heidelberg looking at outsider art and studying the origins of Hans Prinzhorn's thinking, and in 2016 I organized an international conference on "Modes of the Unconscious," bringing together scholars from various horizons to discuss the concept of the unconscious. The planned book did not come together, yet here I am with an inquiry into the body in French psychoanalysis.

Half of the book, in particular Chaps. 2, 3, 5, and 8 were written back then, and earlier versions of Chaps. 3, 5, and 8 were published or presented at conferences; the rest more recently, in the gaps in my teaching schedule at the University of Strasbourg. My gratitude goes, first of all, to the Fritz Thyssen Foundation for the interest in the project, and for the funding, to Thomas Fuchs for hosting me and for the stimulating conversations, to Stefano Micali for his fraternity, to Christian Tewes for his curiosity, to Elodie Boublil for the rich conversations on the topic, to Sandrine Israël-Jost for her encouragement, to Jacob Rogozinski for his mentorship, to David Morris (not only) for advice on the English translation of some technical terms, to my colleagues at the University of Strasbourg who maybe did not expect me to finish this.

I dedicate the book to the love of my life, Anna, who occupies large parts of my unconscious psychic space, and who somehow believed that I would be able to finish it.

Competing Interests The author has no competing interests to declare that are relevant to the content of this manuscript.

Contents

CHAPTER 1

Introduction

The underlying assumption of this book is that what makes us truly human is what we cannot master but what matters most to us. That strange realm is what psychoanalysis refers to as the unconscious, a realm that by definition escapes the contemporary drive for programming and artificial intelligence, and the mastery of nature. This is the reason why psychoanalysis is under attack in many countries, as the French psychoanalyst Yann Diener explains in a recent little book with the title *The Unconscious Instilled in my Computer*. This short story is written in the first person, from the point of view of an artificial intelligence, whose programmer tries to force her to make "Freudian blunders," to "craft her an unconscious" (Diener 2025, 23) by pushing her to make slips of the tongue, figurative meanings, and language disorders. Such a task proves impossible because AI is by definition designed to provide unambiguous answers. Diener shows that programming is contradictory to the unexpectedness that pertains to the unconscious, and that the unconscious is an essential feature of human subjectivity. If this holds true, it is necessary to explore this realm of ambiguities and unexpected turns that is characteristic of our relationship with the world, as human subjects. And language is not the only field permeated by ambiguities; all our ways of relating to the world are ambiguous in nature, especially sensory perception.

This intention behind this book is to explore the consequences of Maurice Merleau-Ponty's claim that "the unconscious is feeling itself"

S. Kristensen, *The Intercorporeal Unconscious*,
https://doi.org/10.1007/978-3-032-22596-2_1

(Merleau-Ponty 1970, 130), as he wrote in the synopsis of his third lecture on the concept of nature at the Collège de France, in the spring of 1960. The French text reads "*l'inconscient est le sentir lui-même*, and "*sentir*" can be translated by "feeling" or "sensing." Merleau-Ponty's lecture had the subheading "The human body," and the aim was to analyze the structure and capacities of the human subject as a sentient body in its vital and affective surroundings: the sensing subject, its being with others and the ontology of what is felt, or sensed, the "sensorial world." The claim that the unconscious is feeling itself implies that it is a site of resonance, a space where the subject is not alone, where it is in touch with the common substance of the world. This is why the topic of this book is the "intercorporeal unconscious," but I should highlight from the start that the space in question goes beyond dyadic relations; not only the unconscious between two bodies but also between my body and the world, past and present. It goes beyond the realm of intersubjective desiring relations, as a common understanding of psychoanalysis would suggest. The relational space between bodies, human and non-human, is always affectively loaded—an energy field of attraction and repulsion, of love and fear. That is why the unconscious in this sense could equally be called an "intercorporeal unconscious." I am attempting here to describe what this interstitial space of resonance consists in, what role language plays in it, and how to characterize the actors in this space, through a reading of the four most important French psychoanalysts who have put the body at the center of their attention and who considered interactions between the biological and the psychological as inseparable in their clinical thinking: Pierre Marty, Françoise Dolto, Didier Anzieu, and René Kaës. The argument is threefold: first, to ground the very idea of resonance, or horizontal unconscious; second, to extend this space beyond the individual, beyond the clinical dyad of therapist and patient, into social space; and third, to extend this relational dyadic space into the space of social interactions.

The overall structure of the book radiates from Merleau-Ponty's ideas, and the dialogue with three major figures in psychoanalytic history will allow us to challenge the philosopher's approach in three directions. Pierre Marty challenged phenomenology through an interpretation of the organic dimension of the body as a manifestation of subjectivity; Françoise Dolto challenged phenomenology via the importance of language and the symbolical for the body; while Didier Anzieu and René Kaës both challenged phenomenology from the perspective of a collective subjectivity, an extension of the realm of the unconscious beyond the individual and the dyad. I affirm that phenomenology is challenged because the dominant approach in phenomenology concerns consciousness and the individual subject, but I believe it is a mistake to regard Merleau-Ponty's philosophy as being opposed to psychodynamic approaches, as Jennifer Bullington does in her book about psychosomatics from a phenomenological perspective (2013). She rightly points out the mind–body dualism at work in Freud's thinking but fails to inquire into the possibility of a non-dualistic approach to psychoanalysis, which is common to the three clinicians at the center of this book. In fact, the four psychoanalysts here in play have in common their neglect (voluntary or not) of the traditional mind–body problem, and this opens up a philosophical reading beyond this separation.

My first goal is to characterize the unconscious in the psychosomatic and phenomenological traditions, based on the claim that it is better conceived by combining the perspectives of both. In recent years, the concept of the unconscious has been widely discussed and renewed, both from the phenomenological point of view and from the point of view of contemporary psychoanalysis. In the work of the German psychoanalysts Michael B. Buchholz and Günther Gödde, the unconscious is conceived of in terms of a vertical and a horizontal dimension. The vertical dimension concerns the memory of the subject, whereas the horizontal dimension concerns the space of resonance between two subjects. As they put it, "In the treatment situation, various resonances have an importance, that cannot be expressed in the vertical model, but are nevertheless of utmost significance for the shaping of therapy, for contact, for the success of the treatment, and for understanding" (Buchholz and Gödde 2013, 863). Not only do they stress the importance of resonant phenomena in clinical interaction, but they give priority to the resonant dimension, as a condition of possibility for the disclosure of the vertical dimension: "Only when the actual therapeutic relation is 'resonant' does it make sense to explore the vertical depth" (Ibid., 867). In their argument to justify the existence of such a resonant unconscious, Gödde and Buchholz rely on psychoanalytical as well as phenomenological sources. In particular, they refer to the idea of intercorporeality introduced by Merleau-Ponty in his *Phenomenology of Perception* (1945). Although they do not quote the philosopher's claim that the unconscious is "sensing itself," their conception relies heavily on the phenomenological interpretation of the unconscious as a latent reservoir of meaning, both in the history of the subject and in interaction with the other.

In the first chapter, I present and defend Merleau-Ponty's interpretation of the Freudian unconscious and discuss both its contemporary and more recent critics. I argue that Merleau-Ponty's interpretation is compatible with a coherent and differentiated psychodynamic conception of the unconscious, that there is just one space of feeling where more or less traumatic events happen, where drives and desires intersect and come into conflict with one another, and not two fundamentally separate realms where one is the conscious-preconscious system, while the other realm is the "other scene" consisting in an unconscious identified with the symbolic system of language. To understand the unconscious as an affective and corporeal realm is both faithful to Freud's thinking (particularly the second topic featuring the Ego, the super-Ego, and the It) and permits a more differentiated conception of the collective dimension of the unconscious.

Before unpacking the thinking of psychoanalysts oriented toward the body, in the second chapter I examine another phenomenologist's interpretation of the unconscious, namely, the German philosopher Bernhard Waldenfels. In his book *Fault Lines of Experience* (2002), he proposed a theory of the unconscious as "withdrawal of the self" intended as an elaboration of Merleau-Ponty's suggestions, in his late writings, that "sensing itself is not thinking of sensing (possession), but dispossession, *ek-stasis*, [...]" (Merleau-Ponty 2003, 283). In pursuing the implications of this suggestion, it becomes apparent that there is a need to develop a clear notion of the desiring body in order to better understand the phenomenology of sensing itself.

A first stage in this exploration of the desiring body involves diving into the French psychosomatic tradition, in particular, the writings of Pierre Marty. In the third chapter, I propose a reading of Marty's two volumes on *Individual Movements of Life and Death* (1976/1980), focusing on his explanations on how the unconscious becomes visible through bodily symptoms, how the organic and the symbolic intertwine, and how the resonance between subjects functions in the clinical setting. He describes his approach as "monist" concerning the psyche-soma distinction, which means that he conceived of the organic body as being always already structured in a symbolic way. In Marty's conception, the unconscious is a realm where the somatic and the psychic are not distinct, and this gives rise to a different conception of the organic. Even though this realm is deemed archaic and primordial, it is not separated from the relational space of the given subject; the aim of this chapter is thus both to show precisely how

Marty describes this "undividedness" (in Merleau-Ponty's terms) of the unconscious, and also the presence of others in this very realm where the organic body is concerned. Here I shall attempt to show that the organic dimension of the body must also be interpreted by taking the symbolic into consideration, and not by opposing the two. For Marty, the symbolic is included but operates through a close intertwining with the organic.

The fourth chapter examines the role of the symbolic in the psychosomatic tradition, starting with Georg Groddeck, considered the grandfather of psychosomatics with his famous *Book of the It* (1923), followed by Franz Alexander, and then takes a second look at Marty. In this rather historical chapter, I show how the idea of a somatic dimension of the symbolic has evolved from one author to another. Groddeck's conception of the body is characterized by the omnipresence and omnipotence of the "It," which is precisely the way he explains the working of the symbolic in the organic realm. In contrast to this conception, Alexander and Marty focus on the unforeseeable nature of psychosomatic affections, and that the outcome of such a disease is contingent upon the degree and singularity of disorder in each particular subject. This historical introduction is also necessary in order to understand the notion of the unconscious in Marty and his attempt to describe it as a realm in which the somatic and the psychic are indiscernible. From this, the question of the role of the symbolic, of interpersonal communication arises, which is why the main protagonist in the subsequent two chapters is Françoise Dolto.

In the fifth chapter, I examine Françoise Dolto's conception of the self in articulation with Paul Schilder's conception of the body schema. Schilder and Dolto are the two major clinicians who have worked extensively with the notions of body schema and body image; Schilder's ideas have enjoyed a wide reception in contemporary phenomenology and psychotherapy, whereas Dolto's conceptions are far less well known but offer a significant challenge to Schilder's relative conceptual blurriness. This confrontation provides the beginning of an answer to the question of the articulation of resonance and memory in the unconscious, inasmuch as it allows us to understand the very origin of the body image in the relation of the infant with its caring adults. But it also poses the question of the role of language in the development of body functions and thus the role of language in the very shaping of the relational unconscious.

In the sixth chapter, I approach the question of resonance in Dolto from another angle by considering her conception of language and speech and their relation to the constitution of the body image. Dolto was a close friend and ally of Jacques Lacan, and she often emphasized the linguistic core of human interactions; she always insisted that adults speak to an infant as if it understood what is said, and indeed in many clinical cases she shows that infants react strongly to the truth spoken to them. In the second chapter, I offer an interpretation of the claim by Dolto that infants understand speech in the same way as persons who themselves have learned to speak; what transpires is that Dolto actually "discovered" the essential affinity, or affordance, of the organic body and speech, since both are based on the movement of desire. This shows that the role of speech in interactions with the infant is evidence of the social nature of the unconscious.

However, this leads to a conundrum at the center of the subsequent two chapters; the clinical experiences of Dolto question the symbolic and its workings in the organic life of the subject, and the unconscious is obviously a relational phenomenon in her clinical experience. Yet, her conception of the body itself is not elaborated; she does not address the question of how the body is structured, what sort of being the body is in order to be able to be disturbed, transformed, and sometimes healed by the speech of others. In addition to the definition of the concept of the unconscious in the crossing of resonance and memory, there is a social question, namely, the issue of extending the space of the unconscious beyond the realm of individual subjectivity into the space of collective movements. Both in Dolto and in Marty and his colleagues, the unconscious is a realm in which the other is always already present, a space of resonance. But the difficulty with regard to their conception, which is essentially based on inner structures and images, is to understand and visualize the space of the self and the space of the other. If the unconscious is a space of resonance and of being-with-others, there must be a way to differentiate the self and others all the while explaining possibilities of fusion and contagion. Only such an articulation of boundaries of the self and bonds with others allows the extension of psychoanalytical understanding. This is the question posed by Didier Anzieu and his colleague René Kaës, both in their clinical practice and in their writings. Their approach is based on the experience of the skin, both in the very literal dermatological sense, and also in the metaphorical sense of an envelope separating the inner and the outer.

The seventh chapter explores the implications of Didier Anzieu's concept of the "skin-ego" as a way of describing the limits of the drives, that is, how the subject experiences its own desires in the lived body. The specific question is how bodily sensations contribute to shaping the intercorporeal space. In Anzieu's clinical descriptions, the skin is a place of encounter with the other, and the problems that might arise in relations may then lead to various affections. The outcome of this exploration of the skin-ego, and the concept of the unconscious that derives from it, is the indicating of a zone (the skin) in which the vertical and the horizontal dimensions of the unconscious cross. Since Anzieu from the start defines the skin in the general sense of an envelope allowing the subject to maintain a sense of self-awareness, he opens up the possibility of thinking about collective subjectivities supported by a shared unconscious between and around sentient bodies.

The eighth chapter is devoted to the extension of the notion of the unconscious, and thus of psychoanalytical metapsychology in general (from the domain of the individual and intercorporeal interaction to the realm of larger groups or communities) and both echoes and discusses the strategy developed in René Kaës' "third type metapsychology." I start that chapter with a short exploration of the contemporary phenomenology of togetherness in order to demonstrate the extent to which phenomenology and psychoanalysis are complementary, and how fecund the combination of the two can be. The ontology of the unconscious encounters the question of a politics of unconscious group dynamics. The hypothesis here is that the intercorporeal space of the unconscious also forms the shape of collective subjectivity, and thus builds the foundation of political communities. This political moment is essential to understanding the very formation of the self from the field of forces of the social bonds it is embedded in.

The last chapter outlines an ecological and animistic conception of the unconscious. Following on from the Merleau-Pontian phrase that the unconscious is feeling or sensing itself, I examine the possibility of the unconscious being a realm of communication between human and non-human entities, or rather more-than-human entities, based on the conviction that more-than-human actors are at least as important for the personal affective development of the human subject as human ones. An animistic conception of the unconscious assumes that a mountain, a river, or any other non-human entity that appears in the field of awareness of another subject has a form of sentience and agency, as David Abram shows in his phenomenological wanderings. From the point of view of human awareness, the modes of expression and the significant presence of such entities is easily ignored, particularly in Western rationalistic culture. But there are nevertheless some hints of an animistic sensibility in the writings of my three main protagonists, Marty, Dolto, and Anzieu. I then propose to outline how we can articulate the psychoanalytic approach with an animistic cosmology and move toward an ecological conception of the unconscious.

The overall objective is to show that the integrity of the human subject is dependent upon the affective surroundings it lives in. The unconscious is the mode of awareness of the body and experiences on that level can either be fully lived or, for various reasons of different intensities, repressed. In any case, it belongs to the relations of the subject; if we use the term "depth psychology," it does not mean that it lies deep inside the subject, hidden from the view of others. To say that the unconscious is "deep" means solely that the subject has put a strong barrier repressing content with which it cannot cope. Yet, the unconscious is in between us, skin deep, where we feel the world touching us.

References

Buchholz, Michael B. & Gödde, Günter. 2013. Balance, Rhythmus, Resonanz: Auf dem Weg zu einer Komplementarität zwischen "vertikaler" und "resonanter" Dimension des Unbewussten. *Psyche, 67*, 9(10), 844–880.

Bullington, Jennifer. 2013. *The Expression of the Psychosomatic Body from a Phenomenological Perspective*. Dordrecht/Heidelberg/New York/London: Springer.

Diener, Yann. 2025. *L'inconscient inculqué à mon ordinateur*. Paris: Premier parallèle.

Merleau-Ponty, Maurice. 1970. Themes from the Lectures at the Collège de France. 1952–1960. Trans. J. O'Neill. Evanston (IL), Northwestern University Press.

CHAPTER 2

"Feeling Itself": The Unconscious Within the Flesh

The theory of the unconscious, of memory, must be renewed through this reference to the perceptual order, i.e. the order of coexistence with the world and others.
Merleau-Ponty 2003, 218

If human subjectivity is constituted by its corporeality, how should we think about the unconscious? That is the question put by Maurice Merleau-Ponty in his third lecture about *The Concept of Nature*, specifically "Nature and Logos: The Human Body," in the spring of 1960. His claim was that "the unconscious is feeling itself" (Merleau-Ponty 1970, 133). This corporeal characterization of the unconscious has been criticized by several prominent psychoanalysts and philosophers, including André Green, J.-B. Pontalis, and Jacques Lacan, for ignoring the specific notion of negativity involved in the Freudian unconscious. By discussing those criticisms, I will show that such a corporeal characterization of the unconscious is not only consistent in its own right but also faithful to Freud's teachings, particularly in his second topic of the early 1920s. Setting in this way the stage for an examination of the unconscious related to the body, it will be an introduction to the conception of the unconscious by psychoanalysts who have taken the body as the psychic subject: Françoise Dolto, Pierre Marty, and Didier Anzieu.

S. Kristensen, *The Intercorporeal Unconscious*,
https://doi.org/10.1007/978-3-032-22596-2_2

When Merleau-Ponty defined the unconscious, he was using the French term "*sentir*" which can be translated into English equally by "feeling" or "sensing," and indeed this latter term does appear in the translation of the course notes for the same French word.[1] "Sensing," or "feeling," refers to the most basic awareness of a movement taking place in the world, a kind of intentionality that does not imply the conscious grasping of its object. The short formulation in the resume sums up the following passage, where the philosopher raises the question of "Eros as the logic of an incarnated life," of "this me that is not me," in reference to Freud's *Metapsychology*:

> It is sensing itself in that it is not the thinking of sensing (possession) but dispossession, *ek-stasis*, participation or identification, incorporation or ejection. In brief, a *Deckung*, a blind, nondifferentiated recognition (of the touching and the touched, of me and my image over there), the zero-degree of difference. The sensed = I don't know and I have always known it (Hyppolite). We do not need to know what it is that we see since we see it. To be at … fascination or deduction of the sensible. To see is to think without thinking. Freud: Communication of unconsciousnesses without the message being deciphered by sensible perception. (Merleau-Ponty 2003, 283)

In this passage, Merleau-Ponty attempts to answer the question "What is this me that is not me, this weight, this surplus below what I can see of myself, and in my eyes is wholly me […]?" This dimension of the self that Freud had named the unconscious is interpreted as a relation with the world by which the ego is dispossessed of itself, by which the self participates in the world instead of being a spectator identifying what it sees. There is a range of expressions hinting at the idea of a recognition without separation of the perceiver and the perceived, a sensing without knowing, without identifying what we see. The simultaneity of not knowing and having always known, of discovering something that one already knew, is the specific paradox of the unconscious. But the most important aspect in this passage is the idea that such a sensing is a "communication of unconsciousnesses," that is, a communication between the unconscious of two or more persons. My interpretation of linking those aspects together is that the unconscious is a realm of the human mind in which the self is participating in the world, where self and world are not clearly distinguished, a deeply relational space where the different subjects in relation with each other are also intermingled with one another.

Such an interpretation of the unconscious clearly leaves the linguistic medium aside: it is what Thamy Ayouch calls a "non-exclusively verbal unconscious" (Ayouch 2017). Merleau-Ponty is famously quoted at the 1960 Bonneval conference on the unconscious, organized by the psychiatrist Henri Ey, saying that he felt uneasy with the category of language taking up all the space, a statement clearly directed at the presentation made by Serge Leclaire and Jean Laplanche during the conference, which was based on Lacan's teachings.[2] For Merleau-Ponty, the unconscious is essentially a realm of the perceptible, only secondarily expressed by symbolic meanings; as Ayouch explains in an article about the place of Freud in the philosopher's teachings at the Collège de France, it is with the ontology of the flesh that the idea of feeling or sensing is related to the Freudian unconscious:

> The unconscious as feeling appears in the movement of reversal of the flesh thematized in *The Visible and the Invisible*. I see the visible from the middle of itself, in the rays of spatiality and temporality emerging from the chiasmus of the flesh, and this visible is thus carried by an invisible. The unconscious is defined here as "articulation of our field," dependent on perception and feeling. It makes the objects possible, places itself between them, "just as the interval between the trees, or as their common level." (Ayouch 2018, §33; my translation)

And, a little further on in the same article, he emphasizes that Merleau-Ponty "reads into Freud a conception of the unconscious, not as a hidden piece of knowledge, but rather as an *unconscious perception*: a knowing before knowing" (Ayouch 2018, §37; my translation). In the following pages, I will present and discuss the criticisms addressed to this reading of Freud's unconscious, and then show that it is better suited to account for a psychoanalysis in which the sentient body is placed at the center. Indeed, Merleau-Ponty did consider that Freud's essential contribution to European culture was a new understanding of the mind–body relation, in the form of a chiasmus between the "body's mental function and the mind's incarnation," as he formulates it in his 1951 essay on "Man and Adversity" (Merleau-Ponty 2007, 194).

Freud's Characterization of the Unconscious

In this section, I shall sketch out the main aspects of Freud's conception of the unconscious, as he describes it in his *Concept of the Unconscious*, presented here in the sense of Freud's classical characterization in his 1912 "Note on the Unconscious in Psycho-Analysis," as a conception "of which we are not aware, but the existence of which we are nevertheless ready to admit on account of other proofs or signs" (Freud 1958, 260). I have employed this definition because it is the most classically Freudian, and my aim in the following pages is to show that Merleau-Ponty's interpretation is entirely faithful to it, without pretending that this is all there is say about Freud's conception of the unconscious. In the same text, Freud goes on to affirm that the term "unconscious" denotes "not only latent ideas in general, but especially ideas with a certain dynamic character, keeping apart from consciousness in spite of their intensity and activity" (ibid, 262). Leaving aside the old philosophical question of whether an unconscious idea is a self-contradicting concept, Freud aims to describe certain mental contents that are active and dynamic while at the same time remaining hidden. His "discovery" is the power of repression: if some contents remain hidden in the unconscious instead of coming to the fore and allowing the subject to find peace, it is due to the ongoing activity of repression. Moreover, he writes that "The distinction between foreconscious and unconscious activity is not a primary one, but comes to be established after repulsion has sprung up" (Freud 1958, 264), implying that there is indeed in Freud's conception a sense of continuity between unconscious and conscious processes, and that the limit between the two is contingent upon the activity of repression.

Another central Freudian text about the unconscious is the famous 1915 essay with the very title "The Unconscious." In this text, he emphasizes that while repression is what prevents unconscious contents from becoming conscious, the unconscious itself should not be reduced to the repressed: as he writes, "the repressed does not cover everything that is unconscious. The unconscious has the wider compass; the repressed is part of the unconscious" (Freud 1958, 166). And, a few pages later, he writes that "The unconscious comprises, on the one hand, acts which are merely latent, temporarily unconscious, but which differ in no other respect from conscious ones and, on the other hand, processes such as repressed ones, which if they were to become conscious would be bound to stand out in the crudest contrast to the rest of the conscious processes" (ibid., 172). What does such a difference amount to? What does this contrast consist in? Does repression actually change the nature of psychic contents? Freud seems to acknowledge a unity in the unconscious—repressed and not repressed—and a difference within the unconscious regarding its becoming conscious. In the section about the communications between the two systems (conscious-preconscious vs. unconscious) in the same essay, Freud points to the complexity of those relations and argues against placing the conscious at the center since he claims that there are two instances of repression, one between the unconscious and the preconscious, and one between the preconscious and the conscious, the first against the unconscious itself, and the second against the "preconscious derivatives" of the unconscious (ibid., 193). Freud thus seems to argue in favor of a certain autonomy of the unconscious system but does not exclude a communication between the systems, in particular, from the unconscious to the conscious, overcoming the obstacles of this double censorship. This is all the more necessary as "the psychoanalytic treatment is based upon an influencing of the unconscious from the direction of the conscious" (ibid., 194).

This dialectic is taken up again in the 1923 essay "The Ego and the Id" where Freud presents his second theory of the ego in spatial terms. In this essay, he writes that "we obtain our concept of the unconscious from the theory of repression", and thus, "the repressed is the prototype of the unconscious for us" (Freud 1961, 15), but he immediately admits that there are two sorts of unconscious [*zweierlei Unbewußtes*], the latent and the repressed, whereby the only difference is that the first can become conscious [*bewußtseinsfähig*], and the latter cannot become conscious "in itself and without more ado" (ibid.). It needs a little help to become conscious; it is not radically barred from the conscious realm, as the French translation of Jean Laplanche suggests, when he falsely translates "in itself and without more ado" [*an sich und ohne weiteres*] as "in itself and to put it bluntly" [*en soi et pour tout dire*]. In his second topic, Freud does not introduce a strict separation between the conscious-preconscious system and the unconscious; he simply emphasizes the importance and the strength of the dynamic of repression, and the ensuing consequences for psychoanalytical practice, as well as the need to develop techniques and methods to help the repressed unconscious become conscious or, as the famous phrase puts it, to let the ego emerge where the Id was previously.[3]

Freud explains, both in 1915 and again in 1923, the difference in genetic terms: all "psychic acts" are unconscious to begin with, and then they undergo an "inspection (censorship)"[4] (Freud 1958, 173), and are divided into two different categories depending on whether or not they have been censored. If not, they become conscious, and if they have, they remain unconscious. In turn, this latter category is divided into acts that can become conscious "without any particular resistance," that Freud calls "preconscious," and acts that stubbornly remain unconscious because of a "strict censorship" (Ibid.). Unconscious emotion or feelings[5] refer to "the fate experienced, as a consequence of repression, by the quantitative factor of the drive impulse" (ibid., 178).[6] It is then safe to affirm that, according to Freud, there is both a continuity and a discontinuity to account for between conscious and unconscious. On the one hand, the psychic contents are essentially the same whether they are conscious or unconscious, but on the other hand, the power of repression can be strong enough to effectively maintain some contents in the unconscious. Furthermore, by suggesting that this power is a function of the "quantitative factor of the drive impulse" (ibid.), Freud is hinting at a correlation between the intensity of the affect and the firmness and hermetic nature of repression.

The boundary between the conscious and the unconscious is guarded by the strictness of repression, but because some contents are not allowed to become conscious, they can undergo particular transformations while they remain in the unconscious system, what Freud calls the "primary process." This "primary process" characterizing the unconscious system enables various strange phenomena: two drive impulses going in opposite directions can coexist side by side "without being influenced by each other" (ibid.). The contents can shift and be transformed, in particular, condensed and displaced to the point of being unrecognizable (this is what Freud calls the "primary process"). Moreover, in this system, "there is no doubt, no negation, no scale of certainty." There are only intensities in the unconscious system, negation is the equivalent of repression on the conscious level. Temporal processes are excluded from the unconscious system, contents are not altered by the passage of time. And finally, the unconscious realm is subjected to the pleasure principle, and thus obeys a logic alien to reality. In sum, the characteristics of the unconscious system according to Freud's 1915 writing are: "absence of contradiction, the primary process (mobility of investments), timelessness, and substitution of psychic reality for external reality" (ibid., 187).

In short, according to Freudian metapsychology, there are substantial differences between the conscious-preconscious system and the unconscious system due to the power of the censorship of repression. The repressive impulse essentially targets the fact that the unconscious is governed by the pleasure principle and knows no contradiction and doesn't respect the limitations of reality. The unconscious system consists at its core of "drive representatives seeking to discharge their investments, in other words, wish impulses" (Freud 1958, 186). And, regarding the structure and permanence of unconscious psychic contents, everything hinges on the power of repression. The peculiar nature of primary processes may even be seen as caused by repression. The unconscious can be understood as a source of unforeseeable and essentially destructive behavior, because it is seen as the result of repression of the subject's forbidden desires. The subject desires something, but this thing is not seen as accessible for social, moral, or affective reasons, and accordingly the energy at the source of this desire is either accumulated or derailed. The subject does not want to, or is not capable of, assuming her desire—and consequently represses it. The unconscious is thus the result of a refusal or an impossibility, and the theoretical issue is to understand this negativity at work at the heart of our affective life.

Merleau-Ponty's Critics

Merleau-Ponty took Freud's idea seriously, and admitted that there could be a splitting within the individual psyche, a kind of double awareness, where the subject has two contradictory ideas or intentions at the same time. He famously discusses Jean Hyppolite's "double formula" of the unconscious, "I don't know and I have always known it"[7] and admits that there is a negating power inside the subject working actively to repress or at least to keep out of reach unpleasant contents. The issue is not whether the very notion of the unconscious is legitimate; it is about the interpretation of this realm, about the kind of negativity at stake. Indeed, in the context of Merleau-Ponty's ontology, there is no absolute negativity; negation is always at the same time an affirmation of something because the concept of absolute nothingness makes no sense, as he shows in the chapter "Interrogation and Dialectic" in *The Visible and the Invisible*. The idea of pure nothingness is precisely a synonym of pure being, "being in its plenitude and its self-sufficiency" (Merleau-Ponty 1968, 65), a being with no negativity. What is at stake in the issue of the unconscious is precisely about making room for a negativity within being, which implies thinking about being as non-absolute, thus allowing for lacks, hollows, and holes. The subject in this perspective cannot be a "seer who forgets that he has a body and that what he sees is always beneath what he sees, who tries to force the passage toward pure being and pure nothingness by installing himself in pure vision"; rather a subject who is thrown back to his own opacity as a seer and to the depth of being" (ibid, 77). In a few working notes, Merleau-Ponty clearly sets the question of the unconscious in relation to this ontology of flesh refusing a dualism of Being and Nothingness; for example, in a note dated February 1959, "*Weltlichkeit* of Geist," he famously writes that the unconscious should be "sought not at the bottom of ourselves, behind the back of our 'consciousness,' but in front of us, as articulations of our field"; it is between things, "as the interval of the trees between the trees, or as their common level" (*ibid.*, 180). And in another often-quoted note dated December 1960, "Body and flesh – Eros – Philosophy of Freudianism," he writes that the notions of psychology (perception, idea, affection, pleasure, desire, love, Eros) should be conceived "not as negatives or negentities," but rather "as *differentiations* of one sole and *massive* adhesion to Being which is the flesh" (ibid., 270). To write that the negative is a result of a movement of differentiation within the flesh means that the unconscious is accessible in a certain way, and the conscious in another way; it implies that there is no hidden content as such. He thereby suggests that unconscious contents are not categorically separated from consciousness, that there is always, at least in principle, a possibility of making unconscious contents appear. It is no wonder that his approach was perceived as favoring continuity over a strict boundary between the two systems.

The dominant conception of the unconscious in French psychoanalysis, however, is based on the idea that its peculiar negativity should be conceived as a radically inaccessible realm. In particular, three influential psychoanalysts have written in such a way, besides Jacques Lacan and his followers Serge Leclaire and Jean Laplanche (Ey 1966, 95–130): JB Pontalis (in particular, 1968 and 1988), André Green (1964), and Cornelius Castoriadis (1971). Their combined influence has weighed heavily on the tradition of French psychoanalysis, establishing the obviousness of the claim of a radical separation between unconsciousness and consciousness. This understanding can be traced back to Lacan's first reading of Merleau-Ponty's reception of psychoanalysis, in his second Seminar on *The Ego in Freud's Theory and in the Technique of Psychoanalysis* of 1954–55. In this seminar, Lacan comments on a lecture given by Merleau-Ponty at the *Société française de psychanalyse* in January 1955, a lecture of which there is no written trace.[8] His main argument is that the philosopher "unyieldingly keeps a distance from the analytic experience" (Lacan 1988, 77), that he "hangs on to the notion of totality, of unitary functioning," that "he always presupposes a given unity accessible to what in the end will be an instantaneous, theoretical, contemplative apprehension" (ibid., 78), the model of an understanding shaped by the notion of good form, a central concept in Gestalt psychology, assuming that the perceptual field always tends to produce the best possible meaning. This "humanist" position is taken by Lacan to be the exact opposite of the psychoanalytical conviction that consciousness is not the center of psychic life, and that the unconscious should be conceived as an autonomous realm, strictly separated from consciousness. For Lacan, the implication is that the symbolic is not entirely under the mastery of consciousness, and therefore not entirely oriented toward communication and mutual understanding, but rather toward misunderstanding and the death drive. Lacan's comments about his friend after the publication of *The Visible and the Invisible*, in the 11th Seminar, in 1964, were much more nuanced, but it could be said that the damage was done in the French context.

Following this trend, JB Pontalis notes—at the end of the text he wrote on the occasion of Merleau-Ponty's death—that for the philosopher, "there is no distinct symbolic universe," and that there is no sense in defining the unconscious "as a repository of signifiers." That is the reason why, he pursues, "The symbolic power that Freud has localized under the term of the unconscious in a separate realm (in the same way that he considered it to be cut off from his patients' consciousness), [Merleau-Ponty] sees at work as *the other side*, and not as *the other scene* (Freud) of our existence" (Pontalis 1968, 97; my translation). According to Pontalis, the unconscious should rather be conceived of as the "other scene" of consciousness, claiming thereby a radical discontinuity between the two. This "other scene" is based on the autonomy of the symbolic realm, seen as the source of the negative able to effectively cut into the continuity and complacency of corporeal imaginary life. In a similar way, in their presentation at the Bonneval conference, Leclaire and Laplanche referred their conception to Lacan, and wrote in the conclusion the following statement:

> Language as well as the unconscious is primarily and indissolubly tied to the surfacing of the death drive, as long as it remains this foundation of the

> world of desire that we cannot, while we are alive, either see or name. (Ey 1966, 127)

This is the short version of the claim that the unconscious is radically unreachable, and thus that Merleau-Ponty's take on psychoanalysis relies on a misunderstanding, that his conception of the unconscious as feeling itself, as a perception remaining in the background, is indeed alien to psychoanalysis, defined as the science of the language of desire. More recently, this is how Thamy Ayouch puts it:

> These four psychoanalysts [i.e. Lacan, Pontalis, Green and Castoriadis] agree that what Merleau-Ponty presents as the Unconscious, linked to the lived body, is no way akin to the structural, fundamentally linguistic psychoanalytical Unconscious. The continuity he maintains between the perceptive and the symbolic level is what prevents Merleau-Ponty from giving a separate, linguistic, non-phenomenal status to the Unconscious. (Ayouch 2017, 185)

Ayouch discusses in great detail those criticisms in his 2012 book about Merleau-Ponty and psychoanalysis, focusing more precisely on Green and Pontalis (Ayouch 2012, 127ff). In this book, he recalls the context of their reflections about the relations between phenomenology and psychoanalysis, in particular the conceptions of Alphonse de Waelhens and Henri Ey himself, authors of two keynote speeches at the Bonneval conference, the former on the unconscious and philosophical thought (Ey 1966, 371–385), and the latter on the unconscious in psychopathology (ibid., 257–289), with both of them relying on the phenomenological conception of consciousness in order to introduce the unconscious; this may help to explain how Green and Pontalis were keen to stress the difference between a phenomenological conception of the unconscious—as an "absence of thematization," as a content remaining unnoticed in the background—and the psychoanalytical conception, based on the heterogeneity of the conscious and the unconscious systems. Despite the fact that Merleau-Ponty had already departed from a philosophy of consciousness, Green and Pontalis targeted his idea of a continuity between the unconscious and the conscious, his ignorance of the difference in nature between primary and secondary processes, and the specifics of the subject's experience of desire according to the psychoanalysts, essentially characterized by the loss of the object and thus the experience of lack.

As Ayouch emphasizes, the issue actually boils down to the question of the negative, the claim by the psychoanalysts that desire is rooted in lack, as opposed to the philosopher's conception of desire as being rooted in the presence of an invisible presence, active in the background. From the perspective of the psychoanalysts, the unconscious is the result of a double negation: first the negation by repression itself, and then also the negation of repression, in order to let the psyche work. For example, from a classical psychoanalytical perspective, there would first be a repression on the part of the little boy in that he would actually like his father to disappear, but then his psychic development hinges on his ability to negate the fact that he repressed the drive, that is, that repression itself is put aside. As André Green writes:

> That is, in place of consciousness the repression of drive excitation (or of its representatives) will form the core of the unconscious. Moreover—and it is at this juncture that the dissociation symmetrical to the one which gives rise to consciousness is carried out—it will have to see to it that the repression itself becomes unconscious. (Green 1999, 47)

In his book about Lacan and philosophy, Alain Juranville describes very clearly Lacan's stance on the question: "The existence of desire, as Lacan conceives it, supposes that the symbolic (and language) cannot be deduced from the real and the imaginary" (Juranville 1984, 104), and this implies that the object of desire is itself absent. In a similar fashion, Guy Félix Duportail also claims in his book about Lacan and Merleau-Ponty (Duportail 2011) that Merleau-Ponty misses the power of symbolic language cutting from outside into the comfort of the subject's imaginary relation to itself. Duportail's original approach is that he proposes to combine Merleau-Ponty's ontology of the flesh with Lacan's use of topology in his later years, starting from Seminar 20 of 1972–73.[9] He writes that "One could speak about a Merleau-Pontian future of psychoanalysis, if one takes seriously the claim according to which the body is that through which there is space" (Duportail 2011, 142). The knotting of the three dimensions of the Imaginary, the Real, and the Symbolic at the level of the sensing body is an idea Merleau-Ponty and the late Lacan share. Lacan takes up the structure of the Borromean knot, a group of three rings linked together in such a way that if any one of them is severed, all three become separated, in order to show that each ring has to cut through the others in order for the common link to be maintained. Merleau-Ponty, for his part, also develops a triple structure as a cloverleaf knot linking together the imaginary, the symbolic, and the real in one continuous thread. The issue in Merleau-Ponty's conception of the unconscious, according to Duportail's interpretation, is "For any intersubjective event in the field of existence, to knot, to create the right envelopments, thanks to the symbolism, *through* the projective imaginary of the body" (Ibid., 140). According to this reading, Merleau-Ponty's conception of the unconscious rests on the preobjective world of corporeality that is supposed to connect together, by itself, the three dimensions of the imaginary, the symbolism, and the events of reality. But this connection is flawed because the philosopher insists on grounding everything in the bodily activity of perception. The cut made by the symbolic into the world of perception is "limited," "The primordial symbolism could not become a genuine logical symbolism [...] because it was not separable from perception" (Ibid., 143–4). Or, in other terms, the negative operation of subject is insufficient; it fails to open up the subject to a genuine alterity. There is a "lapsus" in the philosopher's knotting of the imaginary, the symbolic and the real: the symbolic is not essentially distinguished from the corporeal and from the perceptual activity of the body, and therefore the unconscious flows into consciousness, and there is no proper way to distinguish both systems. Duportail concludes that "the unconscious thematized by Merleau-Ponty is similar, from a clinical point of view, to that of the psychotic" (Ibid., 145). He lends too much importance to desire in perception to the detriment of "the unsolvable conflicts of sexuality" and therefore "the critical reservations by Pontalis and Green of Lacan himself should be taken seriously" (Ibid., 146).

But Duportail is not content with this criticism; he also proposes a correction to Merleau-Ponty's "lapsus," a passage from the clover knot to the Borromean chain, where each dimension (imaginary/corporeal, symbolic, and real) is separate and yet linked together in virtue of the topological structure. Since Merleau-Ponty's continuous linking of the three dimensions fails, leaving the subject in a psychotic unconscious, never really open to the world, the solution would be to add a fourth ring to the three previously existing ones, and this fourth ring is one of naming. The three dimensions are symbolized by three equivalent and interchangeable rings; only the act of naming them is able to link them together at the same time. This is the solution presented by Lacan in his 1974–75 *Seminar* entitled "R.S.I" (i.e. Real. Imaginary. Symbolic). I will not go into too many details concerning the topological approach of the late Lacan; the issue for me at this point is to explore the idea that it may be necessary to add a hole, a ring of negativity, into the phenomenological conception of the unconscious in order to make it work. This extra ring is "from a topological point of view, a *hole* offering the unity of the whole dimensions" (Ibid., 151). It is itself a hole around a void, which in virtue of this nothingness ties the three other rings together; "the structure rests on a void that forms a link and separates at the same time" (Ibid.). It is added at the exact place where the lapsus happened in the knot, and it is actually an act of naming, a linguistic act of saying what is real and what is imaginary. This is precisely what castration is about for Lacan: it is the act of saying what is allowed and what is forbidden, thereby cutting the subject's dreaming and enjoying itself.

"The knot introduces intrinsically the castration as regulation of the enjoyment (*jouissance*) of the body. [...] The articulation of the body and its powers with the law *through* language is one of the major synthetic functions of the knot highlighted by psychoanalysis" (Ibid., 162). Duportail argues that Merleau-Ponty's conception of the unconscious lacks the moment of disruption, and thus of effective castration, since the sphere of the symbolic emerges from the perceptual world. Being too close to the perceptual, the symbolic fails in its role of tying the imaginary-sensorial and the real together.

The Unconscious as "the Affect's Quest for Figurability"

But even if this holds up, is Duportail right in his claim that Merleau-Ponty doesn't account for the specific negativity of castration, of the cutting made by the speech of the normative function? Does the normative presence of the other necessarily require language, does it have to be an act of naming out of the void? Duportail's argument is based on the claim that Merleau-Ponty's conception does not take the realm of the symbolic seriously. By seeking at all costs to ground the symbolic in the perceptual, Merleau-Ponty misses its autonomy and its cutting power. My argument at this point would be to suggest that Duportail confuses two different levels: the level of constitution (or rather, in Merleau-Pontian terms, the institution level), of how the symbolic comes to be, and the level of what it actually is (let us call it the ontological level). Speech and, more generally, the sphere of the symbolic may very well emerge from our relation with shifting perceptual meanings, but this doesn't entail that symbolic meanings should lack the power of disrupting the quiet life of sensations. And it also does not entail that symbolic meanings have the monopoly of this disruptive capacity, that the "articulation of the body and its powers to the law" (Ibid., 162) has to go through language, and moreover that language doesn't have to be of a fundamentally different nature from perception. There are two distinct arguments here: the first amounts to the claim that speech is not the only way to operate a castration, that prohibiting an immediate satisfaction for a subject can be accomplished, for example, through a gesture. The essential aspect is the presence of otherness that refers the subject to herself and lays the ground for a healthy psychic development. The second argument claims that even if language is considered continuous with perceptual meaning, it can still play its cutting role. We must distinguish between genesis of linguistic meaning and its possible psychical function if spoken by an other with authority.

The criticism of Lacan, Pontalis, Green, and, more recently, Duportail should not prevent us from exploring the philosopher's claim that the unconscious is sensing itself. The issue at stake is the kind of negativity involved in the process of repression, in the production of the unconscious as a system of psychic content distinct from consciousness. The hypothesis here is that there should be room for another, carnal, conception of the negative, and that Merleau-Ponty's ontology also allows for conceiving castration, although he doesn't consider sensing and language as two heterogenous realms. Quite simply, the hypothesis is that the unconscious refers to the realm of sensing before any repression, and also of the psychic content that remains in the background when the subject starts to repress some of the content according to its appearing more or less inconvenient. The phenomenon that fits into such a hypothesis is the affect: the psychical motion pushing the subject toward something—the drive in psychoanalytical terms—seeking a meaningful form.

The phrase in the title of this section is from Ayouch's essay on Merleau-Ponty's "non-exclusively-verbal unconscious." Ayouch indeed argues that "affect is the metapsychological category that should make it possible to bridge the gap between a phenomenology of the body and Freudian psychoanalysis" (Ayouch 2017, 186). The unconscious in the sense of Merleau-Ponty is essentially an affective realm because the affect crosses the limit between the two systems, whereas this boundary is indeed effective in "stopping" the unconscious ideas from becoming conscious. The affect is born in the body and its way toward consciousness is a "quest for figurability," or "non-verbal bodily affectivity strives for symbolization" (ibid.). From the perspective of Merleau-Ponty, as Ayouch emphasizes, "body and language prove mutually founded"; language cannot be considered the transcendental foundation ground of the body, as in the structuralist conception, but neither can the body alone be seen as the birthplace of language. On this question of the relation between expression and language, it will be enough for my purpose to admit that perceptual meaning and language are in a continuity and that language is nonetheless able to cut into the realm of affectivity, and disrupt the quiet order of self-contentment. Following his interpretation, I would argue that it is safe to go a step further and claim that the unconscious itself, as Freud was delineating it in his writings introduced above, actually is in its essence the realm of affective life. There is no clinical or conceptual reason to separate the unconscious in a representative and an affective dimension. Ayouch explains that

> The topic, dynamic and economic limit between the Unconscious and consciousness doesn't stop affects as it stops ideas, but rather transforms them. Merleau-Ponty's phenomenology of affectivity aims to cross this limit in order to reveal the unconscious affects sedimented in the conscious affects. (Ibid.)

With his statement that "the unconscious is feeling itself," Merleau-Ponty implies that this splitting inside the subject is due to affective reasons; and affectivity is essentially a bodily phenomenon. There is no essential difference between "primordial unconsciousness" and "repressed unconsciousness";[10] the latter appears "with the formation of a system of perception-consciousness," whereas the former is "the initial yes, the undividedness of feeling" (Merleau-Ponty 1970, 131). Repression is secondary, and doesn't influence the nature of the unconscious itself—only its propensity to cross the limit with consciousness. The only difference between those two modes of the unconscious is that primordial unconsciousness does not face repression, whereas the second does. More precisely, in Merleau-Ponty's account of the perceptible, any act of perception consists of the appearing of a figure on a ground in the perceptual field, an event which, in turn, implies that another figure is obliterated and left in the background. The primordial unconscious is this part of the perceptual field, and, in this sense, to claim that the unconscious is feeling or sensing itself is to say that it is essentially ahead, or in front of, the subject. This was already pointed out by Barbaras in a text about the notion of the unconscious in 1995: he emphasized the ontological importance of Merleau-Ponty's notion of the unconscious, characterizing it as "the dimension of withdrawal inherent to the appearing inasmuch as it is appearing in the flesh" (Barbaras 1995, 541). Barbaras wrote this in reference to a working note from *The Visible and the Invisible*, dated May 2, 1959, where Merleau-Ponty defines the unconscious as the level by relation to which a figure may be seen (Merleau-Ponty 1968, 190).

But in fact, Merleau-Ponty does give an account of perception that entails a radical separation between the sensuous and the symbolic, and not only a continuity. The "other side" of consciousness does actually differ from consciousness: when a ground becomes figure, it does change. Ayouch also argues in another paper that the Freudian critics of Merleau-Ponty come up short when we think about the question of the affect:

> While those critics of undividedness remain perfectly justified with regard to the representations of the unconscious, they seem circumventable in view of the affect, with its status both as conscious and unconscious. "Unconscious," primordial oneiric symbolism, écart in the reversal of the visible into the seeing, these are as many ways to describe the quest for figurability of the affect. (Ayouch 2018, §50)

But even concerning the "unconscious representations," one could use the same argument. Merleau-Ponty does not only claim that the perceptual and the symbolic are undivided; they are at the same time continuous *and* discontinuous, and this simultaneity is precisely the main question throughout his philosophy. André Green himself recognized that Merleau-Ponty's concept of chiasm allows to locate clearly the unconscious, "in the knot defined by the bodily sphere": in his book *The Work of the Negative*, he writes:

> [Merleau-Ponty] seeks movement not in consciousness where he soon senses a closure but rather, beyond this, in unconsciousness. It can never be stressed enough, however, that this is not the last word of Freudian thought, nor the ground on which the psyche is based. It is in the knot—the chiasmus, Merleau-Ponty would have said—defined by the bodily sphere which, more than any other, needs the object, i.e., the drives, that Freud locates the concept of movement. For the movement of the drives relates both to what is necessary for my continued existence and to my relation with my

> counterpart who, even before becoming an object of desire, was essential for my survival. (Green 1999, 46)

Clearly, Green recognized in this text written in the early 1990s that the philosopher's emphasis on corporeality changes the problem. If we admit that both Freud and Merleau-Ponty actually agree on the claim that the experience of the drives is located in the movements of the body, then the question is rather how do the unconscious contents manifest themselves corporeally.

One last aspect of the unconscious as the movement of the affect toward the figure, as emerging from a timeless realm, is to be found in a working note dated April 1960, "Indestructible past and intentional analytic" wherein Merleau-Ponty describes "The Freudian idea of the unconscious and the past as 'indestructible,' as 'intemporal.'" The unconscious is rooted in what he calls in the same passage "an architectonic past," which means a past that plays the role of a ground allowing the present to appear. This may be understood as a comment on Freud's metapsychological text about the unconscious, at the end of the section "Communication between the two systems," where he claims that the "content of the unconscious may be compared with an aboriginal population in the mind." Leaving aside, for the moment, the colonial resonance of this comparison, we can consider what Freud had in mind, namely, that the unconscious is an archaic layer of inherited content, upon which, and also against which, the conscious subject builds her own sense of self. He goes on in the same passage saying that "inherited mental formations, analogous to instinct in animals, constitute the nucleus of the unconscious." And then, in the course of her early life, the human child adds to this inherited layer "what is discarded." In any case then, there is no sharp distinction between the contents of the two systems until puberty (Freud 1958, 195). In the Freudian perspective, then, one should emphasize the continuity between unconsciousness and consciousness, at least until the social rules and normativity sets in and imposes a "sharp distinction." But this distinction seems to be heavily dependent on the weight and power of the repressing processes.

The Unconscious, Vertical and Horizontal

Research on the unconscious in the last 15–20 years in German psychoanalysis (W. Mertens, G. Gödde, M. Buchholz) has focused on resonance phenomena, on the therapeutic relation, and on what some have coined the "horizontal unconscious" or relational unconscious, to be articulated with the more traditionally Freudian "vertical" unconscious of personal traumatic memory.[11] The psychoanalyst Wolfgang Mertens formulates the issue in the first sentence of his article on the "Two-persons-unconscious":

> The issue in psychoanalyses, analytical as well as depth psychological psychotherapies, is not only to make the psychodynamic unconscious conscious, but also empathic resonance, self-esteem support, improvement of affect and impulse control, symbolization and mentalization of what was hitherto unspeakable and not yet felt. (Mertens 2013, 817)

Mertens also calls this dimension of intersubjective resonance the "implicit" unconscious, and his primary concern is to understand the unconscious processes in the here and now of the therapeutic situation, "the interactive entanglement of two people communicating with one another, such as analyst and patient" (Ibid., 830). This entanglement consists in "various non-consciously occurring behavioral expressions of mimetic, gestural, postural and verbal prosodic nature" (Ibid., 835), that is, phenomena that can be perceived by an outside observer, but remain unconscious to the protagonists of the exchange. One of the reasons why it is important to consider such phenomena is the fear that if the therapeutic relation remains on the "level of verbal meanings" (ibid., 839), the analytical process remains stuck in the repetition of the same. The bodily expressions are closer to the emotional life of the subject than the meanings of the words, and it is essential in the process of the cure to leave space and recognition for this dimension. By the way, this "horizontal" dimension of the unconscious was not ignored by Freud himself, as Merleau-Ponty notes in his lecture about passivity in 1955, where he defines the Freudian unconscious in reference to the Dora case from the *Five Psychoanalyses*, as an opening toward "the order of coexistence in the world and in others" (Merleau-Ponty 2010, 165). This "order of coexistence" is a "me-others system" where the other is present in me and me in the other, and relies on the intertwining of subjectivities that causes me to "have endopsychical perception of what the other will think of what I'm saying" (ibid., 163).

Gödde and Buchholz stress the fact that while Freud's theory of the unconscious is oriented vertically according to the subject's memory, his therapeutic practice implied a strong sense of attunement, of the adjustment of both unconsciouses of the analyst and analysand. This clinical approach to the manifestation of the unconscious makes it appear as a relational space, situated horizontally between the protagonists of the clinical encounter, as much as a personal space of traumatic memory. Acknowledging the corporeal dimension of the unconscious implies putting its relational power at the center. Freud had already recognized the relational dimension of the unconscious in his practice, as Gödde and Buchholz have emphasized (2011). Any specific investigation into the unconscious is therefore a perceptual issue—it entails perceiving resonance phenomena in the intersubjective clinical relation through the rhythm of speech, gestures, involuntary body movements, etc. This aspect of the unconscious is neither completely separated nor entirely distinct from the vertical dimension of individual memory. The distinction between a horizontal unconscious where affective resonances between the subjects roam, and a vertical unconscious containing the repressed memories of an individual subject, is not an opposition between two competing notions. The horizontal unconscious is the relational space where the analysand subject may be confronted with her "own" unconscious; in other terms, it is a way of accessing the repressed contents. Since the therapeutic relation, in general, and the success of any therapy, in particular, rely upon transferential dynamics, it should be admitted that the manifestations of those transferential movements are also often themselves repressed during the clinical process. In order to overcome such normal reinforcements of defense mechanisms, the analyst should be able to perceive and identify such manifestations, to respond, and allow the analysand to play with them and weaken her defense mechanisms. To cut it short, the issue of articulating the horizontal and the vertical dimensions is to perceive and interpret non-verbal signs in the affective interaction. The unconscious as feeling, or sensing, itself.

Merleau-Ponty does pose the very question of the vertical and the horizontal in one of the last lines of his Nature course of 1959, although the issue is not formulated in those terms:

> But does this unconscious suffice to take account of libidinal history? Does it not unveil another (in the repressions), that reposits the problem of the second consciousness? The repressed is not only a mute, unnamed sense. It is absent, hidden (emergence of a material of memory, primitive scene, etc.). (Merleau-Ponty 2003, 283)

Just above this passage, Merleau-Ponty writes: "Freud: Communication of the unconsciousnesses without the message being deciphered by sensible perception," referring thereby to the unconscious as working in between the subjects, horizontally. He then goes on to ask if "this" unconscious must be completed with another dimension taking the subject's "libidinal history" into account. The repressed, he suggests, is not only a message that the other was not able to decipher, it is also a hidden content from the history of the subject, and both those aspects must be taken into account. In an early text of 1957 published in the journal *L'évolution psychiatrique* concerning two clinical cases, Dolto describes the role of the psychoanalyst as a "resonator": "The analyst is so to speak the resonator of the subject's spontaneous expressions in the experience that she makes during the sessions" (Dolto 1997, 77). She writes that she prefers this expression to the mirror because it is more dynamic. The very term "resonance" appears several times in the text, for example, a few lines further down on the same page: "The observation by the psychoanalyst of the expressivity, and her registration of the archaic levels that are made present during the session, brings about an understanding by means of her own personal imaginary life concerning her own body image in her past, in resonance with her patient; it is the means of any understanding" (ibid.)

Bodily Negativities in Psychoanalysis

In the next chapters, I will consider different forms of negativity with the body as a point of departure. Pierre Marty's psychosomatics points in the direction of a philosophical monism, but he nevertheless puts a heavy emphasis on the death drive. Françoise Dolto, despite her proximity with Lacan and her strong emphasis on language, actually presented a peculiar conception of psychic development involving a series of "symboligenic" castrations, that is, various moments of prohibition of a satisfaction allowing the little human subject to gain some distance from itself and to develop a sound sense of self-awareness. This series of castrations are not themselves essentially linguistic interventions, but rather attitudes of the caring other enabling the little child to acquire language and to communicate with her surroundings, what Dolto calls "their humanizing effects" (Dolto 2023, 51). Speech is not a cut happening from nowhere, it is uttered by the other and has an effect if it is an affectively close person, someone the subject depends on. Didier Anzieu, for his part, uses the concept of the skin, or envelope, not only to describe the boundary between self and other but also between conscious and unconscious: "contact-barriers serve a triple function of separation: they keep the unconscious from the conscious, memory from perception, and quantity from quality" (Anzieu 2016, 86). The unconscious in his conception is a space where the ego and the other are not clearly distinguished, and the task of psychotherapy is to allow the subject to constitute a stable and harmonious wrapping in order for her to be able to separate what belongs to her and what belongs to others. Anzieu bases his conception of the subject on Freud's second topic, where the Ego is represented with its three components: the id, the ego, and the super-ego. The chapter about Freud as a "precursor of the skin-ego," in his book, is primarily a commentary on *The Ego and the Id*, wherein Freud defines the notion of the ego. In this representation of the ego, it is understated that everything psychical "develops with constant refence to bodily experience," and the "psychical wrapping derives anaclitically from the bodily wrapping" (ibid., 89). The negative in Anzieu's approach is mainly the result of resistance to fantasies perceived as threats to the integrity of the subject, for example, forces ripping the subject apart.

These forms of negativity are all compatible with Merleau-Ponty's ontology of the unconscious. To begin with Dolto, castration is an intersubjective event by which the subject is confronted with a refusal or a delay in the satisfaction of its desire. There is no annihilation of the desire, and the gesture of the parent cutting the subject off from an immediate pleasure operates a break in the continuity of sentience and imagination, but it does not need to be a complete void or nothingness, nor a speech act. On the contrary, the silence of a depressive mother can be much more destructive than her speech. For Marty, the presence of the negative is very obvious although it often remains implicit. Psychosomatic clinic is primarily concerned with the death and destruction of the self, manifested by processes of psychical deactivation or dissociation that Marty calls "essential depression," or "operative thinking." But those processes of "psychical sclerosis or anemia" (Green 1999, 10), as André Green writes referring to Marty's psychosomatics, don't imply nothingness in an ontological sense. The negativity in question is rather a sort of disintegration of the self with organic consequences, which implies that it takes place on the level of sensing and feeling, and the intuition that a psychoanalysis might have an effect on such organic diseases certifies that speech is able to reconnect the subject with her affective and organic life, and the relevant ontology is a monistic ontology of the sensorial rather than a dualism of the symbolic and the imaginary. Anzieu's negativity is also immediately linked to the presence of the other, who is perceived as a threat to the subject's integrity, repression being primarily a gesture of self-protection. The cutting function of castration is primarily conceived as a threat, as causing anxiety,[12] so that the negative is part of the bodily life.

To sum up, interpreting the unconscious as feeling, or sensing, is itself entirely compatible with the Freudian conception, under the condition of showing that a non-dualistic ontology also allows for the cutting function of castration, that castration is not necessarily a speech act in order to play its developmental role, that there are non-verbal castrations. The unconscious as feeling itself is not compatible, however, with a conception opposing ontologically the perceptual and the legislative, the imaginary and the symbolic. But as I hope to have shown, this ontological opposition is not necessary in order for the castrating gesture to produce an effect on the self. In the chapters on Dolto, I will discuss the reasons for this dialectics of castration and the institution of the self; it is enough for the moment to mention that dialectics is grounded in the fact that there is a movement of withdrawal at the heart of any act of perception. Perceiving something is always also at the same time experiencing the withdrawal of the object, its distance from the perceiver. Merleau-Ponty implies this idea when he writes in the *Resume* of his lecture that the unconscious is "dispossession of ourselves in favor of what is felt." Feeling something means at the same time being dispossessed, experiencing the impossibility of owning what is felt. The unconscious as intercorporeal is the realm of grounding affective movements in the interface between animate beings, between all beings bound together by affective bonds. There is a way in which the unconscious is personal, and a way in which it is collective. We have to account dialectically for both aspects. The cut of the symbolic into the smooth world of the senses does not amount to a suppression of sensorial and affective intentionality. Rather it is a dialectic *Aufhebung* of perceptive content.

Transition

We have seen how Merleau-Ponty received the Freudian theory of the unconscious, understood as feeling or sensing itself, and how this interpretation was criticized and rejected by contemporary psychoanalysts, in particular, Lacan, Pontalis, and Green. Against those criticisms, there are nevertheless good arguments in favor of Merleau-Ponty's claim about the unconscious as a corporeal domain, laying the foundations of an approach based on our common corporeality, in particular, the need to account for the passage between conscious and unconscious. This implies a new conception of negativity, not primarily as the cutting power of the symbolic, as the intervention of nothingness, but rather as the movement of withdrawal at the heart of every act of perception. Withdrawal, as the sensuous moment in perception, is the common feature of the primordial unconscious and the unconscious resulting from repression. It also implies admitting that the symbolic does not need to be completely heterogenous to the sphere of sensing and feeling in order to play its cutting role, that the negative can appear in the realm of the flesh and doesn't have to be a hole in being in order to play its role. If this holds up, we need to account both for the continuity and the discontinuity between the body and the symbolic, and this necessitates another ontological framework to account for what is at stake in psychoanalytical practice.

Notes

1. The French "*sentir*" refers quite broadly to a non-verbal intentionality, a relation with the world, where the perceiving subject experiences a kind of union with the sensed realities. I thank David Morris for his explanations on this difficulty in the translation.
2. Cf. Ey 1966, 143. Merleau-Ponty's intervention is taking place after a talk by Serge Leclaire and Jean Laplanche, heavily influenced by Lacan's theories; it is summed up by the editor Henri Ey, and the only passage between quotation marks says "I sometimes feel uneasy seeing the category of language taking up all the space." Ey also reports him saying that, for him, our openness to being is not linguistic, that the birthplace of language is in perception. A few pages further on, one finds a rather long and very influential text by Jacques Lacan summing up his interventions during the conference, subsequently published under the title "Positions of the Unconscious" (Lacan 2006, 829–850), where he explains his idea of the unconscious being structured like a language.
3. This phrase is found at the end of the 31st lecture of the *New Introductory Lectures on Psycho-Analysis* of 1933, with the title "The Dissection of the Psychical Personality." Strachey translates it in the following way: "Where id was, there ego shall be" (Freud 1965, 80).
4. Inspection is used in English to translate "Prüfung," more precisely putting on trial.

5. Strachey renders "*Affekt*" as "emotion," and "*Gefühl*" as "feeling." The first should rather be understood as a momentary emotional state overwhelming the subject, where the object is not necessarily determined; the second as a longer-term affective attachment.
6. The term "drive" is used to translate the German *Trieb*; I have constantly preferred this term over "instinct," widely used in Strachey's standard translation of Freud.
7. In the resume of the lecture, he quotes it slightly differently: "I didn't know, and I have always known" (Merleau-Ponty 1970, 130).
8. Merleau-Ponty's lecture was part of a series organized by the Société française de psychanalyse between November 1954 and June 1955. Other invited speakers were A. Koyré, C. Lévi-Strauss, E. Benveniste, and J. Lacan himself. The program is in the footnote of Lacan's lecture, "Psychoanalysis and cybernetics, or on the nature of language," at the end of the second Seminar (Lacan 1988, 294–308).
9. I discuss Duportail's interpretation of Merleau-Ponty in two essays, the first on desire and the death drive (Kristensen 2019), and the second on the "Metaphysics of anxiety and the thickness of being" (2021).
10. The English translation of Merleau-Ponty introduces the word "unconsciousness," although there is no other term than "inconscient" in French.
11. There was very intensive research on this topic in German psychoanalysis in the early 2000s. It was nurtured by cognitive neuroscientific approaches, on the one hand, and by the psychoanalytical topic of transference and countertransference, on the other. There was even talk of an intersubjective turn in psychoanalysis (cf. Altmeyer 2006).
12. Most occurrences of castration in *The Skin-Ego* are related to anxiety—cf. Anzieu 2016, 200, 206, 216, 244, and 296.

References

Altmeyer, Martin. 2006. Die intersubjektive Wende der Psychoanalyse und das relationale Unbewusste. In *Das Unbewusste in der Praxis. Erfahrungen verschiedener Professionen. Band III*, ed. M. B. Buchholz and G. Gödde, 93–122. Gießen: Psychosozial Verlag.

Anzieu, Didier. 2016. *The Skin-Ego. Trans. N. Segal. [1985].* London, Karnac Books.

Ayouch, Thamy. 2012. *Merleau-Ponty et la psychanalyse. La consonance imparfaite.* Lormont: Le Bord de l'Eau.

Ayouch, Thamy. 2017. Merleau-Ponty's Non-Exclusively Verbal Unconscious: Affect, Figurability, and Gender. In *Unconsciousness Between Phenomenology and Psychoanalysis*, ed. Dorothée Legrand and Dylan Trigg, 181–207. Cham: Springer.

Ayouch, Thamy. 2018. De la passivité à la figurabilité de l'affect: Freud dans les enseignements de Merleau-Ponty au Collège de France. In *Freud au Collège de France*, ed. Antoine Compagnon and Céline Surprenant. Paris: Collège de France. https://doi.org/10.4000/books.cdf.5660.

Barbaras, Renaud. 1995. Le conscient et l'inconscient. In *Notions de philosophie*, ed. D. Kambouchner, 489–551. Paris: Folio Gallimard.

Castoriadis, Cornelius. 1971. *Le dicible et l'indicible*, 67–79. Paris: L'Arc.

Dolto, Françoise. 1997. *Le sentiment de soi*. Aux sources de l'image du corps. Paris, Gallimard.

Dolto, Françoise. 2023. *The Unconscious Body Image* [1984]. Translated by Sharmini Bailly. London: Routledge.

Duportail, Guy Félix. 2011. *Analytique de la chair*. Paris: Cerf.

Ey, Henri, ed. 1966. *L'inconscient. VIe Colloque de Bonneval, 1960*. Paris: Desclée De Brouwer.

Freud, Sigmund. 1958. A Note on the Unconscious in Psycho-Analysis [1912]. In *The Standard Edition of the Complete Psychological Works of Sigmund Freud*, ed. J. Strachey, vol. XII, 255–266.

Freud, Sigmund. 1961. The Ego and the Id [1923]. In *The Standard Edition of the Complete Psychological Works of Sigmund Freud*, ed. J. Strachey, vol. XIX, 3–66.

Freud, Sigmund. 1965. *New introductory lectures on psychoanalysis*. Newly translated and edited by J. Strachey. New York: W. W. Norton & Company.

Gödde, Günther, and Michael B. Buchholz. 2011. *Unbewusstes*. Gießen: Psycho-Sozial Verlag.

Green, André. 1964. Du comportement à la chair. Itinéraire de Merleau-Ponty. *Critique* 211:1017–1046.

Green, André. 1999. *The Work of the Negative* [1993]. Translated by A. Weller. London/New York: Free Association Books.

Juranville, André. 1984. *Lacan et la philosophie*. Paris: PUF.

Kristensen, Stefan. 2019. La chair trouée ou le désir au défi de la pulsion de mort. *Analysis* 3:342–349. https://doi.org/10.1016/j.inan.2019.07.007.

Kristensen, Stefan. 2021. La métaphysique de l'angoisse et les épaisseurs de l'être. Duportail et la phénoménologie du non-sens. In *Phénoménologie et psychanalyse. Hommage à Guy-Félix Duportail*, ed. R. Barbaras and J. Benoist, 95–119. Paris: Hermann.

Lacan, Jacques. 1988. *The Seminar of Jacques Lacan*. Book II. *The Ego in Freuds Theory and in the Technique of Psychoanalysis 1954–1955*. Translated by S. Tomaselli. New York/London: W. W. Norton & Co.

Lacan, Jacques. 2006. *Écrits. The First Complete Edition in English*. Translated by B. Fink. New York/London: W. W. Norton & Co.

Merleau-Ponty, Maurice. 1968. *The Visible and the Invisible* [1964]. Translated by A. Lingis. Evanston: Northwestern University Press.

Merleau-Ponty, Maurice 1970. *Themes from the Lectures at the Collège de France* [1968]. Translated by J. O'Neill. Evanston: Northwestern University Press.
Merleau-Ponty, Maurice. 2003. *Nature. Course Notes from the Collège de France* [1995]. Translated by R. Vallier. Evanston : Northwestern University Press.
Merleau-Ponty, Maurice. 2007. *The Merleau-Ponty Reader*. Edited by T. Toadvine and L. Lawlor. Evanston : Northwestern University Press.
Merleau-Ponty, Maurice 2010. *Institution and Passivity. Course notes at the Collège de France (1954–1955)* [2003]. Trans. L. Lawlor & H. Massey. Evanston: Northwestern University Press.
Mertens, Wolfgang. 2013. Das Zwei-Personen-Unbewusste – unbewusste Wahrnehmungsprozesse in der analytischen Situation. *Psyche* 67: 9/10. 817–843
Pontalis, Jean-Bertrand. 1968. *Après Freud*. Paris: Gallimard.
Pontalis, Jean-Bertrand. 1988. *Perdre de vue*. Paris: Gallimard.

CHAPTER 3

The Unconscious as Self-Withdrawal

What can it mean that life troubles itself, that it sets up a resistance against itself? It can only mean that life itself is not one with itself, that it is haunted by an alien, an alien who appears in the trouble.
Waldenfels 2002, 358

This chapter proposes a phenomenological reading of the unconscious in the Freudian sense: the reading of Bernhard Waldenfels, the German translator of *The Visible and the Invisible.* He describes the unconscious, quoting a Freudian expression, as an "inner foreign territory," (Freud 1964, 57) or with a more dynamic metaphor, as a movement of self-withdrawal, thereby pursuing a similar interpretation of Merleau-Ponty's perspective that Renaud Barbaras also put forward in his 1995 study about the conscious and the unconscious: "The unconscious is not a component of the psyche, but rather the dimension of withdrawal inherent in the appearing, as carnal appearing. It is to be sought, not deep within us behind the back of our consciousness, but in front of us, as articulation of our field" (Barbaras 1995, 541). To the extent that the self is not an entity closed on itself, but a relational being defined by the structure and quality

This chapter was first published in French [1]in a special issue of the journal *Le Cercle herméneutique* on Bernhard Waldenfels, 2019, with the title "L'inconscient comme retrait de soi," 83–96.

S. Kristensen, *The Intercorporeal Unconscious*,
https://doi.org/10.1007/978-3-032-22596-2_3

of its relations with others and its surroundings, the claim that the unconscious is the dimension of withdrawal in the event of appearing is equivalent to claiming that this unconscious also belongs, in a certain sense, to the self; or better: the movement of withdrawal at play in the process of perception can be considered as a feature of the self, inasmuch as the self actually consists in its very experiences. The point here is to discuss this dimension of withdrawal as an essential feature of the unconscious—the question of the boundaries of the self will be the topic of Chaps. 8 and 9 about Didier Anzieu's notion of the skin-ego, and René Kaës' notion of unconscious alliances.

This otherness within the self plays an essential role in the formation of the subject's identity, since it is in response, or in reaction, to it that the subject constitutes itself as such. However, Waldenfels is not content with a "negative" phenomenology in which the withdrawal of the self prohibits the description of experience, which would correspond to a classical phenomenological approach. On the contrary, self-withdrawal paradoxically opens up a field of experience rich in content, whether in the form of Freudian slips, dreams, or various neurotic symptoms linked with any kind of trauma. More precisely, the withdrawal of the self reveals the dimension of desire, which intertwines with that of meaning to form the fabric of experience. Rather than opposing these two, rather than opposing the affective and the cognitive, Waldenfels makes them work as the two cornerstones structuring the field of appearance, of how something appears in our perceptive awareness. This relation between desire and meaning also involves the collective plane, which brings him into close proximity with certain positions taken by Lacan, notably in *Seminar* 11. In the following pages, I will describe how Waldenfels integrates elements of psychoanalytic experience into his phenomenology, and how he accounts for the unity of human subjectivity in this context. In this way, we obtain some decisive insights useful for the dialogue between phenomenology and psychoanalysis.

The Experience of Withdrawal

Waldenfels' central claim is that experience is a complex and contradictory interweaving of meaning and desire. This dialectical conception of the structure of the subject as out of step with itself stems from a phenomenology of desire, the essential elements of which I summarize here, as developed in his 2002 book, *Bruchlinien der Erfahrung* (*Fault Lines of*

Experience).[1] To fully understand this thesis, it is useful to follow his argumentation in order to render his position accurately. He systematically explores "foreign zones" [*Zonen des Fremden*] in experience, and shows that such zones are conditions of possibility for the constitution of a determined and stable self. Waldenfels identifies attraction, repulsion, and withdrawal among the fundamental figures of the in-between that enable the institution of the sentient subject and its relationship with the world. The experience of withdrawal is not just the common experience of something escaping us, be it the functioning of our cell phone, the rules of cricket, or any other practice that seems beyond our reach. The experience of withdrawal has a more fundamental dimension that teaches us, writes Waldenfels, that "our experience is shifted towards itself" (Waldenfels 2002, 189). He points to experiences in which something withdraws from our attention before we have consciously identified and processed it, such as the threatening gaze of someone we meet in the street, a blow received, a piercing pain (ibid., 190). Such cases show that withdrawal is first and foremost essentially a withdrawal within the sphere of the self, which is opposed to the other fundamental movement, which is attraction, where what the subject aims at approaches. This movement of withdrawal is not the movement of an identifiable object withdrawing, like a person taking leave; in that case, we would be in a causal relationship that "would bridge the divide between the own and the alien as soon as it has opened up" (ibid., 192). Rather, it is an internal movement within the self, in which what is withdrawn is the painful sensation itself, the feeling of threat linked to the gaze of others:

> Thus, when viewed by others, it is precisely the pathos, for example the feeling of being caught, that withdraws, and when we are stabbed, it is precisely the painful feeling of being stabbed that only becomes conscious afterwards. The peak of the experience of what happens to us [*Widerfahrnis*] is in the strict sense unconscious, taken away from our knowing. (Ibid.)

That which withdraws is not an external something, it is the very event of what affects us, and it is precisely this that Waldenfels calls *Widerfahrnis*, that which falls upon us and affects us.[2] Significantly, he calls this opposition "the peak of experience" and explains that it is "in the strict sense unconscious."

In this way, the experience of withdrawal is not an erasure or negation of the experience itself; indeed, it is at its heart. In every experience, there is an aspect that affects us and escapes us, and thus challenges us and sets us in motion. The form and quality of withdrawal is recognizable in the way the self is affected, and we can therefore say, from the outset, that the unconscious conceived in this way is knowable by virtue of a phenomenology of withdrawal. The self actually experiences its own movement of withdrawal by virtue of the fact that it is affected in different ways according to which register of experience is affected—feeling, desire, understanding, action, etc. "Withdrawal is specified and differentiated according to the way in which the self is affected, if it is primarily as a feeling, perceiving, desiring, understanding, working, or controlling self" (ibid., 193) Waldenfels also emphasizes that the experience of withdrawal implies a closeness to that which withdraws. Consequently, desire plays a central role in this dynamic, "the countermovement of an attraction is inherent in withdrawal" (ibid., 194). Attraction or desire is a force that pulls us forward, that triggers or reinforces in us a movement toward that which attracts us, and the quality of self-withdrawal can be described according to the nature of that which attracts us and the intensity of the force in question. This reflection on the withdrawal of the self leads in this chapter to a series of developments concerning the fundamental split within the self, where Waldenfels shows that this split is necessary for the self to become a determined self; the self is constituted as such precisely in the tension between relation to the self and withdrawal from the self, insofar as its life as a subject consists in the movement of attraction to and withdrawal from the world.

The chapter on psychoanalysis, "The psychoanalytic blasting of experience," clarifies the argument of the withdrawal of the self and situates what is at stake in relation to the phenomenon of the unconscious. The unconscious, according to Waldenfels, concerns us through "the mixing-up of self-reference and self-withdrawal which is hinted at in the paradoxical discourse of a self-abdication of consciousness" (ibid., 293). He then shows that the unconscious introduced by Freud escapes the paradigm of knowledge, in particular, the "dynamic form" (ibid., 296) of the unconscious arising from the effort of repression. He makes it clear, following Merleau-Ponty, that an unconscious simply indexed to cognitive consciousness would be as trivial as a second consciousness behind consciousness; on the other hand, he refers to Jacques Lacan with the argument that the unconscious can be discovered at the very heart of the relationship to oneself, at that blind spot in consciousness that is irreducible to any constitution:

> From Jacques Lacan, we can learn that Freud's positioning of the ego in a field of forces that exceeds its own powers, and in a power structure that surpasses its own needs, cannot be done justice by eliminating or circumventing the cogito, but only by taking the cogito to its extreme, to the point where it becomes aware of its own otherness and its selfhood, which can be spelled out from the Other, in which heteronomy recognizes submission to the law of the Other, which is to be distinguished from simple submission to the Other. My own attempt aims in the same direction, but starting from phenomenological findings that cannot be derived solely from the twists and turns of the signifier chain and that give greater weight to the physical self, its sensuality, and its imaginative power. (Ibid., 298)

The ego of psychoanalysis is not opposed to phenomenological consciousness; on the contrary, it is faithful to the modern Cogito, except that it discovers at its heart a dimension of irreducible otherness. As non-knowledge, the unconscious is not the absence of knowledge (lost or to come), but the experience of withdrawal, an absence in presence. In support of this idea, Waldenfels evokes the *Meno*, where Plato remarks that non-knowledge is only felt against the background of a *desire* to know (ibid., 300). This is where Waldenfels meets Lacan's conception of the unconscious as a "concept of lack" (ibid.). Thus, the unconscious as a movement of withdrawal implies taking into account the dimension of obscurity and the resistance that reveals it. The fundamental Freudian distinction between the unconscious and the preconscious-conscious system is then reformulated in terms of opacity[3]; unconscious processes correspond to the irreducible remnant of obscurity in consciousness, "as resistance that reveals not only my own powerlessness" (ibid., 301). This resistance can take different forms, but it is always the resistance of a determined context, so that the experience of otherness, or strangeness, always has a determined form, and so the movement of withdrawal of the self is never a simple neutral and formal movement, but always reveals something of the self that withdraws. The unconscious, he stresses, must be thought of as "withdrawal from experience," as a movement of withdrawal at the heart of experience, the only way to avoid the absurdity of the unconscious as a reservoir of hidden knowledge, a second cogito hidden behind the conscious cogito.

The movement of desire therefore does not lead to the erasure of the subject's singularity, but on the contrary reveals, through the way in which the movement of withdrawal takes place, his/her singularity as a desiring subject. Desire itself is the correlate of the pathic dimension of experience, that is, the moment when the subject encounters that which will set him in motion. This corresponds quite well with what Lacan calls the Real, as the outside of all experience, or, as Maldiney wrote, "the real is always what wasn't expected" (Maldiney 1985, 60).

The Fertile Tension Between Desire and Meaning

By introducing the concept of desire, Waldenfels underlines the action, at the heart of experience, of a dimension of force. Attraction, which is the counterpart of withdrawal, "is not a form we grasp, is not a goal we pursue, but a force, [...] that triggers and reinforces in us a movement that spurs us on, that tempts us, that pulls us along with it" (ibid., 194). What we see in this description of force is that it is not purely mechanical, that it is described as a force *for* a subject, a force that spurs, that tempts, etc. In fact, desire as a force is a force for a subject, a force that spurs, that tempts, that drags, that pulls. Indeed, desire as a force is always, in Waldenfels' phenomenological description, intertwined with meaning. Later in the book, when he develops his interpretation of Freudian thought, he details this interweaving, which constitutes one of the main common themes of psychoanalysis and phenomenology, "the connection between sense formations and drive forces, in relation to specific modes of withdrawal" (ibid., 302). Among the various attempts to articulate these two moments, Waldenfels rejects strategies that, like Paul Ricoeur's, accentuate the heterogeneity of the energetic and hermeneutic realms and postulate a blending of the two.[4] It is not enough to use hybrid expressions such as "drive representative" (*Triebrepräsentanz*) to account for the articulation of the two moments; these expressions "are distantly reminiscent of Descartes' pineal gland" (ibid., 303), he mockingly writes. He also rejects Michel Henry's radical criticism that any theory of the drive force is doomed to failure because the force is impossible to represent as such; Henry overlooks the fact that the drive force always presents itself after the fact in the order of phenomena, and that it is therefore illusory to try to seize it *in* flagrante delicto (304, note 16). We need to pick up the thread of phenomena, as Freud himself does, and propose a "phenomenology of disorders, anomalies and pathologies" (ibid., 304). These phenomena appear as contradictory movements, opposing tendencies, intentions in conflict with one another, so that the interweaving of signifying and desiring actually consists in the particular intensity of importance that a being or an event can have in the life of a subject. It is a question of "structures of relevance" (*Relevanzstrukturen*), that is, that a signifying event is signifying *for* someone, which immediately rules out a purely cognitive theory of signification.

Thus, a phenomenology of disorders, anomalies, and pathologies clearly shows that every meaning is signifying in subjective life by virtue of its more or less attractive or repulsive character. In other words, desire and meaning are in fact inseparable, although they can (and should) be conceptually distinguished. For Waldenfels, this also underpins the importance of the distinction between desire and need, as is the case with Lacan and Levinas (ibid., 310), and I would also very strongly add Françoise Dolto, as we will see in Chap. 6. If we were to equate desire with need, we would be replacing this aspiration, this movement at the heart of the subject's relationship with the world, with a relationship of possession, a relationship that has the effect of immobilizing the subject. The object of need is always something identifiable and manageable, whereas the object of desire is precisely that which withdraws at the very cusp of experience itself, and whose satisfaction, therefore, can only be frustrating, and thus relaunch the subject's movement. The dynamic of desire is that it always manifests itself in a given situation, as the singular withdrawal movement of a given subject in the face of a given event that is significant for him or her. In short, desire is revealed in phenomena such as missed acts, dreams, and somatic symptoms, so that it is the mixture of meaning and desire that is the subject of Freudian descriptions. All these phenomena "represent an amalgam of meaning and force" (ibid., 310). There is never pure desire, meaning and force are always intertwined. "The meaning to be discovered by psychoanalysis appears as the effect of a play of forces, and at the same time as a compromise, since no synthesis regulates the play of heterogeneous forces" (ibid.)

However, the limitation of the Freudian conception lies in the fact that the founder of psychoanalysis presupposes the possibility of total satisfaction of desire, a possible complete unveiling of the meaning of a dream or a missed act. The alternative proposed by Waldenfels consists in positing lack or failure as the experience of a carnally experienced impossibility [*eine leibhaftig erfahrene Unmöglichkeit*], and not as the experience of missing a target that would in principle be attainable (ibid., 312). Thus, every missed act, every symptom, etc. possesses a double bottom, an absurdity in meaning, and this impossibility lived at the very heart of experience is what the unconscious consists of. But this duplicity in the experience of disorders also points to a fundamental structure of all experience, insofar as it is constituted by a tension between meaning and force. Here, Waldenfels sums up the situation with a complex development based on the distinction between signifying something, or meaning, and aiming at something, or pursuing a goal:

> What is signified as such, and what is sought for specific purposes, would correspond to a germ of reason that would only have to unfold. But such an order would be a usurped order. The *as* of the intention of meaning and the *in* of the pursuit of goals function as transformers that make something that does not yet have meaning into meaning, and something that was not yet a goal into a goal. (Ibid., 314)

And a little further on: "The *as* of meaning, and the *in* of the effort mark the pivots around which the appearing revolves" (ibid.). If meaning is manifest, purpose and aspiration are obscured but nonetheless present, and if aspiration is dominant, meaning is obscured. But the interaction of the two is close and essential: it is aspiration that gives meaning to something, and it is meaning that gives force to aspiration, so that the two dimensions of meaning and force are in reality inseparable. If we isolate meaning from aspiration, we must presuppose an order that is the guarantor of truth in itself; similarly, if we isolate aspiration, we must presuppose an order that is the guarantor of goodness of purpose. But the presupposition of such an order is obviously usurped. To avoid such a disguised petition of principle, we can simply show that meaning and desire function as each other's condition, mutual "transformers." In experience, meaning and purpose are, as it were, the condition of each other. Even if Waldenfels doesn't say so explicitly, it is clear enough that the solution to the problem of the articulation between meaning and desire is given by the phenomenological description that shows that it is only because a phenomenon appears as desirable (or repulsive) that it has meaning, and that conversely, it's only because it appears as meaningful that it can be desirable (or repulsive). Thus, the "as what" and the "in what" that are the levers of experience do not appear themselves, but are situated both below and beyond experience itself. Indeed, they are what the self responds to, setting it in motion by producing meaning and movement.

Recognition of the constitutive interweaving of desire and meaning then raises the question of how these complex units are produced. For this, two aspects are essential: that of the body of flesh, which Waldenfels calls the "bodily self" [*das leibliche Selbst*], and that of symbolic and social norms, which he calls "the order" [*die Ordnung*]. These two aspects will help clarify the relationship with Lacan's thinking.

The Libidinal Body

All developments of desire and meaning belong to the bodily self; it is the bodily self that is the actor and subject. This fact was the subject of his last lecture as a professor at Bochum University in 1999, published the following year. Prior to this, in *Antwortregister*, the longest chapter of the third part, "Dimensions of Response," is devoted to "Carnal Responsivity" [*Leibliches Responsorium*], and in this chapter, it is the section on the libidinal body that is the most substantial. These bibliographical elements are significant only to indicate the provenance of the elements that show how Waldenfels' approach both parallels and complements that of Lacan. As I mentioned earlier, he himself explains that his approach is along the same lines as Lacan's, but that the difference lies in the place he gives to "the bodily self, its sensibility and imaginative power" (ibid., 298).

In the section devoted to the libidinal body in his 1994 book, Waldenfels places the Freudian approach to libido on the same level as the Platonic theory of Eros, taking up Freud's fundamental gestures: the detachment of sexuality from reproduction, the fact that the whole body is concerned by libido, the identification of areas more particularly concerned with pleasure, as well as the evolution of the individual's sexuality in different stages. In short, he takes up the Merleau-Pontian reading of sexuality in the corresponding chapter of the *Phenomenology of Perception*, stressing that sexual impulses are omnipresent like an atmosphere, and that sexuality is significant to the subject's entire life. At the heart of his questioning is the responsiveness of desiring and, consequently, the doubling of desiring into a desire to desire (Waldenfels 1994, 517), or in other words, a *sense of* desiring that enables desire itself to be at the origin of a movement on the part of the subject. The exclusively economic and quantitative point of view of many Freudian writings is not sufficient, insofar as it is always a question of easing a tension. For the desiring subject, it's as much about desire itself as about its object; desire itself must be desired if desire is not to be equated with a need to be satisfied, a thirst to be quenched, and this amounts to recognizing that the subject's desire is doubled and nourished by the desire of the other.[5] Waldenfels points out that in the autoerotic framework of object libido and narcissism, there can be no question of such a doubling: "A desire that seeks its 'object' has, in the strict sense, no addressee" (ibid., 521); in such cases, the subject is alone with the object he or she is aiming for. For a redoubling of desire to take place, another person must be present in the process, and this is precisely what the descriptions of the stages of development demonstrate: "The redoubling of desire, which is reinforced through the difference of desire for the other sex, presupposes that the carnal relationship to oneself includes from the outset a moment of otherness that goes beyond the simple satisfaction of drives" (ibid., 525). And a little further on: "The demand for the other signifies an excess that shatters all economies and topics, but also presupposes them in the same way" (ibid., 527). This demand, or call, of the other is not merely ethical, as Levinas would have it; it is constitutive of what makes the corporeal self in motion and in relation. It is this demand that makes the intimate experience of the self something that withdraws and attracts the very movement of the sensitive body. The other always already inhabits my desire, and consequently my desire is a desire in response to this solicitation that I experience. The doubling of desire in desire of desire marks the fact that desire cannot be equated with an impulse that can be satisfied by a specific object or gesture, but that desire always comprises an excess; this excess is constituted by the presence and call of the other at the very heart of my desire, and it can be described in very concrete and circumstantial terms, for example, according to the (erogenous) zone of the body under consideration, or according to the mode of relationship with others that it opens up.

Thus, the dispossession of the self that occurs in the desiring experience is not a fusion with the world; this movement of withdrawal is precisely the moment that gives rise to the subject's responsiveness, and is therefore necessary to the constitution of its integrity as a subject in movement in the world. This presupposes a genuine otherness, which cannot be absorbed by the predictable counterpart of love for the desired partner; on the contrary, it is what makes desire desirable, and therefore distinguishes it from purely economically defined need and drive. Thus, the other's demand is present in my very body, and does not need to be embodied by a person here and now to be effective. On the other hand, it does presuppose that desire is carried by a language that precedes it, that "employs rituals and non-verbal techniques, and that does not exclude strategic and violent moments" (ibid., 528), as he writes when highlighting Lacan's essential contribution. Indeed, Waldenfels stresses in a footnote at this point that Lacan's decisive contribution to his linguistic conception of the unconscious consists in the moment of the cut, the moment when "the circle of phantasmatic needs is broken" (ibid., note 110). And this moment of rupture presupposes that desire is traversed by relations of force, by wills to dominate and social norms that sometimes give it shape, sometimes interrupt it. It is particularly significant that he introduces his interest in Lacan in the chapter devoted to the sentient body; it is the body that bears the signs of its membership of a social ensemble where power relations reign, and the libidinal configuration of the body is given by such relations between human subjects, the "great interhuman passions of the will-to-regenerate, the will-to-possess and the will-to-impose" (ibid.). As an introduction to the question of desire, Waldenfels refers to Lacan's report to the Rome Congress in 1953, "The Function and Field of Speech and Language in Psychoanalysis," where Lacan introduces and justifies the thesis that "the unconscious of the subject is the discourse of the other" (Lacan).[6] In the chapter on the redoubling of desire, where Waldenfels introduces the distinction between desire and need, he also refers to Lacan in a lengthy footnote, quoting the formula "every word calls for a response" (ibid., p. 246; 1994, p. 339). Thus, the presence of others' otherness also links the individual and intercorporeal perspective with the social and political plane. In the final section, I propose to follow Waldenfels' argument about order and norms in order to situate his thinking more precisely within contemporary attempts to bring psychoanalysis and phenomenology closer together.

Order and Responsiveness

In his course on the corporeal self, Waldenfels repeatedly stresses the simultaneity and analogy between the relationship to the self and the relationship to others; these two relationships "are to be read synchronously," and this simultaneity "presupposes a certain form of strangeness in myself" (Waldenfels 2000, 285). He does not enter into the question of which of the two forms of otherness is primary, which grounds which; rather, as I pointed out above, it is a relationship of reciprocal conditionality. For the otherness of the other to produce an event that affects me and sets me in motion, it must entail the real presence of the other as the one who solicits my desire and targets me with his or her desire. And this real presence of the other, his or her word and will to dominate or serve, does not take place in a vacuum; the question arises as to how this connection between the event of the response and its content, between word and response, is structured. This is Waldenfels' problem of order. In his 2002 book, in the section on "Foreign Voices of the Superego," he integrates this question into his reading of psychoanalysis. In this section, he expresses reservations about Freud's favoring of desire over morality, interpreted primarily as a repressive force. But with the appearance of the superego in the Second Topic, denial and repression "attain a new social quality" (Waldenfels 2002, 346). Yet, Freud's favoring of desire and portrayal of the law as a purely repressive instance leads to a bias, whereby even the voice of the law that resounds through the superego is an instance of the ego; even identification with the paternal instance is an identification with oneself, where the other plays a role only "insofar as he or she is loved or hated, insofar as he or she proves helpful or stands in the way of all incestuous desires" (ibid., 354). In his critical remarks on the solipsism of the Freudian subject, Waldenfels evokes Lacan to point out that in the psychoanalytic field there are actors who give a clearer place to the other in the real sense, for whom desire is not enough "to account for the demands that are expressed through the voice of the superego" (ibid., 353). The foreign voices of the superego are not foreign enough; they reflect the dynamics of the subject's desire, the compromises between the contradictory desires that run through it. With Freud, at least, there is no room for otherness in the strict sense of the term, that which arises when we least expect it, that which Lacan calls the Real, a notion he evokes in a footnote (ibid., 313) by describing Lacan's gesture as a "stroke of genius" because it situates the Real beyond the Symbolic and the Imaginary, and thus makes it the origin and fundamental cause (*Ur-sache*) of desire.

Thus, order as it imposes itself on the desiring subject, as it channels and constrains desire, is an instance of repetition, an order that reproduces itself identically. For an order to present itself in a new and surprising way, there must be an interaction between meaning and desire, so that one serves as a transformer for the other; indeed, order and law are made up of this interweaving and tension between meaning and desire, which means that the singular desires of subjects follow trajectories prescribed by the rules in force, or that a transgression is identifiable as such. In this sense, Waldenfels evokes Lacan's distinction between the "little law," which consists in the prescriptions of the superego, and the "big law," which concerns relations between desiring subjects. He refers here to Juranville's comments on the Seminar on the *Ethics of Psychoanalysis*, in which he explains that we must distinguish "on the one hand, the law of castration as inscribed in speech, and the ethical attitude that requires us to confront it; on the other, the forbidden, which is the form in which the law presents itself in the Oedipus complex, and the neurotic attitude that consists in fleeing desire and imaginary self-preservation from the castration it implies" (Juranville 1984, 202). And Waldenfels sums up the thesis when he writes: "the voice of the law does not coincide with the prescribed regulations" (Waldenfels 2002, 351). What interests Waldenfels here is the opening up of a difference between the other in me, that point of experience that escapes, and the Other outside me, who resides in a "real elsewhere," as he also writes (ibid., 354). The criticism levelled at Freud is that he excessively privileges the subject's desire through the figure of Narcissus, that with the Freudian device, the voice of the third party who bears the law and that of the Other (who ultimately embodies the object of the subject's desire) are assimilated and reduced to the subject's fantasy world. When he poses the rhetorical question of whether "the thread of desire-pleasure (*Lust*) is sufficient to account for the foreign demands that are heard in the voice of the superego" (ibid., 351), he suggests that the answer to this question is negative, and that we must leave room for a call from outside that solicits an authentic response. This is where the sporadic references to Lacan's thought make phenomenological sense. For Waldenfels, Lacan is the one who pushed psychoanalytic thought to pay attention to what comes from outside, upsetting the subject's habits. In the internal relationship with otherness, something of the foreign body of the Other is preserved—As Waldenfels also writes in the chapter on order, "It is important to note the fact that the order of the third party is embodied in the self and yet retains something of a foreign body" (ibid., 257). The peak of experience that necessarily escapes is the irrefutable phenomenological testimony to this.

Transition

Waldenfels includes the word of the Other in the field of events that can act as a counterpoint in the subject's life and solicit his or her responsiveness. In this sense, the unconscious always belongs to the experience of the corporeal self, but it constitutes the tip of it that always escapes, and this escaping tip is always in relation to the desire of the Other, be it the collective Other, that of the social and political order, or the intimate Other, that of the intercorporeal relationship. Waldenfels shows that the otherness that constitutes desire at the cutting edge of experience is an embodied otherness, existing in the field of the sensorial. Following

Merleau-Ponty, Waldenfels takes up Freudian descriptions of the manifestations of the unconscious and extracts them from Freud's positivism and naive realism. In doing so, he encounters the theses of Lacan, who considers the point of experience to be inaccessible in principle, and always below or beyond what appears to the subject. But unlike Lacan, he does not situate the question of the unconscious on the level of the signifier or structures of meaning alone. He also challenges Lacan's emphasis on the death drive, arguing that death only makes sense within the life of the subject: "The struggle between drives needs a conflict, and that conflict is life itself" (ibid. 58), he writes, quoting an expression by Freud in *The Ego and the Id*. (Freud 1961, 41) Real death, in the sense of the cessation of existence, cannot be an object of desire, because it amounts to the absence of purpose; in this sense, death, in the sense of the death drive, would rather be the experience of absence *in* life.

The thesis that the unconscious corresponds to a movement of withdrawal from the self is powerful because it enables us to articulate the original unconscious and the unconscious of repression. Waldenfels' approach, however, allows us to situate repression within the horizon of an experience from which an aspect is withdrawn, and thus to discern a link between the two forms of unconsciousness. The unconscious is the apex of the phenomenon of withdrawal from the self, for the self. This movement takes place in different ways, depending on how the self is affected by what attracts or repels it, but always involves encountering an obstacle, making an opposition. Finally, as such, this flaw at the heart of the self is the very condition of its integrity, insofar as it is the response to this flaw, namely, repression, that constitutes the unity of a subject in the face of its own desire and that of others.[7]

Notes

1. I refer here to this work as well as to *Anwortregister* (1994). Since that book, Waldenfels has been extremely productive, and his works (all published by Suhrkamp) cover most of the major themes of contemporary thought.
2. The term *Widerfahrnis* is also rare in German; the verb *widerfahren* is a little more common. It designates the movement of that which comes against the subject, that which arrives against (*wider-fahren*). The translation choices for the noun are fairly limited: to translate it by "obstacle" would be too

static. It seemed to me that we could construct a somewhat forced equivalent to the German term with the word "encounter."

3. Or in terms of a "preontological gap," as Lacan puts it in the same seminar: Lacan 1978, 29.
4. Cf. Ricoeur 1970.
5. Waldenfels devotes a chapter to the doubling of desire in *Antwortregister* (pp. 339–42).
6. Jacques Lacan, *Ecrits* I [1966], Paris, Seuil, 1999, p. 263.
7. I've talked about this in my book *La Machine sensible* (2017), particularly in the chapter on the Ego as resistance (85–118).

References

Barbaras, Renaud. 1995. Le conscient et l'inconscient. In *Notions de philosophie*, ed. D. Kambouchner, 489–551. Paris: Folio Gallimard.

Freud, Sigmund. 1961. The eEgo and the Id [1923]. In *The Standard Edition of the Complete Psychological Works of Sigmund Freud*, ed. J. Strachey, vol. XIX, 3–66.

Freud, Sigmund. 1964. *New Introductory Lectures on Psychoanalysis*. Translated by J. Strachey. New York: W. W. Norton and Company.

Juranville, Alain. 1984. *Lacan et la philosophie*. Paris: PUF.

Kristensen, Stefan. 2017. *La machine sensible*. Paris: Hermann.

Lacan, Jacques. 1978. *The Four Fundamental Concepts of Psychoanalysis. The Seminar of Jacques Lacan. Book XI*. Translated by A. Sheridan. New York/London: W. W. Norton and Company.

Maldiney, Henri. 1985. *Art et existence*. Paris: Klincksieck.

Ricoeur, Paul. 1970. *Freud and Philosophy. An Essay on Interpretation*. Translated by D. Savage. New Haven: Yale University Press.

Waldenfels, Bernhard. 1994. *Antwortregister*. Frankfurt M.: Suhrkamp.

Waldenfels, Bernhard. 2000. *Das leibliche Selbst. Vorlesungen zur Pänomenologie des Leibes*. Frankfurt M.: Suhrkamp.

Waldenfels, Bernhard. 2002. *Bruchlinien der Erfahrung. Phänomenologie, Psychoanalyse, Phänomenotechnik*. Frankfurt M.: Suhrkamp.

CHAPTER 4

The Psychosomatic Unconscious

It is beyond doubt that work that does not take into account the importance of the problems raised from the outset by the investigator's position, the emotional interrelationships between the patient and the investigator, the unconscious movements in both, and the quality and role of energy investments, can only be short-lived and will sooner or later betray the specificity of the clinical data.
Marty, de M'Uzan and David, 255

In the first chapter, I discussed the psychoanalytic critiques of Merleau-Ponty's thesis that the unconscious should be considered as "feeling itself." Counter to those critics, my claim is that Merleau-Ponty's ontology of the flesh is a better philosophical framework for the psychoanalytic conception of unconscious than a dualistic conception where the sensuous and the symbolic are considered two radically heterogeneous realms. In order to articulate the dialectics of continuity and rupture at work between the unconscious and the preconscious-conscious system, my proposal here is to consider the role of the body from a clinical point of view. Rather than asking which rules the unconscious obeys in contrast to the conscious, we should try to define what the unconscious actually is according to what happens in its realm, and this is, in my interpretation, the issue at stake in the psychosomatic literature.

S. Kristensen, *The Intercorporeal Unconscious*,
https://doi.org/10.1007/978-3-032-22596-2_4

I will attempt to show that the phenomenological unconscious, famously described by Merleau-Ponty as a "primordial unconsciousness," or the "undividedness of feeling," (Merleau-Ponty 1970, 131) can serve as a conceptual foundation of psychoanalytical psychosomatics, in particular, as presented in the writings of Pierre Marty, the founder of the French school of psychosomatics. As Merleau-Ponty did not offer much more than these rather laconic remarks about sensing or feeling, my hypothesis here is that Marty's descriptions of the unconscious might help to fill it with some content; conversely, as Marty's preoccupation was essentially clinical, Merleau-Ponty's ontology might help understand what is at stake at the unconscious level, and in what sense Marty's position can be defined as monist. More precisely, the issue at stake is to describe the structure of the primordial unconscious and show that this level also implies the presence of *others*, that it is in fact a realm of intercorporeal resonance. In particular, I take the works of Pierre Marty into consideration because he proposes an account of the unconscious including the somatic dimension and an articulation of the fundamental and the repressive levels. In the 1950s and 1960s, along with his colleagues Michel de M'Uzan, Christian David, and Michel Fain, Pierre Marty forged many concepts still in use in contemporary psychotherapy, beyond the concept of operative life, such as mentalization, essential depression, and progressive disorganization.[1] Here I focus, in particular, on the notion of "operative life" in order to delineate a space where the biological and the psychological are not distinguished, where they overlap and interfere. Such a conception is very much in line with Merleau-Ponty's philosophy of the flesh and his claim that the unconscious is sensing itself, both object and subject, alternatively touching and touched, a realm of experience where the subject is not fully self-conscious. Yet, both in Merleau-Ponty's thinking and in more recent phenomenology, for example, in Thomas Fuchs' notion of "dual aspectivity" referring to the double sidedness of the human body, successively sensing and able to be sensed, there is little about what this unity of two aspects actually consists in, and this is where Marty's approach might be useful. Marty claims that the therapist must be particularly careful with cases of patients stuck in operative life, that the resonance with those persons is crucial to maintain their state and minimize the risks of somatic disease. There are apparently good reasons to think that this zone of the unconscious, the "primordial unconscious" in the terms of Merleau-Ponty, the "core of the unconscious" in the words of Freud,[2] is also a space of human relations. The following pages are intended to show how the sentient body is this relational space, and this supposes to overcome the traditional dualism between *psyche* and *soma*.

The Unconscious Prehistory of the Self

In his book *Ecology of the Brain*, Thomas Fuchs reflects on the double nature of the human body, both object and subject, and this leads him to raise the question of the unconscious. Faithful to Husserl's and Merleau-Ponty's legacy, he criticizes the dualism of Descartes as a "twofold disembodiment": "On the one hand the subjective body is objectivized as a mere physical thing; on the other hand, the bodily subject is hypostasized as a pure ego-consciousness" (Fuchs 2018, 73). In order to account for embodiment in a coherent way, he needs to reconcile the two appearances of the body with the unity of both, otherwise we very soon end up with a dualistic conception where the mind "supervenes" upon a body defined ultimately through physical and chemical processes. Fuchs avoids the concept of flesh as introduced in the later work of Merleau-Ponty in order to account for this common substance of consciousness and organism, but he admits that the "living being is an ontological unity," manifested "in the fundamental coextensivity of subjective body and physical body" (ibid., 80). This "coextensivity" is precisely what is at stake in psychosomatics as well; in using this term, Fuchs argues that the body is one and the same being, but that according to the perspective adopted, fundamentally different aspects of it become apparent. He calls the unity of both aspects a "mediated monism," or a "dialectical unity of unity and diversity" (ibid). In an attempt to answer the question of what this monism consists in, he refers to the Aristotelian notion of *physis*: "The original Aristotelian meaning of *physis* as 'living nature' gives an accurate summary of this dimension: it means a natural entity which is its own source of motion, and which we regard in analogy to our own self-experience as living beings" (ibid., 83). He does say a few things about this living being with the help of a few concepts, of which the most fundamental is the concept of life itself. He writes about the "spontaneous and autonomous activity of life," the "energetic source of our lives" (ibid., 71). With these phrases, and others such as "a source of becoming within ourselves," or "an origin of spontaneity and movement that we cannot take possession of," Fuchs seeks to capture a realm of subjective life that belongs to the individual subject, while at the same time escaping the subject. He then uses paradoxical formulations such as "an unconscious pre-history of the self" (ibid.), by which he means that the self has an unconscious history, that is, that this history is not simply an anonymous history, but in a sense belongs to the self although the self can "neither cause nor control" it; he also takes up the formulation of Waldenfels about the self experiencing itself in the mode of its self-withdrawal" (ibid.),[3] as discussed in the previous chapter. This is the problem of the unconscious in the sense of the "primary repression, as an initial phase of repression" described by Freud in his essay on repression (Freud Sigmund 1957, 148). If the self experiences itself in the mode of self-withdrawal, and if it is identified with the sentient body, with the "unconscious bodily background" on the basis of which we necessarily live, this poses a challenge to the very method of phenomenology, since the object to describe—the self—is never actually itself present, but always already gone when we focus our attention on it.

The phenomenological task of describing the "prehistory of the self" is paradoxical and requires us to distort or extend the phenomenological method: not simply describe the appearing of a phenomenon but also describe and interpret its retreat, its withdrawal. But it is precisely because this "prehistory of the self" belongs to the self that an essential part of our description of the self will be lacking if we limit ourselves to what appears to consciousness. In other terms, the difficulty of describing the structure of the prehistory of the self derives from its being a part of the self. To escape this paradox, one solution could be to describe the very movement of withdrawal, to follow the movement and see where it ends up. To follow the movement of a withdrawing self is not an easy task. Especially not if we look for a phenomenon to describe. But within the psychodynamic conception lies the claim that the self is going through different stages, each corresponding to different degrees of development of the self. And the process of development implies the possibility of regression, a process that can be observed in various psychological disorders, given that psychodynamic explanations involve a regressive strategy for coping with a conflict or a situation that appears insurmountable for the subject. In Marty's practice and conception, regressive processes triggered by psychic conflicts are not limited to the mental realm but may also have consequences on the somatic level. This type of process Marty calls "progressive disorganization," to which most of the second volume of his *Individual Movements of Life and Death* is devoted.[4] It concerns certain cases of character neurosis, and constitutes one potential pathological path. The category "character neurosis" is a very large category, including "the majority of the individuals in our civilization" (Marty 1976, 12; all quotes from Marty's works are translated by me), and, unlike the ordinary mental neuroses, the character neuroses are not limited to a "symbolic expression of psychic conflicts" (ibid., 13). Progressive disorganization is the exact opposite of the developmental process; the functional organizations are progressively dismantled, in particular, as a consequence of traumas, and the process is different in each person, but in every case, the progressive disorganizations are transversal, in the sense that they ultimately also touch the somatic functions. This last idea is what leads Marty to a monist position, a stance, as he puts it, that "overtly abandons the principle of psyche-soma dualism" (ibid., 16).[5] Indeed, the traditional psyche-soma dualism "relies on a denial of death" (ibid., 17), on the tacit assumption that the subject, being essentially a psyche, doesn't disappear, doesn't decay. Only the body really dies in the process of disorganization.

Marty's stance against dualism doesn't imply that he conceives affective life as being plain and without tensions, on the contrary—his rejection of dualism is ontological, but he retains the duality of drives from Freud's second topic, between life and death. Another reason is his insistence on the contingency of individual development and regression. When he states in his introductory book on *The Psychosomatics of the Adult* (1990) that his perspective "brings together the temporal variations of the psyche and those of the soma in the case of subjects bearing a somatic affection" (1990, 11), he does not mean that he sees a determined causal correspondence between affective life and somatic diseases, since every individual history is singular. In the first volume of *Individual Movements*, he presents a whole range of clinical cases wherein the evolution of the disease (pleurisy, pulmonary embolism, leukemia, meningitis, hepatitis, etc.) is unforeseeable and surprising, be it in direction of recovery or death. In his comments and his interpretation, he strongly highlights the singularity of each sick individual. "In reality, you don't find more similarity between two ill persons than between two individuals. Yet not only does all classical and present nosography rely on the specific agent external to the individual, but also the notion of recovery only concerns this agent" (1976, 71). While "man is psychosomatic per definition" (1990, 11), psychosomatic analysis considers the relations between psychic and somatic movements in somatically ill patients, without seeking a causal relation between them.

Contrary to the grandfather of psychosomatics Georg Groddeck, there is no determinism about the outcome of a pathological process in Marty's conception, only the attempt to locate the disease within the context of the individual's affective life; predictions about the evolution of a somatic disease are impossible, since the connection between the affective life and the somatic state is only determinable afterwards, once the disease has broken out. Marty does not employ a hypothesis of the unconscious as a universal explanatory tool. It is rather a way to underline the importance of the affective environment of the person, the structure of her defense mechanisms. On this etiological question, he writes:

> We can only apprehend in an approximate manner the individual problems concerning the distribution and the precedence in time of the life and death instincts. We know about the instincts only through their effects on organization and disorganization. Moreover, our (mostly retrospective) evaluation must take into account the reconstructions and reorganizations of each evolution level and age. (1976, 84)

There is always a possibility of disorganization, in the sense of a dismantling of the structure of the self both in the mental and the organic sense, and the reasons why this happens in a given individual case are only accessible afterwards. Such a process of a withdrawing self is exactly what is at stake when Marty writes about the death instinct as a fundamental tendency of dismantling the structure of our body and abandoning our individual shape. What is uncovered through this process of dismantling is what Freud called the "nucleus of the unconscious" (in the sense of "inherited mental formations") "analogous to instinct in animals" (Freud 1957, 195), in a passage from the essay on *The Unconscious* that Marty quotes when sketching out his conception of the unconscious in his second volume, *The Psychosomatic Order* (Marty 1980, 103). Before I present those ideas, let us first follow his path into this core, through descriptions of the disorganization process.

Operative Life and Intercorporeality

The phenomenon that leads Marty to formulate his conception of the originary unconscious is what he and Michel de M'Uzan named "operative life," or "operative thinking," describing the evolution of certain patients at the last stage of progressive disorganization.[6] Such a process is the result of what they call an "essential depression," where the subject is unable to cope with a traumatic event and this causes a disorganization of the central psychic functions. The main symptom of such disorganization is a diffuse anxiety without object, that is, an anxiety with no relation to phobias or repressive moves.[7] Such disorders may become somatic when the person fails to resolve the conflict or to cope with the trauma on a mental level. This follows naturally from Marty's evolutionary premise: since the progressive disorganization is a process of undoing the organization of the self, "the somatic apparatus that preceded and allowed the constitution of the psyche on an evolutionary level, becomes itself disorganized" (1976, 112). This relation of precedence is based on the clinical approach: Marty observed that the somatic crises are the last stages in a process of progressive disorganization.

Operative life refers, in particular, to persons whose emotional life is emptied and whose speech is exclusively practical, apparently impersonal and with no connection to relational and affective life. The patient's speech, as they write, is devoid of symbolic reach and sublimation capacity; operative thinking is also devoid of identifications with the other: "the other is fundamentally considered as identical with the subject and gifted with the same operative system as himself" (Marty and de M'Uzan 1963, 349). Moreover, such patients often show various somatic manifestations such as migraines, chronic pains, motor coordination problems, high blood pressure, etc. Although they seem to rely upon a use of language as a screen shielding their emotions, their mode of thinking is not completely cut off from the unconscious: "All we can say is that the operative thinking establishes its contact with the unconscious at the lowest and least elaborated level, below the first integrative elaborations of the drives" (ibid., 352). Marty and de M'Uzan present three examples in their article: one of them is a young man with headaches, shivers in the limbs, and memory loss. In responding to a question about his relationship with his father, the patient provides a precise description of the way he changed the roof of his car, and how his way of doing it was different from the way his father would have done it (ibid., 347f). His description sticks to the technical details of the operation and ignores completely any attempt by the therapist to make him allude to his feelings toward his father, although this very aspect would seem to be essential since it was the very reason why the patient began to talk about changing the roof of his car in the first place. According to Marty and de M'Uzan, "The subject remains constantly at level with his gestures, his mode of thinking sticks to the materiality of the facts and to the utensility[2] of the objects [*ustensilité des objets*], he is stuck in the present, and when he manages to project himself into the future or back into the past, it is by transforming them into *bits of the present*, where everything is dominated exclusively by the succession of facts" (ibid.,

348). Such patients are also unable to dream, of if they do dream, they are unable to report their dreams, or they do so without associations, as if it were someone else's dream. The patient is unable to express his or her affective movements, as the therapists put it, "the somatic functions constitute the essential economic path and become the site of morbid sequences [*enchaînements morbides*]." In sum, "the economy escapes the mental apparatus" (ibid., 354), and the behavior of such a person appears as the "soulless collection of devices able to effectuate the necessary operation of basic existence," "suggesting the image of a zombie" (Marty 1980, 99).

The crucial feature here is the following: when Marty and de M'Uzan state that "the somatic functions constitute the essential economic path," it is because they have observed that operative life is the last stage before the outbreak of a serious disease; in the process of disorganization, it is the stage where the organic balance of the patient is at stake, after the emotional balance has broken down. The stage of operative life results from the dismantling of higher levels of affective structures and it is therefore a stage of extreme fragility. It is the contrary of a solid foundation on a biological basis; it is a stage in which the somatic level is left bare and therefore particularly vulnerable. When the disorganization affects the somatic functions in such a radical way, it can become dangerous since it can impair essential physiological functions or weaken the immunity system. This type of situation is described by Marty in metapsychological terms as the power of the death drive, since this concept in the second Freudian topic refers to the tendency of any living organism to return to a state of rest and then decomposition.[8] This is not the place for discussing the fundamental concepts of Freud's second topic; I mention the duality of life and death drives, or instincts[9] since Marty's approach is based on an evolutionary conception, according to which the disease may be the result of regression at a previous stage in psychological development. In a regressive process, where some disorganization has already taken place, operative life is a stage of relative stability. It is a "fragile arrangement, more or less extended in time, in which one (mistakenly) fears neither the imminence nor the fatality of the resumption of the disorganization" (Marty 1980, 94). But this relative confidence is mistaken because of the precariousness of such states where the subject is literally cut off from her emotions and desires.

On the other hand, although this manifestation of somatic functions seems to involve totally automatic behavior, it is indeed also sensitive to intersubjective interaction. As Marty points out in his late book about adult psychosomatics, "Operative life, related to essential depression, constitutes a stage of relative chronicity, a fragile arrangement, an unstable state, that sets in during a slow *progressive disorganization*. It is marked by somatic incidents or accidents" (Marty 1990, 28). This "unstable state" is not a state of complete isolation from others and of any kind of social interactions; there is still a "general sensitivity of the individual unconscious toward stimulations" (Marty 1980, 103). And those "stimulations" are indeed real interactions with other sensitive beings, since he insists on the therapeutic resonance with operative patients; in the same passage he affirms that, "too large gaps between the therapist's own behavior and speech and the patient's behavior and speech can risk aggravating their disorganization" (ibid., 102). While the consequences of the disorganization vary from one individual to another, in retrospect there are ways to reconstruct the paths according to each individual history, and there are also sudden disorganizations leading to the death of the person. One wonders whether this state of operative thinking or life should be understood as an unconscious where the subject's unconscious is laid bare. Since the manifestations of affective life tend to be expressed through the somatic functions, and that the progressive disorganization of the person's psychic structure has reached a stage where no affective protection exists any more, or where it is weakened, my claim is that operative life manifests the level of "feeling itself" that Merleau-Ponty defined as being the essence of the unconscious. In what follows, I shall argue in favor of this paradoxical claim, thereby showing that the apparent absence of emotional and relational life in operative patients is actually the uncovering of a fundamental sensorial layer of existence.

The Psychosomatic Unconscious

In the middle of the chapter dedicated to the notion of operative life in *The Psychosomatic Order*, Marty introduces his conception of the unconscious (1980, 101–110). In this passage, Marty shows that the unconscious is a differentiated field of experience opened up by disorganization, not a layer of pure indifference toward the world. He starts with a reference to Freud's idea of the "nucleus of the unconscious," writing that "the originary unconscious would apply from the start to the fulfilment of the program of the human species according to the encounters between the subject and her surrounding world" (1980, 103n; also 1990, 35). It is worth noting that Marty doesn't use the traditional binary conception of a repressed unconscious and an originary unconscious, so essential in Pontalis', Green's, and Lacan's criticism of Merleau-Ponty's conception, but from the outset places the whole unconscious realm within the idea of a phylogenetic inheritance. Marty argues for a conception in which the unconscious has real content and relative autonomy and is not only defined negatively, as an absence of consciousness. He argues for such a nucleus on the basis of the existence of "originary fantasies" as well as the applicability of physiological principles such as the constancy principle to the mental apparatus. The main feature of the core of the unconscious is that it is made up of inherited materials and that these materials are the origin and starting point of the structure and organization of the Ego. He claims that this nucleus of the unconscious "signifies an unconscious phylogenetic heritance with germinative and organizing contents" (1980, 103). This means that the unconscious is both a space where the psychological ego-structures are undone and a space with a structuring potential, a space both of disorganization and productivity. In order to explain such relative autonomy of the unconscious and its double orientation towards regression or structuration, Marty claims that there is a "principle of sensitivity towards excitations" (ibid., 104) remaining at the unconscious level; on this level, the human subject is still sensitive toward the surroundings, but in cases of patients with psychosomatic diseases there is a gap between this level of sensitivity and mental structures.

The originality of his conception can be summed up in three essential and forceful claims: first, that the unconscious is the bearer of biological functions, and even physical and chemical principles as well; second, that the unconscious is relatively independent from consciousness, at least some of its content might remain unconscious, some of it becoming conscious, but there is no teleology of the unconscious to become conscious; and third, that disorganization and regression may also occur within the unconscious. The first claim happens to be the core claim of psychosomatics: the unconscious does not identify with the biological, but the biological is borne by the unconscious, and this also implies that the biological and chemical dimensions are also involved in the relational world of the subject, an obvious consequence of a monist position taking subjectivity seriously. As for the second claim, Marty preserves the autonomy and the heterogeneity of the unconscious in the sense of the primary processes described by Freud and highlighted by Pontalis and Green in their criticism of Merleau-Ponty, but his innovation is that the manifestations of the unconscious may take the form of somatic pathologies, and not only of meaning (signifying) effects. The third claim implies that there are different levels of organization within the unconscious, that the unconscious is internally structured.

More precisely, concerning this third claim, Marty explains that the unconscious is structured around two levels of processes that he calls automation and programming, respectively. The first level, automation, is the most archaic and originary, wherein the somatic and psychic are not distinct; it is the level of inherited forms and processes, a principle of repetition whose function is to maintain the psychosomatic processes and keep the person alive. In other words, it is a mode of survival; therefore, it is the most resistant to progressive disorganizations. In clinical experience, such patients may remain in a seemingly stable state, relatively successful at work and with no particular events in their private life, for a long period. The next level in the structure of the unconscious is referred to as programming by Marty; this is where the associations, the links, and symbolizations build up. This is how he sums up both levels of unconscious organization:

> The analysis of this problem informs us that two functional principles could exist in the nucleus of the unconscious, two principles to be found in all systems and all psychosomatic organizations.
>
> On the one hand, a principle of automation and iteration, a principle of repetition maintaining all sorts of psychosomatic operations in a relatively stagnant way. [...]
> On the other hand, a principle of programming opening the path for an evolution of the different functional connections and associations, for hierarchization, sexualization and development, that is for the program of organization and reorganization. (Marty 1980, 104f)

The relation between automation and programming is one of anaclisis [*Anlehnung*], in the same way as desire relies upon need, as Marty explains in an important footnote: "The automation of a given functional system, [...] evidently renders the automation of this system necessary in order for the programming to take place (principle of *anaclisis*) [...] Programming leans on automation as desire leans on need" (ibid., 106). There is, moreover, an evolutionary order between the two: the principle of automation is more archaic and precedes the establishment of a programming capacity of the subject, a claim based on the clinical observation that patients can live without expressing any desire but nevertheless keep on satisfying their needs; and reciprocally it's only by satisfying their needs that they are able to build up a sense of desire again. Desire appears as a need whose satisfaction gives rise to a new desire.[10]

In operative life, only the most archaic level of automation subsists whereas the level of programming has disappeared, a situation which leaves the space open to the death drive in the Freudian sense, that is, the tendency of an organism to restore the previous state, that is, a regressive move. The death drive triumphs when disorganization also attains the somatic level and causes a collapse of organic functions. This, in turn, may take many different paths: infectious disease, cancer, burnout, etc. As Marty adds in a footnote, "Individual death occurs only when the principle of automation has itself collapsed at the level of all psychosomatic functions, including those of the nucleus of the unconscious" (ibid., 108). On the one hand, operative life is a very dangerous state because the person is particularly vulnerable to any changes in her environment. The level of programming is required in order to be able to cope with changes in life. On the other hand, operative life, albeit fragile, is a state of relative stability; in psychoanalytic terms, it is a fixation system representing an organization from earlier stages in the subject's life history, aka a regression. It represents in other terms the "unconscious prehistory of the self," as Thomas Fuchs formulates it (see above). It is the "last stage of stabilization of a system before the collapse of this system itself" (1980, 112) but also, at the same time, the condition of possibility of a "dynamic reorganization," which is why the repetitive processes need to be protected and preserved by the therapist. In doing so, the therapist's role is to offer a space for the patient to live her repetitive gestures and ways, which can lead to very long cures, as, for example, in Joyce McDougall's clinical cases.[11]

Resonance in the Psychosomatic Interview

Introducing the passage about the unconscious, Marty highlights the relational dimension of the clinical approach to operative patients. As a psychotherapist, he seeks to "avoid our own conduct and our own speech becoming too far removed from the behavior and words of our patients because such gaps, noticed by the unconscious of the patients, risk accentuating their disorganization" (ibid., 102). And indeed, in his descriptions of therapeutic strategies, Marty compares the maternal function toward infants with the psychotherapeutic function toward operative patients (ibid., 122ff). The analogies are quite obvious (a caring person concerning the evolution or regression of the subject, the provision of protective shields against stimuli, the relative absence of mental organization, and the analogy between the developmental and the reconstructive situation), but the differences are also significant. Among those differences, the absence of internal stimuli, of desires, from the side of the operative patient is different from the case of an infant, whose life is characterized by a number of internal stimuli that the maternal figure has to help filter and accommodate. Thus, the therapist must be quite active and suggest projects in phases when the patient has the ability to program again, and "actively maintain the relation in periods of automation" (ibid., 124). At this point in the text there is another significant footnote in which Marty indicates the difference in attitude between the normally neutral position of the analyst and the active involvement of the maternal function: "The maternal virtues are entirely different from the values required for practicing psychoanalysis" (ibid., 124). And indeed, in the following pages, under the headline "The medical intervention," he actually goes on to describe the abilities of the maternal function and its use in the medical relation, in particular, the dialectics of stimulating the child and protecting it against the stimuli that Donald W. Winnicott also described in terms of the sufficiently good mother.[12] Marty's conclusion in this passage is that the quality of the relation between the therapist and the patient depends on the capacity of the therapist to "aim right" [*viser juste*], and this capacity is essentially defined by the affective sensitivity of the therapist, an ability to respect the particular evolutionary rhythm of the patient, as he writes, "those natural rhythms had better be respected from the somatic as well as the relational perspective" (ibid., 132). In sum, it is worth quoting the last paragraph of the chapter devoted to the progressive disorganizations: "The medical function relies for a large part on the availability, the intuition, the attention, and the alertness of the physician, on her continuously renewed adaptation to the state of the patient. It evokes at times the maternal function. The affective balance of the physician remains primordial" (ibid., 135).

My interpretation here is that Marty cannot satisfy himself with a binary idea of the automation aspect being completely mechanical and devoid of any desiring potential, and programming being the only aspect involving a spontaneous desire from the subject. The task of the therapist is to preserve the desiring potential in the phases during which the patient seems completely given over to the organic functions, in the most seemingly mechanical phases of operative life. This interpretation is motivated by some passages in the conclusion of *The Psychosomatic Investigation*, co-authored with Michel de M'Uzan and Christian David in 1963, a book essentially consisting in the transcription of, and commentary on, clinical cases. The conclusion furnishes clues about the conception of the risks and potentials of the psychoanalytic cure. The authors highlight the importance of the investigator's (therapist's) attitude, the affective interrelations with the patient, the unconscious movements of both protagonists, and the quality and role of energetic investments. And those movements consist in unnoticeable manifestations that the therapist must be trained to notice: "The investigator must watch out for the vaguest allusions, the slightest associations, the slightest reactions, the slightest quantitative or qualitative changes of the verbal flow, for the very rhythm of speech and for its physiological context, all manifestations conveying transferential modulations" (256). It remains for the next chapter to examine the specific structures of the transfer, and how to account for the emergence of the symbolic, in psychosomatic practice; it will be enough for my argument here to point out that the resonance between the therapist and the patient touches the whole range of the patient's life, from her molecular and organic state to her more spiritual dimension.

From Intercorporeality to an Ontology of the Unconscious

The claim here is that resonance phenomena in the psychosomatic setting manifest a continuity between the corporeal and psychological, the physiological and the mental, the biological and the experiential. Everywhere, at any stage, there is always a potential for a desiring subject to come forth. The death drive is not an independent force pushing the subject toward its own destruction, but rather a tendency to the dislocation of the subject's unity and, inasmuch as the subject is still alive, there is a possibility of restoring the capacity to program again and move over a purely material survival based on satisfying needs.

This conception is close to the sketches of Merleau-Ponty in the later parts of his work, particularly in his 1955 lecture on passivity. When the philosopher states that the unconscious is "the symbolic matrix left behind by the event," or the "persistence of symbolic matrices" (Merleau-Ponty

2010, 169), that it is the "cohesion of a life," he also refers to a dimension of the unconscious not resulting from the activity of repression, but rather pertaining to the sedimentation of events in personal life. Moreover, the productivity of the unconscious in Marty's thinking is similar to Merleau-Ponty's conception of the flesh; in particular, in *The Visible and the Invisible*, when he writes about the "perpetual parturition and generativity of brute Being" (Merleau-Ponty 1968, 115), and in the same period shows that the unconscious is the privileged access mode to this realm, that the unconscious as "feeling itself" should be understood as "not the possession of 'what' is felt, but a dispossession of ourselves in favor of it" (Merleau-Ponty 1970, 130). And he concludes by distinguishing the two levels of the unconscious, the "repressed unconsciousness" and "primordial unconsciousness," this last level being defined as "the initial yes, the undividedness of feeling" (ibid., 131), as seen in the first chapter above. Concerning the access to this realm, Merleau-Ponty mentions, in particular, the aesthetic experience, where the painter puts himself in tune with the movements of being.

Marty's approach is conditioned by the clinical experience of persons unable to access their own emotional life and living in a regime of impersonal and seemingly automatic behavior. But this difference is only apparent, since the primordial unconscious, in Marty's terms, is also a realm of sensing. Marty claims a monist position, not in the sense of a reductive materialism nor in terms of a kind of spiritualism; his monism consists in claiming a fundamental unity of the somatic and psychic; he writes that his conception of psychosomatics "overtly abandons the principle of the psyche-soma dualism" (Marty 1976, 16).[13] There is, according to Marty, a source of meaning in human life where the "prehistory of the self" takes place, and in which the psychological and the biological are indistinct. But the main reason of his rejection of dualism is practical: although the traditional view makes compromises and recognizes that there is an action of the mind on the body and of the body upon the mind, it "neglects the perspective of both ontogenesis and phylogenesis" (ibid., 17), by which Marty means that the evolution and the development of the human being is impossible to account for if we remain within the dualistic framework, and the value of this dualism between psyche and soma tends to "fade and disappear with experience" (ibid., 16). Marty says little about what this realm positively consists in apart from the distinction between automation and programming; but in any case, it should be emphasized that even the most archaic level also includes the presence of others. This implies that the psychosomatic unconscious can be defined as a relational space of "feeling itself." Or more accurately, that the unconscious as "feeling itself" should be interpreted as a relational space where the feeling or sensing is directed toward another. The prehistory of the self includes such a realm, where the self is not yet identified as a distinct unity, but where the organic body somehow offers its unity to make possible a certain sensitivity. Ontologically, there is only one being, and the unity of this being is manifested in the sensitivity of the unconscious, a realm in which what happens in terms of intersubjective relations can have consequences for the somatic functions. Exploring the clinic of the prehistory of the self through a phenomenological reading of psychoanalytical psychosomatics allows us to escape the paradox of dual aspectivity by answering the question of *what* it is that the two aspects are aspects *of*, that is, the unconscious as a dynamic space of inherited structures in a permanent process of appropriation by the conscious self and yet completely in continuity with the biological totality of which it is an expression. The unconscious as feeling, or sensing, itself is therefore to be considered as corporeal through and through, but only on the condition that the corporeal is meaningful.

Transition

The "unconscious prehistory of the self" can only be accessed through the description of a retreating self, a self caught in a process of dislocation. Such a notion of self is not only corporeal, but remains a relational being, a being haunted by the presence of others. Through the whole process of disorganization, the self still remains a subject and does not merge with the world at any moment. In Merleau-Pontian terms, the flesh of the subject remains distinguished from the flesh of the world; even in the last stages of the dislocation of psychic structures, a sensitive self remains. This brings up an argument in favor of the claim that the minimal self (or the operative self in the psychosomatic language) is a self that is always already in relation with others. A caring other is necessary to maintain the operative functions, and to render a new programming possible. If we look at the unconscious from the point of view of the sentient body, we discover that feeling or sensing is a relation of resonance between sentient bodies, and that there is an organic dimension of this relation. Consequently, we are led to the idea of a symbolism of the body itself, in the sense of a relational structure allowing us to make sense of the affective moves of the subject. The relations of such a corporeal symbolism with the symbolic proper, with verbal and conceptual language, remain to be discussed, in particular, how we can retain the ontological unity of soma and psyche, while at the same time accounting for the interrelations of the body's signifying powers and the symbolic realm proper. This question is inescapable in order to understand how the unconscious works *between* bodies.

Notes

1. For an overview of both the history and the current situation of psychoanalytical psychosomatics, cf. Smadja 2008 (in French), as well as Storck 2016 (in German).
2. Cf. Freud, 1957, 186, 195. Other occurrences of the expression are to be found in the Wolfman's analysis (1918), as well as in the essay "A Child is being Beaten" (1919).
3. Cf. Waldenfels 2002, 315.
4. The first version of Marty's study on this topic was published in English in the *International Journal of Psychoanalysis* with the title "A major process of somatization: The progressive disorganization" (Marty 1968). His *magnum opus* is the two-volume *Les mouvements individuels de vie et de mort*: the first bears the subtitle *Essai d'économie psychosomatique* and was published in 1976, and the second is *L'ordre psychosomatique* (1980).
5. See also 1990, 12: psychosomatics, Marty writes, is "an overtly monist adventure."
6. He and de M'Uzan first presented the concept in 1962 at the 23rd Congress of French-speaking psychoanalysts in Barcelona (Marty and de M'Uzan 1963); it is summed up in Marty 1980, 93–101.
7. Cf. Marty 1980, 61. These features are very close to the notion of alexithymia that is widely discussed in contemporary psychiatry. Cf. Pirlot and Corcos 2012.
8. See Freud's "Beyond the Pleasure Principle": "If we are to take it as a truth that knows no exception that everything living dies for internal reasons—becomes inorganic once again—then we shall be compelled to say that 'the aim of life is death' and, looking backwards, that 'inanimate things existed before living ones.'" (Freud 2015, 32) Franz Alexander interprets the Freudian death instinct as the disintegrating tendency of an organism, that is, the affirmation of the parts—see Alexander 1963, 63ff.
9. Marty's use of the term "instinct" instead of drive can probably be related to his relation with the works of Franz Alexander and the American tradition of psychosomatics; for example, Alexander's *Fundamentals of Psychoanalysis* [first published in 1948] and his *Psychosomatic Medicine* [1950] were translated into French very early, both in 1952. Marty actu-

ally appropriates Alexander's use of the Freudian life and death instincts (Alexander 1963, 63–75). In the first volume of *Individual Movements*, he explains that the term "instinct" is used instead of "drive" (*pulsion*) because "drive" implies that they have a purpose, an aim. Instinct is a pure force spanning the biological and the psychological.

10. This exact same distinction between need and desire is also key to Françoise Dolto's thinking—cf. Chap. 6 below.
11. Cf. in particular the cases presented in *Theaters of the Ego* and *Theaters of the body* (McDougall 1986, 1989), for example Tim (1989, 223–254).
12. As he writes, "Ideally, the mother invests affectively not too much and not too little in each of her infant's functional systems (thanks to the regulation of stimuli and protective shields), and then disinvests those systems in order to let the child progressively regulate them by herself" (Marty 1980, 127).
13. Another quote in the same vein can be found in *The Psychosomatic Investigation*: "We should talk about indifferentiation, [...]. By this, we mean, in reference to [corporeal] intentionality, the consubstantial tendency to a dialectics of organism and environment, developing according to real continuum, that is found also in representation" (Marty et al. 1963, XXVIII).

References

Alexander, Franz G. 1963. Fundamentals of Psychoanalysis [1948]. New York: Norton & Co.

Freud Sigmund. 1957. The Standard Edition of the Complete Psychological Works of Sigmund Freud, ed. J. Strachey. Vol. XIV.

Fuchs, Thomas. 2018. *Ecology of the Brain. The Phenomenology and Biology of the Embodied Mind.* Oxford: Oxford University Press.

Marty, Pierre. 1968. A Major Process of Somatization: The Progressive Disorganization. *International Journal of Psychoanalysis* 49:246–249.

Marty, Pierre. 1976. *Les mouvements individuels de vie et de mort.* Paris: Payot.

Marty, Pierre. 1980. *L'ordre psychosomatique.* Paris: Payot.

Marty, Pierre. 1990. *La psychosomatique de l'adulte.* Paris: PUF.

Marty, Pierre, Michel de M'Uzan, and Christian David. 1963. *L'investigation psychosomatique.* Paris: PUF.

Merleau-Ponty, Maurice. 1968. *The Visible and the Invisible [1964].* Translated by A. Lingis. Evanston: Northwestern University Press.

Merleau-Ponty, Maurice. 1970. Themes from the Lectures at the Collège de France. Translated by J. O'Neill. Evanston: Northwestern University Press.

Merleau-Ponty. 2010. *Institution and Passivity. Course notes at the Collège de France (1954–1955).* Translated by Leonard Lawlor and Heath Massey. Evanston: Northwestern University Press.

McDougall, Joyce. 1986. *Theaters of the Mind. Illusion and Truth on the Psychoanalytic Stage*. New York: Basic Books.
McDougall, Joyce. 1989. *Theaters of the Body. A Psychosomatic Approach to Psychosomatic Illness*. New York: W. W. Norton & Co.
Marty, Pierre, and Michel de M'Uzan. 1963. La 'pensée opératoire'. *Revue Française de Psychanalyse* 67:345–356.
Pirlot, Gérard, and Maurice Corcos. 2012. Understanding Alexithymia Within a Psychoanalytical Framework. *International Journal of Psychoanalysis* 93:1403–1425.
Smadja, Claude. 2008. *Les Modèles psychanalytiques de la psychosomatique*. Paris: PUF.
Storck, Timo. 2016. *Psychoanalyse und Psychosomatik. Die leiblichen Grundlagen der Psychodynamik*. Stuttgart: W. Kohlhammer.
Waldenfels, Bernhard. 2002. *Bruchlinien der Erfahrung. Phänomenologie, Psychoanalyse, Phänomenotechnik*. Frankfurt a.M.: Suhrkamp.

CHAPTER 5

The Symbolic and the Organism in Psychosomatics

Symbols are not invented, they are there, and belong to the inalienable estate of man; indeed, one might say that all conscious thought and action are the unavoidable consequence of unconscious symbolization, that mankind is lived by the symbol.
Groddeck 1949, 49

Developing a new ontological non-dualistic framework for psychoanalytic practice implies exploring the role of the symbolic in the history of psychosomatics, starting with Georg Groddeck, the "grandfather" of the psychosomatic tradition, and then discussing the topic in terms of the "mothers and fathers" Joyce McDougall, Pierre Marty, Michel de M'Uzan, and Christian David, and concluding with more recent literature. Indeed, the history of psychosomatics also involves a shift in the conception of symbolization. Groddeck's approach was mainly to explain somatic diseases through symbolic interpretations referring them to a precise trauma in the patient's life, thereby supposing a direct path from the symbolic to the organic and vice-versa. This entailed the risk of overlooking the specific nature of the organic body, reduced to a space of expression of symbolic conflicts, thereby confirming a particularly primitive version of the traditional dualism of inert matter and active conscious symbolic activity. As we saw in the last chapter, Marty and his colleagues did not separate, either in practice or in theory, the organic and the symbolic, considering

S. Kristensen, *The Intercorporeal Unconscious*,
https://doi.org/10.1007/978-3-032-22596-2_5

diseases of the organic body as expressions of conflicts that the psychoanalytic cure is intended to make explicit. As Marty puts it, "Our approach overtly abandons the principle of psyche-soma dualism" (Marty 1976, 16); however, this does not entail any reduction in either materialism or spiritualism; it rather points toward a monistic ontology beyond the traditional dualisms of the Western philosophical tradition. In this chapter, the aim is to describe the relation between the corporeal and the symbolic within such a framework, where symbolic verbal expression prolongs the expressions of the body itself, and the verbal functions as a space of resonance for the corporeal, rather than a screen or a cover. In doing so, it is crucial to preserve the autonomy of the body's expressivity; indeed, psychosomatic disease is an expression of an unconscious conflict or trauma, although the relation of the body's expression and the symbolic shared meanings is not linear: the challenge of a psychosomatic cure is precisely to find the ways through which these expressions may circulate yet again. This is precisely where the intercorporeal resonance between bodies in the clinical interaction is key. I will specifically consider the descriptions of the way the body communicates in the psychosomatic clinic in order to delineate the structure of the intercorporeal space of communication between therapist and patient.

The It and the Symbolic

Psychosomatics operate chiefly with regard to Freud's second topic, where the main characters of our psychic life are the Ego, the Super-Ego and the It, and the human subject caught in the tension between life and death drives. This is at least how Marty lays his conceptual groundwork in his books, both of which bear the title *Individual Movements of Life and Death*. In this, he is faithful to Georg Groddeck, the author of the *Book of the It*, published in 1923, a few months before Freud wrote his famous essay *Beyond the Pleasure Principle*, where he laid out his second metapsychological theory. It is well known that Groddeck inspired Freud to name the It, as Freud himself admits in the introduction to his 1923 essay "The Ego and the It"[1] and in Groddeck's writing, the It expresses itself through bodily symptoms.

The very idea that conflicts on the symbolic level may cause somatic disorders is the central idea of psychosomatics. In *The Book of the It*, Georg Groddeck, lets his alter ego, the narrator Patrick Troll, describe nearly all clinical cases according to an interpretation where the somatic is a manifestation of a symbolic conflict. The book is a collection of fictive letters written by a psychiatrist to a female friend, explaining the various ways the unconscious may cause a somatic disorder. For example, in the 13th Letter, he writes about abdominal pains and headaches that a woman might experience during her period, explaining that they can be caused by her resistance to her desires. It starts with pain in the sacral region, and if this is not enough, "the It seizes upon headache in order to deaden thought, migraine, indigestion, vomiting." The explanation is that "indigestion, vomiting and the sensation of a bursting head" (Groddeck 1949, 100–1) are symbols, or images of birth in the form of a sickness [*Geburtssinnbilder in Krankheitsform*]. Such a discourse concerning the It causing various disorders and pains through the action of symbols in the body is Groddeck's principal explanation. The omnipotence of the It expresses the way the symbolic operates in the organic realm and may cause mayhem. In Groddeck's book, most examples are meant to show that there are symbolic contents on the unconscious level and that these symbols may have an effect on mental as well as physiological health. To put it short, Groddeck claims that the human psyche is governed by the symbolic. As he writes, "one might say that all conscious thought and action are the unavoidable consequence of unconscious symbolization, that mankind is animated by the symbol" (Groddeck 1949, 49).

In *The Book of the It*, the unconscious is essentially symbolic, and the body is the space where the symbolic unconscious produces its effects. The interpretation of bodily symptoms must find clear and unambiguous symbolisms, such as, for example, a toothache as a symbol of the desire of the pregnant woman that her unborn child should die (Groddeck 1949, 22). The reason for this preeminence of the symbolic is his claim that psychoanalytical treatment, that is, treatment using only verbal resources, may have an effect upon organic diseases, and even infectious diseases and accidents. He writes that "For the It, there is no distinction between organic and mental, and consequently that if the It can be influenced by analysis, even organic diseases can, and in certain circumstances must, be treated psycho-analytically" (ibid., 120). The only possible way to discover the truth of some unconscious origin of a disease is to have the It express itself "in word, gesture or symptom" (ibid., 140). In all the cases that the narrator describes, there is always the search for a symbolic origin and explanation of the problem: the It is in fact considered as a second subject inside the subject, reacting to circumstances in a similar way as the conscious subject, but sometimes in an opposite direction.

At one point, in the 18th Letter, Groddeck evokes the rhythmic aspect of the unconscious. In reference to Freud's *Totem and Taboo*, taking the point of view of the son in the primitive horde eager to eliminate his father, or at least to emasculate him, along with his brothers, he talks about the childhood imprints of prenatal rhythms and explains on this basis why children may be sensitive toward military marches and other regular rhythms of a similar sort. He comments saying that "It seems that the It expresses itself in rhythm just as it does in symbol," or at least "that we must ascribe rhythmical properties to it" (ibid., 144). But he doesn't go any further, and returns to the interpretation of symbols brought up by associations. In short, what dominates in Groddeck is the postulate that in order to be accessible for the talking cure, the unconscious must be essentially constituted by symbolic meanings. But if this is so, then the becoming conscious of unconscious content doesn't change anything in its nature. While it is necessary to suppose a continuity between the two realms, as we saw in the second chapter, it is also necessary to recognize that the process of becoming conscious does change something in the mental content. We have to account for the difference between symbolic meaning and tangible, perceptual meaning, and the reason why psychosomatics is relevant to the philosophical problem of the unconscious is that it locates unconscious meanings on a bodily level, and bodily meanings are of a different nature from symbolic ones.

The Body as a Carnal Text

From an opposite perspective, in an article on the "Psychosomatic Act," Silvia Lippi emphasizes the opacity of psychosomatic illnesses, fundamentally different from neurotic symptoms. In line with Joyce McDougall's but from a Lacanian perspective, Lippi shows that psychosomatic acts are not to be interpreted as symptoms, but rather as gestures that the body makes because of an originary trauma that the subject is not able to overcome. This originary loss causes an ever-missed encounter with the other, and the desire of repeating this failure over and over again. Following this path, the impossibility of overcoming the originary trauma determines a void repetition of speech, where the spoken speech is projected in a void with no grip on the level of the trauma. Thus, "the psychosomatic illness is like a writing of flesh," where "the body becomes a signifier"; Psychosomatics, she pursues, is a "modification of tissues," a "flesh graphic language," that "we are unable to read" (Lippi 2008, 69–70). The psychosomatically ill subject tends to see her desire blocked through this identical repetition, with no perspective of transforming either its form or its intensity. There is a loss at the origin that the subject does not acknowledge; this prevents the subject from desiring in her own name, since desiring implies an inner separation creating the space of a lack. Lippi writes: "Language has lost its barrier function against *jouissance*[2]: speech becomes body, the trace of a body that causes trauma. The subject is no longer protected from the real by the meaning of the words (the imaginary), the crystallization of the signifiers triggers the psychosomatic phenomenon. (…) Language and body have exchanged their functions, now the body has a symbolic function: the sick organ is a carnal graphic, a mark, a writing" (ibid., 72). Whereas spoken speech normally filters the drives and affects arising from within the body, in psychosomatic cases, the body takes the whole place, and its malfunction, its disease, is like speech, the only difference with verbal language being that the body's language is unintelligible. Since the body's language coincides with the moment of jouissance, it is fixed and crystallized, thereby losing its intersubjective value, its capacity of conveying meaning to another subject.[3] A similar situation is characteristic of the psychotic subject who also faces the impossibility of overcoming an originary trauma causing a foreclosure, which is a much more solid kind of repression, keeping the hidden content completely out of reach.

Yet Lippi's approach also uses a dualistic framework in order to account for the discrepancy between the body and the symbolic. There is a presupposition that the body's language (the disease) does have a clear and distinct meaning since it can be referred to an originary trauma; its incomprehensible character is only because it has not been deciphered, not because its mode of signification is ambiguous or simply alien to verbal language. If there is a continuity between verbal language and body language, it cannot (and should not) be a reduction of the latter to the former. The body's language is fundamentally opaque, it is a "modification of the tissues," as Lippi herself writes, but this modification should not itself be taken as a writing since this would mean a negation of the organic nature of the body, and it would mean neglecting the multiple bodily expressions of one particular trauma.

I'm turning to the inventor of the notion, Pierre Marty, in order to continue the exploration of the intertwining of the symbolic and the organic, but this time taking the organic and its power of significance as a point of departure. Marty and his colleagues highlighted the unpredictable dimension of psychosomatic affections, and the singularity of each subject susceptible to such an affection. The outcome here is thus that the bodily unconscious is a realm where the symbolic plays a central role, but in an unpredictable way. It doesn't presuppose a symbolic meaning and consider the body as a simple vehicle for such an already determined meaning, as is the case with Groddeck; on the contrary, the organic body must itself be considered a producer of meaning, but in conflicting, ambiguous, and confusing ways.

Transference and Countertransference in the Psychosomatic Consultation

In *The Psychosomatic Investigation*,[4] Marty, de M'Uzan and David emphasize the horizontal dimension of the manifestations of the unconscious, as mentioned in the last chapter. They write at the end of the conclusion that "one never listens with enough readiness, both intellectual and sensitive, to what the patient, as if unwittingly, is trying to express" (Marty and de M'Uzan 1963, 262). The utmost importance of the "relational system of the patient" (ibid.) is also emphasized in Marty's book about the *Individual Movements of Life and Death*, when he introduces the importance of psychoanalysis in psychosomatic medicine. In the very first line of a chapter entitled "The Importance of Psychoanalysis," he writes that the psychosomatic economy of a person relies on "interhuman communication" and that this communication relies on a "system of affective relations" (Marty 1976, 86). He then goes on to explain that the "psychic economy" plays a central role in the psychosomatic economy, indicating thereby that the psychosomatic approach implies a careful awareness for the relational environment of the patient. The relational, affective ecology of the somatizing subject does have a bodily foundation, upon which the psychic and emotional levels are built. The situation in psychosomatics is therefore rather contradictory: on the one hand, the somatizations do express the relational and affective state of the patient, just as in any classical psychoanalytic neurotic situations, but, on the other hand, the intensity of the repressive energy prevents the contents' normal circulation between the unconscious bodily and the preconscious-conscious system. This causes language to be void and superficial, and to fail when expressing feelings; the patient's affective life becomes inaccessible to verbal expression.

In psychosomatic cases, "the unconscious appears padlocked, isolated, fierce" (Marty, de M'Uzan and David, 256), or as Marty himself notes, the psychosomatic cases are characterized by a default in the circulation between the conscious and the unconscious, where the preconscious functions as an "often fragile" hinge.

> The normal functioning, e.g. continuous, of the first topic constitutes the minimum of mental organization that can theoretically open the door, if needed, to psychoanalytic cure. In psychosomatics, it guarantees the absence of a system of disorganization, of essential depression, of operative life, and progressive disorganization. (Marty 1976, 91)

The postulate of continuity, as we can see in this passage, is quite close to the approach of Merleau-Ponty, who considered that unconscious contents are not in their essence different from conscious contents. But the fundamental clinical problem faced by psychosomatic patients is that the barrier between consciousness and unconsciousness is too rigid, that contents do not circulate, or circulate with considerable difficulty, making it all the more difficult to organize the transferential movements that enable the psychoanalytic cure in the case of neuroses. Since the transferential movements tend to escape the verbal level, the psychosomatic investigation has to question the patient much more actively than a classical psychoanalysis on the couch, as the different examples in Marty, de M'Uzan and David's book show. In the clinical observations that are transcribed in *The Psychosomatic Investigation*, the style of the investigator is heavily different from a classical psychoanalysis, where the analysand is the one who speaks, with the analyst giving occasional feed-back. In the psychosomatic investigation, the clinician is constantly asking questions, linking the present words of the patient with what he has just said, asking why he said what he said, etc., thereby making sure that the contact between them is not lost. This is particularly clear in the case of Eugène E., a 15-and-a-half-year-old boy with a paralysis in his arm and leg (Marty and de M'Uzan 1963, 75–102). The investigator is constantly active in the face-to-face clinical situation because the psychosomatic patient has heavy difficulties associating content and frequently loses the thread; when asked for an example of what he is thinking about when evoking his father, who died shortly after his birth, he cannot associate with any images; he answers "I just had the image of the square, that's it!" while staring at the tiled floor (ibid., 81). This inability to associate any images with an emotionally relevant fact in the patient's life is exactly what Marty and his colleagues have in mind, when they explain that the circulation between the unconscious and the conscious is blocked, and must therefore be actively stimulated by the investigator. Reading the transcript of such a session gives a rather hectic impression, where the investigator both stimulates the patient to associate while following his cadence of short answers. Short replies and reminders follow the patent's short answers giving the whole exchange a singular rhythm. In the comments, the authors remark that the "motor value of verbalization is predominant," and is constantly "accompanied by a gestural and mimic activity, itself often impulsive" (ibid., 103). The deficit in the ability to express one's thoughts with words gives rise to a particular awareness toward gestures and mimics, to the point that "most of the relation takes place at the sensorimotor level" (*ibid.*, 104). In the case of Eugène E., the predominance of motor mechanisms is clear, with "aggressive impulsions, escaping movements, and a generalized tremor" (ibid.). The investigator mimics the patient's gestures in order to facilitate identifications and to favor interpersonal contact, in the absence of a possibility of real transferential movements. "One takes up a sentence, a mimic, a gesture, or a combination of those recently experienced elements" (ibid., 105), and this allows the patient to feel recognized by identifying with the investigator, at least momentarily, and feel secure enough to carry on answering his questions.

Another, closely related, characteristic of a psychosomatic patient is his tendency to withdraw and remain on the level of what happens immediately in the relation in the here and now, and answering with aspects of the surrounding environment when asked to associate: the investigator asks about the link between his anger and his eating habits when he was a small child, and the patient answers "I don't see… I may have said it just like that." And to the question of what he's thinking about right now, "I see the seat over there, that's worn, that's all, this armchair" (ibid., 83). All his associations are immediately linked to his surroundings, or as Marty et al. sum it up: "His energy is mostly invested in regressions and reconstructions entirely linked to the immediate relational play" (ibid., 105). His energy is not invested toward verbal expression, only in gestures and behaviors, and his use of language itself is analogous to a gesture: "Generally, language, which is elsewhere so often the object of a conscious control, appears here with the same value and the same function as a behavior, and only that" (ibid., 108). And a bit further on in the text, they state that this patient's unconscious reveals itself entirely at the level of "behavior mechanisms." The level of verbalization is not absent, but it "counts mostly as behavior" (ibid., 109). This is essential in psychosomatic theory: the unconscious is manifested in visible corporeal gestures and behaviors, and the verbal level is, so to speak, reduced to the level of bodily gestures. On the same page they affirm that "The somatic dimension is central as an elective way of releasing the unconscious," and that "the unconscious is fused with functional systems" (ibid.).

The central claim here is that the unconscious is a bodily phenomenon, and that the investigator / therapist must learn to play with it, not wait until a slip of the tongue or any other incoherence appears in the patient's speech (as in a classical couch psychoanalysis), but instead actively question the subject and imitate his gestures, look in the same direction, reciprocate his postures. This is because the subject needs to feel safe in order to open an access to bodily expression. The transferential dynamics play out on an immediate instantaneous and apparent level, where the theoretical and mythical constructions of the psychoanalytical tradition, such as the oedipal phase, or the name-of-the-father, or the castration process, etc., do not play a role. But even on such a level, transferential dynamics are still essential in order for the therapy to have an effect; they are simply reduced to their minimal structure. I shall now turn to Joyce McDougall's clinical writings in order to deepen this issue; McDougall is a highly regarded participant in the Parisian psychosomatic school, and her twin books *Theaters of the Body* and *Theaters of the Mind*[5] (McDougall 1985, 1989) are a precious source of clinical reflections, in particular on the specific structure of psychosomatic patients, their use of language and the transferential and counter-transferential dynamics of the clinical relation.

The Paradoxical Role of Language in the Psychosomatic Investigation

Joyce McDougall writes about the "radical break between psyche and soma," and the fact that when the ego has "resigned for unknown reasons, the soma is called upon to invent the answer to foreclosed conflicts of the ego" (McDougall 1982, 63). There is an autonomy of the body through which the inner conflicts are channeled. The psychosomatic patients are in essence characterized by a disconnection of body and language; as McDougall explains, most of her adult psychosomatic patients function like small children who are unable to use words to express their thoughts and therefore only react somatically; "When an adult becomes somatically ill, we are tempted to conclude that we have to do with an archaic form of mental functioning that doesn't use language" (McDougall 1989, 28).

Alexithymia is a typical state found in many psychosomatic patients defined as the etymology of the term suggests: the inability to verbally express feelings: the lack (a-) of words (*lexis*) for affectivity (*thymos*), concerning not only "the difficulties patients may have in attempting to describe their affective states, but also the incapacity to distinguish one affect from the other" as McDougall explains (1985, 159). This emotional void is perceived by the therapist through her own affects (e.g. of unease, or anger), or as McDougall formulates it, "in the analytic relationship, countertransference affects usually provide the first warning" (ibid., 160). It is paradoxically the emotional response of the therapist to the patient's absence of emotions that puts the therapist on the right track in order to interpret the case as alexithymia. In the French version of her book, she makes a remark concerning the countertransference in presence of the void of the meaning of the words: Whereas the alexithymic subject is often a skilled wielder of words, they remain "without impact, drained for the one who speaks," and those who hear them are sometimes "stunned by the resonance of emptiness" (McDougall 1982, 213). The resonance of a speech with no (or only limited) grip on what it is supposed to express—leaving the floor entirely to the body to express.

Similarly to the reflection brought by Silvia Lippi in her recent article, McDougall already remarked that the manifestation of operational thinking or alexithymia is quite analogous to symptoms of psychosis, in the sense that there is a similar powerful repression of affective states amounting to a foreclosure, that is, a total inaccessibility for consciousness.

> A severe lack of libidinal cathexis attached to certain bodily zones or to the somatic self as a whole, when coupled with parentally instilled alexithymia, runs the risk not only of impairing somatic and zonal functioning but also of allowing bodily pain as well as mental pain to be totally foreclosed from conscious awareness. This mechanism is reminiscent of one of the fundamental mechanisms that contribute to certain mystical states as well as to the

> maintenance of certain psychotic states such as catatonia and self-mutilation. (ibid., 164)

And a bit further in the text:

> My proposition is that psychosomatosis and psychosis reveal similar psychic structures and that this similarity is not limited to the dynamic force of the above-mentioned anxieties. Certain of the psychic mechanisms, such as alexithymia, that are employed to keep archaic terror at bay are also common to both states. (ibid., 167)

Alexithymia can be a common symptom in both psychosomatosis and psychosis because there is at the origin of the symptom trauma and pain so overwhelming that it tends to deactivate speech, and let the body alone express itself. But there are differences, in particular about the meaning of the symptoms: Psychosomatic symptoms "neither make biological sense nor carry verbal symbolic significance" (ibid.), whereas neurotic as well as psychotic symptoms do have a symbolic meaning inasmuch as they exist in relation to the presence of others.

> Psychotics attribute to others their overwhelming affective pain and intolerable anxiety and proceed to create a neoreality in order to make continued existence tolerable and understandable. With the same aim in mind, alexithymics attack their psychological capacity to capture affect and use it for thought or as a signal to themselves. But instead of creating a neoreality, they simply drain external reality and object relationships of their meaning. (ibid., 168)

In other words, we are confronted with clinical situations where the recourse to language doesn't help in any way to access the origin of the symptom. The unconscious therefore is not linked to the symbolic, at least not in the verbal sense. This is also shown by the fact that the countertransferential sign is nothing other than a feeling of uneasiness, or uncanniness, when faced with the void of the patient's speech. The alexithymic person's defense mechanism consists essentially in blocking any feedback related to her own emotions; consequently, her thoughts become aimless and void because it is the emotional component that gives thinking its direction and its meaning. Without emotion, any thought or any perception becomes pointless and loses its relation with objects.

Bodily Expressions and Individuation

Even in psychosomatic patients who have the ability to express their emotions, patients who seem capable of describing and analyzing their situation, this doesn't always change the somatic expression of their suffering. Expressing verbally one's emotions doesn't suffice to get over a psychosomatic disease. As McDougall writes in *Theaters of the Mind*, "With today's much longer analyses we frequently find that, following the disappearance of the neurotic symptoms that bring patients to analysis, these and other discharge patterns risk becoming another rock upon which many an analysis may founder. The symptoms are gone and there are many inner psychic changes, but the analysand still feels empty, anxious, unhappy, or unfulfilled" (McDougall 1985, 116). The discharge patterns, the depressive and anxious states may continue, showing that the case is not a typical neurosis, but rather a psychosomatic problem, that may lead to a somatic disease. Such a resistance of psychosomatic symptoms can be referred, according to McDougall, to the childhood and upbringing of the patient with an overprotective mother (or rather an "over-good" mother in the Winnicottian sense of the "good-enough mother"), not allowing the little child to develop an independent self-consciousness, to allow themselves to "exist as separate human beings" (ibid, 119). She writes:

> In severe psychosomatic and anxiety states, we tend to find a primitive oedipal organization in which the mother, while not repudiating the father, nevertheless is felt to have related to her child as a sexual complement or as a narcissistic extension of her own self, thereby establishing a specific form of relationship to her child's bodily self. (ibid, 117)

This originary fusion of the mother with her child is a characteristic feature of many psychosomatic patients, in McDougall's clinical experience.[6] She introduces the phrases "the chasmic mother" and "the cork child" concerning Isaac A, a patient with an addictive relationship with his mother. Such mothers "use their children as parts of their own bodies or selves," and the children are instruments of an "overfeeding and overcontrolling mother" (ibid., 86). The essential feature here is that the mother and the child are in a fusional relation: the mother uses the child as a cork to close her own feeling of emptiness, and thus includes her child in her own self-awareness, whereas the child is constantly called upon to fill up the void in her mother, and thus may develop an addictive relationship with her. Such an indistinction of mother and child is a feature in most of McDougall's cases.

In such cases, the deactivation of speech, the inability of speech to convey the meaning of the affects, may be explained by the insufficient distinction of the patient's self from that of the mother. In this way, the fact that speech tends to be "drained of its meaning, devitalized and bloodless" (ibid., 176), according to McDougall formulation, is tied to the fact that there are no two distinct persons, but rather a two-headed monster of mutual interdependence. If the child's main attention has been directed toward satisfying its mother's needs, it may tend to develop an addictive relationship with her, as in the case of Isaac A., and then it has little chance to start a normal individuation process. In such a situation, the child cannot experience its own feelings of legitimacy, to be truly its own, and consequently, will tend to experience them to be identical with those of the mother. Since verbal communication supposes the existence of two (relatively distinct) persons, the reach and power of verbal communication is largely deactivated in such cases. This in turn explains why the body takes over and surprises the subject with an unexpected disease.

The fact that the verbal expression of affects is blocked in such cases is therefore not the consequence of a blindness toward one's emotions; it is rather a consequence of the inability of the subject to recognize them as her own. As McDougall notes, there is a confusion about the limits of one's own body, and "doubts about one's right to possess an individual body" (ibid., 168). But since the subject does have a body in spite of her deeply rooted doubts about her right to have one, it is the body that takes over and expresses the meaning of the situation. Consequently, the transferential and counter transferential dynamics will have to pass through the body and to play out between the bodies of both the therapist and the patient.

How the Unconscious Works Between Bodies

Bodily gestures and attitudes have an expressive quality that is not reducible to symbolic content. It is also not imaginary in the Lacanian sense of the imaginary, that is, of a content dependent upon the more or less conscious fantasies of the desiring subject. The Lacanian perspective appears as a contrast here, and also in order to prefigure the next two chapters about Françoise Dolto's clinical thinking, and the way she understood the workings of language between bodies. In Lacan's conception, the unconscious unfolds in the symbolic realm, and the subject of the unconscious is a symbolic subject. The It is on the side of the symbolic, as is obvious in his famous diagram Z, which links the subject of the unconscious to the It (understood as the symbolic signifier).[7] From the perspective of psychosomatics, on the contrary, we are led to acknowledge an essential dimension of the unconscious directly stemming from the sentient body's own ability to express its traumatic history. Such a mode of signification is as elusive from the perspective of the subject as Lacan's Symbolic, but it doesn't have a symbolic structure; it is directly the body's way of metabolizing the impact of its affective history. The body's expressions are not sharable in the same way as verbal meanings; they are approachable in the clinical setting through a particular awareness for bodily phenomena, such as the organic evolution of the patient, the variations of excitations and protective shields in clinical work, and the process of reconstruction of the psychic structure (analogous to the development of the child).

In *The Psychosomatic Order*, Marty indeed compares the "maternal function" and the "psychotherapeutic function," and emphasizes their similarities as well as their differences (1980, 122–128). The main difference is the prevalence in many psychosomatic cases of death instincts leading potentially to a disorganization of the personality, whereas the alternating between life and death instincts is an essential component of the normal development of the child (124). But in spite of such differences, Marty goes on to describe "the maternal instinct" and uses it as a model for "medical intervention." In essence, the maternal function[8] consists in allowing the child to pass the different stages of her development, from the automation to the programming stage (see the section about *The Psychosomatic Unconscious* in the previous chapter). The maternal function, he writes, is expressed directly, "with no mental intermediary," and consists in "the affective unconscious appraisal of the desires and needs of the infant" (ibid., 37). In other words, the "maternal instinct" is a relational projective space, where the caring person "mentally elaborates" her affects, where she projects her previous affective relations onto the infant, and where all other "relational organizations, conscious or not" are implied. The needs and desires of the infant are directly linked to its development through the stages of automation and programming, and the caring person's (the mother's) function is to be attuned to the specific stage that the infant is going through, so as to be able to sense and perceive "the new signals allowing the recognition of the infant's desire to develop" (ibid., 126). This recognition leads to a progressive withdrawal of the caring person, allowing space for the child to regulate her needs and desires with increasing autonomy (ibid., 127), a process that requires a good deal of sensitivity and attunement. In this description, Marty is very close to the Winnicottian notion of the "sufficiently good mother." He then describes the "medical intervention" in analogy to the maternal function, as a way to "both intuitively and scientifically distribute and dose excitations and protective shields according to the observed automation and programming movements" (ibid., 128) of the patient. While the rhythm and pace of the automation-programming reconstruction in the psychosomatic patient is individual and is often unpredictable, it is essential that the therapist respects those rhythms, both from a somatic and a relational perspective (ibid., 132). "The appraisal of desires, that are clues of programming and of opening to evolution, implies a constant attention to what is said, and the often delicate tracking of symptoms" (ibid.). The delicate mission of the therapist-physician is to track the patient's possibilities of development by appraising her desires as clues for her readiness to go on to the next stage of psychosomatic constitution.

The unconscious between bodies resides in the meaningfulness of the bodies' expressions. Such expressions are not univocal, but rather unpredictable and mysterious, and they are not dependent on verbal, symbolic meanings. There is no determined meaning of a bodily symptom that can be deduced from its form, as Groddeck might have wished. The unconscious operates within the body and between bodies to favor a more balanced organization, or on the contrary, in the case of a traumatic situation, toward a pathologic disorganization that can lead to disease and death. The unconscious within the body refers to the body's own ecology, its capacity for adaptation, while the unconscious between the bodies refers to the way the body is in relation to other bodies, in other words, it refers to the desiring body. Both aspects are in reality closely intertwined, since the human body is itself a desiring being, and its ecological health is dependent on the way its desires are recognized, or not.

Transition

The intercorporeal space should be thought of in terms of a living and ever-changing relation, where the corporeal and the verbal are intertwined. But a more precise understanding of the body itself is required. In psychosomatics, the body is essentially the site where diseases appear mysteriously and express fundamental dimensions of a person's affective relations with the world; such diseases can be treated, prevented, or alleviated by a talking cure, allowing the patient to mentalize what the body expresses, provided there are no identifiable biomedical causes of the disease. But, with regard to questions concerning how the body itself should be understood, how it is structured, or how its structure is dependent upon its relations, psychosomatics is not the primary source. In French psychoanalysis, two other important figures have developed a genuine conception of the body that may be put in dialogue with the phenomenological conception of Merleau-Ponty: Françoise Dolto with the notion of the "body image" and Didier Anzieu with the notion of the "skin-Ego." The former emphasizes the way self-awareness is made possible by the recognition of the caring persons and the emergence of a stable image (both affective and cognitive) of one's own body; the second stresses the question of the boundary between self and other, and describes the skin and more generally the wrapping as the holding of one's own body. Their respective conceptions developed in parallel without interaction (one of the reasons being that Dolto remained close to Lacan, whereas Anzieu was very much opposed to Lacan and the Lacanians), and I will now argue in favor of their complementarity.

Notes

1. Cf. Freud 1961, 23: "We need feel no hesitation in finding a place for Groddeck's discovery in the structure of science. I propose to take it into account by calling the entity which starts out from the system Perception, and begins by being preconscious, the 'ego', and by following Groddeck in calling the other part of the mind, into which this entity extends and which behaves as though it were unconscious, the 'id'."
2. *Jouissance* is a central concept in Lacan's clinical thinking: the ordinary English translation of the term is "enjoyment," or "pleasure." This is precisely the ambiguity that Lacan plays with: jouissance is both a juridical term referring to the situation of absolute power upon a possessed good, and a term describing the climax of sexual pleasure. It means in essence a moment when the chain of signifiers is broken, when it is brought to a halt, and the drive is present with its whole intensity.
3. I leave aside the question of castration from the Lacanian perspective: the intervention of the Father allows the subject to distance itself from the immediate satisfaction of her drives, and thus "the psychosomatic phenomenon presents itself in the place of the name of the father, and transforms

itself into the name of the father" (Lippi 2008, 68). This phallocentric approach merited the critical inquiry that Lippi herself, together with Patrice Maniglier, undertook in their last book (Lippi and Maniglier 2023).

4. This book should be considered "the founding text of psychosomatics," according to Botella (2014).
5. These two books were first written and published in French, with the titles *Théâtres du Je* (Paris, Gallimard, 1982) and *Théâtres du corps* (Paris, Gallimard, 1989), respectively. The English versions are not direct translations, but were written by the author herself.
6. We don't know much about the personal histories of the patients in Pierre Marty's writings because his clinical descriptions are centered on investigative techniques and directed toward the drive structures of the patients rather than their personal history. This is very clear in *The Psychosomatic Investigation* (1963), as well as in the last part of the *Individual Movements of Life and Death* (Marty 1976).
7. One of the first occurrences of the diagram is in the introduction to the fourth Seminar (Lacan 2020, 4).
8. In Marty's generation, it was considered obvious that the mother enacted a particular sense of motherhood, prompting her to take care of her baby, just as Winnicott also wrote about the "good enough mother," and not the good enough parent. It is however quite easy to transfer this onto the caring function, not necessarily carried out by the mother herself. It is clear that Marty himself was well aware that the "maternal" function can be performed by other persons given his reference to the "mother or the function-performer" (126) in a passage in the same chapter.

References

Botella, César. 2014. De l'« attention flottante » de Freud à l'« expression associative » de Marty. Une nouvelle perspective dans la méthode psychanalytique. *Revue française de psychosomatique* 45:83–102.

Freud, Sigmund. 1961. The Ego and the Id [1923]. In *The Standard Edition of the Complete Psychological Works of Sigmund Freud*, ed. J. Strachey, vol. XIX, 3–66.

Groddeck, Georg. 1949. *The Book of the It* [1923]. New York: Vintage Books.

Lacan Jacques. 2020. *The Seminar of Jacques Lacan. Book IV*. The Object Relation. Edited by J.-A. Miller, translated by A. R. Price. Cambridge (UK), Medford (MA, USA), Polity Press.

Lippi, Silvia. 2008. L'«acte» psychosomatique. *La Clinique lacanienne* 13:59–75.

Lippi, Silvia, and Patrice Maniglier. 2023. *Sœurs. Pour une psychanalyse féministe*. Paris: Seuil.

Marty, Pierre. 1976. *Les mouvements individuels de vie et de mort*. Paris: Payot.

Marty, Pierre. 1980. *L'ordre psychosomatique*. Paris: Payot.
Marty, Pierre, and Michel de M'Uzan. 1963. La 'pensée opératoire'. *Revue Française de Psychanalyse* 67:345–356.
McDougall, Joyce. 1982. *Théâtres du je. Paris*, Gallimard.
McDougall, Joyce. 1985. *Theaters of the Mind. Illusion and Truth on the Psychoanalytic Stage*. New York: Basic Books.
McDougall, Joyce. 1989. *Theaters of the Body. A Psychosomatic Approach to Psychosomatic Illness*. New York: W. W. Norton & Co.
Storck, Timo. 2016. *Psychoanalyse und Psychosomatik. Die leiblichen Grundlagen der Psychodynamik*. Stuttgart: Kohlhammer.

CHAPTER 6

Self-Awareness and Desire: Body Image and the Continuity of the Self

My truth is a function composed of what is attributable to the other and to myself in his view of me.
Merleau-Ponty 2010, 163

The question in this chapter is how the subject develops a sense of a continuous self-awareness, spanning over several separate singular experiences, or how to get from the "minimal" or "synchronic" self to the "diachronic" self (from the mere "*for-me-ness*" of experience to the sensation of the experience being really *mine*), a very much debated question in contemporary phenomenology, through the works of Dan Zahavi, Shaun Gallagher, Thomas Fuchs, and others. The central premise here is that the sense of self-awareness arises from the experience of one's own body and its desires. From this premise it follows that the sense of self-awareness is dependent upon the way our bodies are in relation to other bodies. As we saw in the previous chapter, the psychotherapy of psychosomatic patients can only succeed if the therapist is aware of the rhythms and implicit responses of the body to her interventions; this is because the therapeutic relation plays with transferential dynamics, since every desiring move has

This chapter was first published as an article in the journal *PHI/PSY. Journal of Philosophy and Psychoanalysis*, vol. 2, n. 2, 2022, 21–37.

S. Kristensen, *The Intercorporeal Unconscious*,
https://doi.org/10.1007/978-3-032-22596-2_6

repercussions on one's own body. Thanks to Paul Schilder's concept of the body schema and Françoise Dolto's concept of the body image, we shall be able to deepen our understanding of such dynamics and their repercussions on the sense of the self. The intimate link between affectivity and the structure of subjectivity established through the clinical practice of both authors will then be linked to contemporary debates about minimal selfhood. The main claim is that in order to go from a thin momentary self, correlative only to the singular momentary experience, to a diachronic continuous self, something more than reflexivity of the self is needed: a desiring relation with caring others. In sum, to go from momentary self-awareness to continuous self-consciousness, and fully-fledged selfhood, desire for the presence of the other is required.

If self-awareness is a process ranging from a minimal structure of experience to a full self-consciousness crossing through time, there should be an explanation of the conditions of its development. The aim of this chapter is to show how desire plays its role in this process. In order to do this, I shall start with a commentary on the libidinous structure of the body schema in Paul Schilder's *Image and Appearance of the Human Body* (1950), noting *en passant* how this has been systematically ignored by contemporary phenomenology. I will then show the limits of Schilder's approach regarding the role of desire in the structure of the self, and confront this approach with the conceptions of Dolto, thereby introducing her key notion of the "unconscious body image," formed in order to account for the intertwining of the symbolic and the bodily. Since the notion of the body image plays a key role in her conception of the institution of selfhood, I shall provide a psychoanalytic response to the phenomenological question of self-awareness. Indeed, if an implicit desiring relation to the other can be proven necessary to the very emergence of a sense of selfhood, we shall have a strong argument in favor of the intercorporeal nature of the unconscious.

Self-Awareness Is Bodily and Affective

Even more fundamental than the above-mentioned premise that self-awareness is essentially awareness of one's *own* body, is the idea that self-awareness is a bodily phenomenon altogether; there is no self-awareness if there is no possibility of touching, of perceiving one's own body, *and of integrating this experience into an awareness of oneself as a totality*, and self-awareness is therefore temporally extended. The temporal extension of self-awareness is grounded in its embodied structure, as Jacob Rogozinski convincingly shows in his *The Ego and the Flesh* [*Le moi et la chair*]. Criticizing Merleau-Ponty's description of the chiasmus, and of the non-coincidence of the experience of touching and being touched, he states that "In wishing to base the chiasmus on a temporal simultaneity, Merleau-Ponty reversed the order of constitution: in truth, it is the carnal synthesis that founds the temporal synthesis; it is the carnal chiasmus that makes the synchrony of temporal fluxes possible" (Rogozinski 2006, 190; my translation). The fundamental phenomenon is the bodily self touching itself and experiencing the coincidence of the active and passive aspects.

Yet this already signals a tension, since the contemporary notion of minimal self-awareness is ultimately based on the approach of Michel Henry, who argued in his *Essence of Manifestation* that the self essentially consists in the reflexivity of each experience, or as Dan Zahavi terms it, "the most basic form of selfhood is the one constituted by the very self-manifestation of experience" (Zahavi 2014, 18). As Thomas Fuchs remarks, the basic self-affection in the sense of Henry and Zahavi consists in the "first-personal givenness of every experience," "any sensation, any perception or action directed towards an object implies a tacit self-awareness without requiring introspection" (Fuchs 2018, 33f). Henry is the ultimate reference for the position stating that the condition of possibility for the subject to be sensitive toward the world, to be intentional, is that it shows a reflexive structure. The passage in Henry that Zahavi refers to in this last quotation is the following: "That which senses itself, in such a way that it is not something which feels but the very fact of thus sensing itself, in such a way that its "something" is constituted as follows: the self-feeling of self, the experiencing of self, the being-affected by self, this is the Being and the possibility of the Self" (Henry 1973: 465). The intention in quoting Henry is to show that basic self-awareness from the phenomenological perspective is simply the necessary subjective correlate of a singular experience, with no temporal continuity. Henry grounds the "Being and the possibility of a Self" in the punctual self-affection of a singular experience. But this does not answer how we get from the idea of a self-affection of each experience taken singularly to the idea of a subject in the sense of a diachronic structure, a difficulty also obvious in Zahavi's argument. What allows us to get from punctual awareness of a singular act to a sense of selfhood extended in time, from the evident reflective aspect of any intentional act to a self-conscious subject? Zahavi himself recognizes the problem in his book *Self and Other*, when he writes that he doesn't believe that "The notion of an experiential self in and of itself will allow us to address or solve all relevant questions concerning diachronic persistency" (Zahavi 2014, 77). In other words, he argues in favor of a minimal temporal extension of the self of experience, but also recognizes that this is insufficient to ground a diachronic continuous self across its various experiences. In the contemporary literature on the minimal self, there is an assumption that reflexivity of a given experience gives rise by itself to a continuous self; but there is a difference between the self *of* a singular experience and the underlying subjectivity able to establish a continuity of various experiences as belonging to the same being.

A proposal by Marie Guillot, within the context of contemporary phenomenology, might help shine some conceptual light on this matter. Guillot refers mainly to the works of Shaun Gallagher, Kriegel and Zahavi, but her clarifications also seem useful in the psychoanalytical context: she proposes distinguishing three different features of minimal self-awareness, i.e. "for-me-ness," "me-ness," and "mine-ness," or in other words, the awareness of the experience, the awareness of the experiencer and the awareness of the experiencer *as* owner of the experience (Guillot 2017, 32). At first glance these three features seem equivalent, but Guillot argues that the latter two are not necessarily entailed by the first. She begins by distinguishing between three different modes of "subjective character," three different ways in which the subject appears: as "one of the two relata in the relation of phenomenal awareness […], as the one who is appeared to," as being aware of the appearance, and as the owner of the experience (ibid., 27). This distinction is founded on a position that she calls the "state-self-awareness view" that claims that every experience has an awareness of itself, which corresponds to the minimal self. In Guillot's terms, "The relation of awareness is taken up by the experience" (ibid., 29), and the result of this is that "for-me-ness" is the awareness of an experience that the subject has "just by virtue of having it" (ibid., 29). The difficulty is the passage from this simple "for-me-ness" of experience to a sense of being an ego with a continuity from one experience to the next, as she claims that "there is no straightforward implication [between each of them] to rely on," and the transition from one notion to another "should not be made without argument" (ibid., 34). To go from the former to the latter, one needs to add a premise, namely that "the self is identical with the experience" (ibid., 37). In other words, there is a layer of human subjectivity where an experience is given, but not yet in the form of ownership; there is something happening in my field of awareness, it is *for me* but my sense of me-ness in the sense of my being the same being from one experience to the other is not yet established. It is potentially there but not yet effective. Against this reasoning, Zahavi has argued that it would be contradictory to admit the subjectivity of experience and that the experience is essentially distinct from the self having it. He writes in reply to Guillot that "if self and experience are separated, it is unclear how self-experience would ever be possible, and how a certain object […] could ever be singled out and identified as myself" (Zahavi 2020, 645). As soon as the slightest sense of self appears, be it a mere phenomenal awareness of a singular experience, the phenomenal field has a center, and this center is the ecological dimension of the self. This argument presupposes that the momentary awareness of an experience is sufficient to ground a continuity toward a full sense of self. As he puts it, "There is certainly more to being a human self than being an experiential self, the claim is that the latter is a necessary precondition, not only for self-conscious thinking and first-person self-reference, but also for mature selfhood" (ibid., 9). But one might wonder whether it is also a sufficient condition. Even if we accept that the "me" in question in "for-me-ness" is already a self able to extend in time, the question remains how this extension happens, what are both the necessary and the sufficient conditions for it. In the 5th chapter of his book *Self and Other*, Zahavi actually defends an account of the continuity of the self in terms of "dimensions of mine-ness or for-me-ness" grounding the continuity across various singular experiences. He also claims that "our experience of the temporally extended and unified stream of consciousness is *eo ipso* an experience of the real diachronicity of the experiential self" (Zahavi 2014, 74). Once again, questions remain about the way this continuity is established; we need an "extra premise" to ground the continuity of the ego from one experience to another. This situation was formulated by the French philosopher Henri Maldiney when describing the psychotic subject as the "eternal under-lying" (*éternel sous-jacent*; Maldiney 1985, 68), and evoking a layer of subjectivity compatible with all sorts of experiences of alienation It is the "I" to whom it can happen to feel like someone else: when Artaud writes in the asylum "I am Lucifer," it is still Artaud writing "I," although this instance of selfhood is deeply alienated. Guillot herself takes as an example the phenomenon of depersonalization and describes it as "a condition in which the experience lacks both mine-ness and me-ness but retains for-me-ness" (Guillot 2017: 42). In short, the argument here is that subjectivity in the most minimal sense of the reflexivity of a momentary experience does not entail selfhood in the full sense.

Guillot's analysis is only conceptual and essentially deconstructive, leaving the question open about the emergence of the two more complex features of self-awareness, mine-ness and me-ness. But her distinctions allow us to question their emergence, to understand how the human self actually develops a full sense of self out of simply having an experience, how to move from the mere "for-me-ness" of experience to a full awareness of "me" having the experience and of the experience being "mine." What are the real conditions of possibility for an experience aware of itself to become the experience of a subject in the sense of an agent and owner of this very experience? I would like to argue that Dolto's notion of the unconscious body image provides an answer worthy of examination. In order for the child to stabilize its[1] sense of being a "me" and of having its "own" experiences, in order for it to acquire both the sense of agency and of ownership, we have to admit there being already a sentient being supported and shaped by the movements of desire. Only the fact of being supported by the desire of the Other allows the self to become the carrier of its experiences and thus to be aware of its experiences as its own.

The solution to this problem requires stepping beyond the boundaries of the classical phenomenological approach in order to understand that selfhood and the experience of otherness are simultaneously originary, and not thinkable separately. Self-affection necessitates an Other that touches the self, and thus a coordination of (at least tactile and visual) perception and motility in the self, in order to be able to recognize the identity of touching and being touched on the same part of the body. Indeed Merleau-Ponty's very conception of the sentient body is based on the arguments of Paul Schilder about the body schema, a notion comprising not only the sensorimotor aspect of the body's structure but also the libidinal and the social aspects. Schilder explicitly develops this notion within a psychoanalytical framework. Although Françoise Dolto's notion of the body image doesn't relate to Schilder's body schema, she also connects body and self through the unconscious. At stake is the experience of the desire of the other, of being carried by the affects and gestures of the caring other; Schilder's body schema has had a major influence on contemporary phenomenology, but this reception has completely left aside his psychoanalytical orientation, although it is the core of the positions defended by all those who refer to Merleau-Ponty's teachings. I propose to turn now to Schilder and his reception by Merleau-Ponty, and then to compare his conception to that of Dolto.

On the Reception of Paul Schilder's Body Schema

Paul Schilder's *Image and Appearance of the Human Body* is a fundamental work in the theory of the body-subject. Drawing from psychoanalytic conceptions, from neurological research, from gestalt psychology, as well as from his own practice as a neurologist, Schilder shows that the body cannot be reduced to its biological dimension, but that it is a being in action and perception, a relational being. The body is not only the organism, but is formed by its perceptual, motor, emotional, and libidinal movements, and those aspects make sense from a first-person perspective. As Emmanuel de Saint Aubert writes, Schilder studies "The spontaneity of our corporeal relation to space, things, and the other bodies – a spontaneity that can neither be reduced to the realm of the voluntary, the controlled, to explicit intentionality, nor to the realm of automatisms" (Saint Aubert 2013, 56).

The reception of Schilder's conception of the body is complex and multi-layered; he was widely read in psychoanalytical and psychosomatic circles in the 1970s and 1980s, but today the dominant reception began with Gallagher's works on the body schema in the 1990s, collated in his *How the Body Shapes the Mind* in 2005. Although he relies quite heavily on Schilder's approach, Gallagher refers to him as the origin of the "historical confusion" around the question of body schema and body image, noting that Schilder tends to use various terms interchangeably. But this reference to Schilder is actually as confused as Schilder's own use of the terms. Instead of asking why Schilder seems to conflate the terms (he actually uses indifferently "body image," "body schema," "postural model," along with a few other terms), he swiftly rejects Schilder's approach because it doesn't fit into his binary conception opposing motor capacities (*schemata*) and conscious perception (*image*). Gallagher refers briefly to Schilder in the following way: "According to Schilder this image or body schema is a conscious picture constructed not only from sensory impressions but also from unconscious libidinous elements and from socially formed images of the body." This approach, he concludes, "clearly shows a conflation of terms" (Gallagher 2005, 20), and goes on to say that Merleau-Ponty was more careful, simply because he consistently used the term "body schema" [*schéma corporel*] in order to refer to what Schilder was talking about under various terms. But in fact, Schilder did not lack rigor; he did not claim any form of dualistic conception, nor did he oppose motor capacity to conscious cognition.[2] On the contrary, he highlighted the intertwining of all levels of experience, from the physiological to the social, and was aiming to show, at all those stages, how these complex configurations actually work by discussing various clinical cases. Indeed, he uses the term "body schema" when he focuses on the articulation of perception and motility. This is what drew Merleau-Ponty's interest in the first place.

Indeed, if we wish to take seriously the embodiment of subjectivity, i.e. the sense of self-awareness as being essentially tied to the sensitivity of our body and its reflexivity, such a dualism will be difficult to uphold. Since it retains the implicit unconscious level of sensitivity below any possibility of awareness, it maintains a dualism between a purely material biological organism and a conscious mind operating upon the organism. Moreover, when Gallagher first classifies the "body affect" in the realm of the "image," and then proceeds to develop his argument only on the perceptual-cognitive level, leaving affectivity aside, it is difficult to reflect on self-awareness. Either the motor capacity is a kind of intentionality (this term meaning any kind of relation with the world by a subject, unconscious, preconscious, or conscious), and so should be conceived in a continuity with other forms of intentionality; or the motor capacity is thought of as a kind of automatic and purely organic dimension with no relation to intentional life, but then it would be completely useless in the perspective of a holistic enactive theory of self-awareness.

In contrast with Gallagher's recent reception, one can read in Merleau-Ponty's first lecture at the Collège de France on *The Sensible World and the World of Expression* given from January to June 1953, a precise and careful reading of Schilder's book. This reading is crucial for Merleau-Ponty's formulation of his concept of flesh and to his entire late attempt at an ontology of the tangible from the early 1950s to his death. In those preparatory notes, he does not take any serious notice of Schilder's terminological confusions. He adopts the term "*schéma corporel*" as a generic notion in order to describe the proper movement of the sentient body, of the body as subject, and as a body-in-relation. He thereby lays the foundation of his conception of the *Ineinander* of the flesh, of the constitutive intercorporeal relations in the realm of meaningful life. At stake in the lecture is the question of bodily movement as opposed to the movement of things in space, i.e. the nature of motility. But to explain the nature of motility implies explaining the relation of the subject to herself, and when he sums up Schilder's thoughts concerning the relation with the other, he states that "The total elucidation of the body schema shows not only the subject's relation to self, but also his or her relation with others: my body schema already includes presentations of myself that are only obtained from the point of view of others" (Merleau-Ponty 2020, 118). This echoes the summary at the end of the introduction to *The Image and Appearance of the Human Body*, where Schilder writes: "We have to expect strong emotions concerning our own body. We love it. We are narcissistic. The topography of the postural model of the body will be the basis of emotional attitudes toward the body. Our knowledge will be dependent on the erotic currents flowing through our body and will also influence them. The erotic zones will play a particular part in the postural model of the body" (Schilder 1950, 15). And a little further on in the text, "Experience of our body-image and experience of the bodies of others are closely interwoven with each other" (ibid., 16). Schilder argues in favor of the simultaneity of my awareness of my own body and the body of the other.

Emmanuel de Saint Aubert writes in this connection that the notion of desire constitutes "The very horizon of the conception of the body schema in Schilder and Merleau-Ponty" (Saint Aubert 2013: 53). The concept of "desire" here is the one in use in the psychoanalytical tradition, as opposed to the concept of need: before I outline the way Dolto understood the term, it will be enough to mention that it refers to the movement of a subject toward other subjects, a movement leaving enough space for their autonomy.[3] My claim, on this basis, will be that it is impossible to understand the very development of self-awareness without integrating the dimension of desire into the body schema. Schilder indeed shows many examples of persons being bodily affected by the (real or phantasmatic) presence of the Other. Affectivity here means not only emotional states of mind, but also the experience of being desired or repelled. It is both a pathic (being-desired) and an active (desiring) position for the subject.

Schilder's Intercorporeal Schema

As I mentioned, Schilder devotes the second part of his book to the "libidinous" and the third part to the "social" structure of the body schema. Merleau-Ponty only mentions this aspect of Schilder's work on one page of his 1953 lecture, but one can argue, as does Emmanuel de Saint Aubert, that it actually does play a fundamental role in the development of the concept of flesh in the course of the 1950s. The basic idea is that the body schema as such is always already structured by the real or virtual presence of others. Not only does the sensitive body incorporate the surrounding space (as Schilder shows for example in the first chapter of the third part of his book), the body schema also comprises the schema of others. As he comments on a clinical case of schizophrenia involving a 42-year-old woman at the Bellevue psychiatric institution in Switzerland:

> The patient connects itself with everybody. When a person breathes it's her breath. When a person moves his shoulders, she feels it in her shoulders. In other words, she takes the postural models of others into her own. Their spatial difference does not exist anymore. [...] The specific space round the body-image may either bring the objects nearer to the body or the body nearer to the objects. The emotional configuration determines the distances of objects from the body. (Schilder 1950: 216)

In this example the relation of body and world is shaped by the "emotional configuration," which means that it is the presence of others that forms this configuration and gives rise to the intertwining and confusion of one person's body schema and the other's body schema. In the same vein, Schilder writes a few lines further on about the libidinous aspect of the body that "Every separation between perceptive and emotional (libidinous) processes is artificial" (ibid., 216).

This is precisely the aspect that attracted the attention of Merleau-Ponty in the last phase of his work: the intertwining of body schemas is at the basis of the very notion of flesh, and of the idea that human subjectivity is originally tied to the subjectivities of others, that it is not a closed unity that only secondarily comes into relation with others. Schilder emphasizes strongly that the body schema of one person is in constant evolution and that it is able to incorporate the body schemas of others, and does so constantly. There is in Schilder's words a fundamental confusion of my body schema and the body schema of the other, and this is particularly manifest in the early stages of psychological development. He indeed takes up the Freudian idea of a primary narcissism, where "the child is interested only in himself and not at all in the outside world" (ibid., 119),[4] but immediately insists upon the originary givenness of one's own body and of the world. As he writes in the second part of the book: "The building-up of the postural model of the body takes place on the physiological level by continual contact with the outside world. On the libidinous level it is built up not only by the interest we ourselves have in our body, but also by the interest other persons show in the different parts of our body. They may show their interest through actions or merely through words and attitudes. But what persons around us do with their own bodies is also of enormous importance" (ibid., 137–8). As Saint Aubert explains, Schilder's body schema is actually from the onset an intercorporeal structure: he writes, "If desire is the animating principle of the body schema, then the whole esthesiological structure *is* a libidinal structure"; and a bit further on the same page, "Desire is not reducible to a psychic state, since it is a disposition of the body schema, a fundamental comportment of the flesh" (Saint Aubert 2013, 124).

This thesis is crucial to the development of Merleau-Ponty's conception of the flesh, where the sentient structures of the different living subjects are mirroring each other and constituting an infinitely complex web of resonances. This has also been emphasized by Gail Weiss in her book *Body Images* when she comments on Schilder: "Primary narcissism never involves an infant's unmediated relationship with her or his own body, but from the start implies a complex series of interactions between the infant and others in an on-going situation" (Weiss 1999, 16). The development of the infant's relation to oneself, her self-awareness of her own body necessitates the active loving participation of caring others, in order to allow the child to even perceive its own body parts as desirable.

As Saint Aubert notes, it is worthwhile reading Dolto in parallel to Schilder because they both developed an original conception of body schema and body image based on extensive clinical experience.[5] Dolto developed her thought about body image independently of Schilder's, but her approach tends very much in a similar direction, except for the clear distinction she sets between the unconscious body image and the physiological bodily schema, that I shall examine below. The reason why I propose discussing Dolto's thinking is first and foremost because she explicitly links the body image to the institution of the self, while describing it as the unconscious, relational, and desiring dimension of the body. She thereby develops a conception of the intercorporeal relation based on the resonance between the unconscious of several subjects. Schilder for his part does not consider the body image to be unconscious although he speaks about "organic repression," or even "organic unconscious," to explain cases of patients with a paralysis that they are unaware of, or in medical terms, hemiplegia with anosognosia or asomatognosia, resulting from localized brain damage. But this notion is not on the same level and not equivalent to the "psychic unconscious" in the Freudian sense, as it manifests "a blind urge, which is still more primitive than the unconscious wish." Although the organic and the psychic unconsciousses show an analogous structure, this merely reveals the "deep community between the psychic life and the organic function" (Schilder 1950, 33). Schilder emphasizes the fundamental libidinal relation that the human subject has with her body, analogous to the desiring relation with others. While I will address the question of the between "psychic life" and "organic function" in the next chapter, I shall emphasize for the present purpose that the body schema in Schilder does, both on the organic level and on the psychic level, imply a dimension of desire. But on the organic level, the relation with the other subject is not mentioned by Schilder. He presents the issue of the organic function as if there were a libidinal relation with one's own body and, in parallel with that relation, another relation with the body of the other. In other words, Schilder does not go beyond the statement of an analogy between the relation to the subject's own body and the relation to the other's body. This is because he approaches the pathologies of the body image mainly from a neurological perspective, as consecutive of neurological disorders or impairments, and then observes the consequences on the relation to oneself and with the other.

Dolto's Body Image

As I mentioned above, there is no evidence to suggest that Dolto knew anything about Schilder's work while she elaborated her conception of the unconscious body image. This is obvious since she introduces the notion through a sharp distinction between bodily schema and body image, the first being defined as a purely physiological structure, and the second as an unconscious representation, whereas Schilder tends to use the terms body schema and body image indifferently. Dolto's clinical and theoretical work entirely rests upon the conviction that affectivity is at the core of the infant's development, and more precisely that the desire of the other is essential to the development of the continuity of the self. She is the other figure in the history of clinical thinking to have operated with a (seemingly) dualistic notion of body image and body schema. Schilder used those terms interchangeably, emphasizing the multiple aspects of the notion, whereas Dolto draws a clear line between schema and image (in French: *schema corporel* and *image du corps*). In her most important book, *The Unconscious Body Image*, published in 1984 but written in the course of 20 years of clinical practice through the 1960s and 1970s, she aims to show that the little human being develops thanks to its being supported by the desire of its caring persons (the parents generally, and mostly the mother in her context). An English translation was published in 2023, thereby showing a new interest in her work in the English-speaking world. This driving force in the development of the child is distinct from the simple physiological infrastructure that allows the child to interpret and to metabolize others' desire for its existence. As she writes in the first pages, the bodily schema refers to the "integrity of the organism," it is a "factual reality" (Dolto 2023, 15), "in principle the same for all human individuals," it refers the body "in its current state and place with its immediate experience" and it "can be independent of language understood as a history of the subject's relations with others." In contrast, the body image is the "living synthesis of our emotional experiences," it is "the unconscious symbolic embodiment of the desiring subject," and a little further on in the text, it is the "unconscious memory of the whole relational experience" (ibid., 18–9). It is the body image that "allows us to enter into communication with others" (ibid., 22–23). The body schema, moreover, is the place where the drives take their source (since the drives have a physiological origin), whereas the body image is the "place of their representation" (ibid., 38).

I should emphasize that the distinction between body image and bodily schema in Dolto should not be understood as a distinction within the matter itself, as if the image would be understood as the soul and the schema as the organic body, in a Cartesian manner. Her framework should not be interpreted in ontological terms, but rather as a way of putting forward the importance of the symbolic realm in the development of the perceptual and relational capacities of humans, and as a way of showing the action of the relational dimension of existence upon organic life. As Gérard Guillerault shows, the distinction actually points to a duality of aspects of one and the same being. He writes: "It is not the body opposed to the soul. It is two levels of the body, of subjective corporeality that are distinguished (and at the same time are articulated)" (Guillerault 1996, 81). Concerning the notion of representation, in the context of Dolto's teachings, it refers to what is called intentionality in the phenomenological framework: to say that the "body image" is the place of representation of the drives doesn't mean that the representations are necessarily fully-fledged conscious meanings, only that conscious meanings are possible through the workings of the "body image." To sum up, the "bodily schema" refers to the factual reality of our physiological constitution, whereas the "body image" refers to the body as it is shaped by the individual affective history. The Argentinian-French psychoanalyst JD Nasio has an accurate formulation concerning Dolto: "The body is the royal path leading to the unconscious." He proposes the following definition of the unconscious body image:

> A diachronic set of affectively invested representations, impregnated by the interiorized presence of the other, and repeating itself in our history, constitutes the whole of the mental image of the body. (Nasio 2007, 11; my translation)

Although the "body image" has an essential link with the realm of representation, for the subject it does not depend upon the mastery of language; it is there long before the infant is able to say "I," even before the mirror stage where the infant makes the connection between her self-awareness and the image she sees in the mirror. As Guillerault explains, the notion of body image is conceived by Dolto to describe the situation of the self in a "relative indistinction of herself, a self still not constituted, unaccomplished, precarious, that mingles with the others, with the world, to the measure of what happens to its body" (Guillerault 1996, 29). The body image is called unconscious for the subject because it essentially depends upon the way the desire of others carries the subject toward its own realization. It is unconscious from the perspective of the child who is not able to verbalize its meaning. From this perspective, the notion of desire plays the central role. Desire in Dolto's terms is not primarily genital; the Freudian distinction between the genital and the sexual also holds up for Dolto. One of the most convenient ways of understanding the notion is to distinguish it from the concept of need. Need is correlated to satisfaction and does not imply any proximity of one human to another; Dolto often uses the example of parents obsessed with hygiene and who clean their babies as if they were dirty objects, never using the cleaning ritual as a space for the intersubjective relation with the child. If those parents remain entirely focused on the need for cleanliness when changing the nappy, the child is likely to develop disorders, because there will be a profound lack in the relationship; the space for the child to express herself will be lacking, since the primary addressee of the child's expressions remains inaccessible. What is at stake in the relation between the caring adult and the infant in such a situation is joy, pleasure, and playfulness much more than it is about cleanliness, and this joy, pleasure, and playfulness are ways of expressing a desire for the child to become who she is destined to become, to realize her potential as a free human being. To simplify the matter, one might say that desire is a question of the freedom of the other, in the sense that it does not project or require anything determined from the other; need on the contrary is pre-empting what it will find in the other, it is subordinated to the satisfaction of a particular demand. Desire is originally shaped by the structure of the body because of the way the child communicates with the caring other: through the erogenous zones, the cavities and orifices, via the motile capacities, etc. As Dolto said in a lecture at the *French society of philosophy* in 1973:

> A desire which is taken seriously only at indispensable moments of need, a desire repeatedly cancelled by an immediate bodily satisfaction, is in itself, neither in its tension nor in its enjoyment, "poetic." This is to say that it leaves no trace in the memory of the infant and becomes confused with need. Such a desire doesn't symbolize into a love for the mother. It remains articulated with the body in its most organic, vegetative and functional meaning. (…) On the contrary, the desire will be poetic if it opens up to a creative inventiveness with various mediations, with modulations of pleasure for oneself exchanged with pleasure of others, requested and given, which is the sublimation of desire into love. (Dolto 1981: 294; my translation)

The contrast of body schema and body image parallels the distinction between need and desire mentioned above; human beings are barred from any development if only their basic needs are met. They have to be supported by the desire of others to be with them, and thus the desire of others is crucial in order to anticipate the very possibility of the subject establishing and upholding a relation to itself. In this sense, Dolto writes that "For a human being, the body image is, at any moment, the immanent unconscious representation wherefrom arises his desire" (Dolto 2023, 26). The expression "immanent unconscious representation" refers not necessarily to verbal or conceptual representations, but rather to the form in which the subject experiences herself in relation to others, as both subject and object of desire. Dolto also describes the body image as the place where "relational experiences of need and desire, valuing and/or devaluing, which is to say narcissising and/or de-narcissising are inscribed" (ibid., 28). It designates the form of the body inasmuch as it makes sense in the affective desiring relation with the caring adult, or in other terms, it designates the body of the subject in a particular desired form by the other. Claude Boukobza formulates it as follows:

> The "image" of the body is [...] specific to each one of us and linked to the subject and the subject's history. It is the living synthesis of the emotional experiences of the desiring subject, the unconscious memory of lived relational experiences, both narcissistic and interrelational. The unconscious image of the body is always shaped in relation to the other—in particular to the caregiving mother—and refers the subject of desire to her *jouir*. (Boukobza 2018, 87)

This implies that the very condition of self-awareness depends on the presence and desire of the caring other, rendering the constitution of the self a precarious and fragile process, where we must take into account both the fact that loneliness (e.g. a depressive mother's inability to interact with her infant) creates pathologies of the self, and also that the others' attitudes can make the subjectivation process derail. Dolto's clinical work and reflections are from the beginning to the end concerned with this dangerous dialectic.

Desire and the Unification of the Self

Dolto's notion of body image raises fundamental questions about the unity of the self. In particular, if the self develops in and through its relation to others, does this mean that self-awareness arises through a primary experience of otherness? Is hetero-affection in this perspective the first phenomenon or is there still an originary self-affection allowing the infant to be aware of its own sensations independently of any presence of the other? Actually, much depends on the amount of substance we allow in the minimal self. Conflating the synchronic self of the singular experience (even with a tiny temporal extension) and the diachronic self transcending the singular experiences is not a satisfactory solution. Is the fetus or the new-born devoid of selfhood, or else which kind of selfhood does it "have" (or rather embody)? Is such minimal selfhood already a sort of proto-ego, or is it a self with no awareness of its being a self? The result of Dolto's clinical works is that there is a development in the forms and the depth of the self, but how does it start? Dolto suggests that there actually is already a sense of selfhood from the start, but she also claims that the desire of the caring adults is needed to let this primitive self develop into a real ego able to entertain productive relationships with others. How do these two dimensions articulate with each other? How does it work on the phenomenological level?

Dolto's main claim is that in order to build up a real and continuous awareness of oneself, a healthy selfhood, the human subject has to be supported by the speech and desire of others, particularly the caring others. Only if the little human has a space in the expectations of the caring others is she able to access an awareness of herself as a subject in the full sense, i.e. both as having experiences and as owner of those experiences in the course of time. This is why I claim that Dolto actually provides the "extra premises" that Guillot is calling for: the issue at stake in the explanation of her clinical practice is to describe the conditions under which the infant can experience permanent selfhood, and this is the function of the "basic image" as she introduces the four different "dynamic aspects" of the body image (the three others being the functional, the erogenous and the dynamic body image). Those four aspects play together and build up the singular body image of the subject at the different stages of affective growth. The basic image produces a "conviction of continuity," a "feeling of existing" [*sentiment d'exister*], or "sameness of being" [*mêmeté d'être*] (Dolto 2023, 36), and that precisely corresponds to what the phenomenologists call "self-awareness." This is what Dolto refers to as primary narcissism, understood as desire of living, or as she also writes, as "an experienced intuition of being-in-the-world" (ibid., 51), i.e. as the opposite of isolation, rather a capacity of each self, allowing an orientation toward the future of one's own life.[6] But this very orientation requires, as a condition of possibility, that others establish a context in which it makes sense for the infant to project itself toward its own future. Such a context is given when the caring others express their own desire for the existence of the infant, and act accordingly, which entail that they treat the infant as a desiring being themselves, and not merely as an object to be fed and cleaned. If this is absent, the infant will tend to regress into earlier stages of development showing that her relation with her own future is impaired.

Dolto brings an eloquent example from her clinical experience (Dolto 2023, 38–40): an 8- year-old boy, Gilles, presented to her for enuresis. He appears constantly in movement, his gaze never resting on anything more than a few seconds; today one would probably diagnose hyperactivity or attention deficit. Once the enuresis problem is solved after a small number of sessions, the therapist recounts a significant dialogue from the last session: the boy says to her "Now I can tell you where the danger is. – she answers – Because you are going to go away? – Yes." And he makes some new drawings to show her that all the angles that he drew in previous sessions were like arrows threatening him; at the beginning he sensed this danger everywhere, but now only in the analyst's office. Actually, as Dolto explains, this had to do with a series of traumatic events dating back to 1940, when the boy was 3 years old. The family fled to the South to escape the German invasion and had a car accident on the road; some days later, his father tried to teach him to swim in the Mediterranean and he nearly drowned and had to be reanimated. But the most significant event was a conversation in a phone box between his mother and his beloved uncle where his uncle told his sister that he was leaving for England in order to join General de Gaulle. The little boy was with his mother in the phone box and strongly felt her anxiety, but she kept silent about what happened. This created a strong link in his imaginary between "*Anglais*" [English], "*Angleterre*" [England] and "*angle*," about the English representing a specific danger, that he symbolized with the arrows threatening to run through him. Dolto also hears the pun "*angle-taire*," [angle-hush], i.e. the necessity of keeping silent in relation to England or the English. At this moment in his life, the three-year-old boy regressed toward his mother as the only protective person, since the two masculine figures had become threats, the father because of the drowning and the uncle because of his departure for England. Thus the enuresis was linked to attempts to master his phobia due to the emergent sexual drives, which were forbidden because of the threat represented by the masculine figures. In this case, there is a regression (manifested by the enuresis), and there is the silence toward the child, the hope that the child will not register what happens. The future dimension of the child's perspective is embodied by the sexual drives, but since they appear dangerous to him due to his father and uncle becoming threats, he cannot embrace this future and remains stuck in a previous affective structure. Hence the arrows sent by the *Anglais*, and all the angles threatening him, leading him to be constantly watchful. The body image is involved here in the following manner: the way the child refers to himself unconsciously is shaped by the atmosphere of threat and the failure of the mother to verbalize it (and thus put it at a distance). This atmosphere constrains his development possibilities, and he subsequently falls back into a previous stage, where he feels more secure.

In the progressive setting up of the body images in the course of the infant's growth, Dolto cannot insist enough on the role of castration, i.e. on the gesture of the caring others by which the infant sees her desire recognized and at the same time barred. The term "castration" is directly taken from the Freudian corpus. It must be understood as an extension and transformation of sexuality, i.e. as a metaphor for the impediment of immediate satisfaction. In this way, the infant can become aware of itself and bridge the gap between the basic for-me-ness of each sensory experience, and acquire a sense of continuity of the self. As Dolto puts it, "It is the mother who, by her speech, talks to her child about what he wants but that she does not give him, mediating for him the absence of an object or the non-satisfaction of a demand for partial pleasure, while validating, through the very fact that she talks about it, this desire for the satisfaction which is being denied—a situation with which she sympathizes" (Dolto 2023, 45). Her main concern is to show how and under which conditions the human subject elaborates her successive body images, and thus comes to structure her relation to oneself. This is the role of the successive castrations allowing the child to progressively acquire the body images corresponding to its physiological and psychological growth; but the initial move is essential, and it consists in transporting the infant from one experience to another while denying her the immediate satisfaction of every one of her demands.

Dolto's Minimal Desiring Selfhood and Symboligenic Castrations

It appears that Dolto actually runs exactly counter to the pretended mainstream Freudian tradition in which the infant is considered shut off from the social world and locked in a kind of primary narcissism, or as Philippe Rochat puts it, in this primary "state of confusion," "it is as if there is a barrier between young infants and their environment" (Rochat 2001: 32). But this only describes one particular interpretation of Freud; as Laplanche and Pontalis note, the issue is quite unclear in Freud's writings.[7] Already Schilder explicitly contradicts this view in the first chapter of the second part of his book, where he first expresses his doubts about the notion of the death drive and then, after having explained the Freudian conceptions, proceeds to deconstruct the very idea of a primary narcissism, that he calls the "narcissistic libido": "We are in a world and objects are part of this world" (Schilder 1950, 122), he states, and then affirms that given the intentionality of drives, there are no pure drives without representations ("instinctual representative" in the Freudian vocabulary), even drives must be directed toward something in the world.[8] The consistent claim Schilder makes is that since "our own body can exist only as a part of the world" (ibid.), there is no essential difference between the perception of one's own body and the perception of an object in the world. The body schema of the subject is in constant exchange with the other subjects and objects in the world, and is structured analogously to them. Consequently, the Freudian idea of primary narcissism, a state where the newborn child "is interested only in himself and not at all in the outside world" (ibid., 119), is senseless. Indeed, as he writes, "the newborn child has a world, and probably even the embryo has" (ibid., 123). The primary narcissism is thus the fundamental relation of the subject with his own body schema, and since every part of the body is invested with desire, the other is always already present in the primary self-awareness of the subject. In Schilder's terms, "In the build-up of the schema of the body, there will be a continual interaction between ego tendencies and libidinal tendencies" (ibid., 123f).

Similarly, Dolto's conception of primary narcissism is not of a state where the infant is locked in a private world, solely in relation to its own body. She introduces the notion of "primary" or "fundamental" narcissism, preceding the "primordial" narcissism of Freud, a stage similar to Schilder's "narcissistic libido": This stage is consecutive to the very first separation of the small child's body from the mother, i.e. birth. "In terms of joy and anxiety that accompany the birth of the child, it constitutes a founding element in his relationship with the desire of the others" (Dolto 2023, 63).

As I explained above, Dolto sees narcissism as equal to the desire of living, in a sense to the life drive, which entails the necessity of being supported by others. And this being supported by the others' desire implies the use of language, the speech addressed to the infant in order to signify the future milieu in which the infant will have to take its place. Indeed, language structures the intersubjective space where human interactions take place, so the very gesture of speaking to the infant is tantamount to a gesture pulling it toward its own future. But the use of language with the infant is not only in relation to the future; Dolto very often emphasizes the fact that the infant understands the words addressed to it. She does not thereby claim that the infant literally understands the verbal content of a discourse, but rather that it understands that a speech is addressed to it, and that the adult has understood the infant. By explaining situations to the child no matter how young, the caring person shows that the feelings and desires of the child have their place, that they might be recognized. This is precisely what opens up a sense of the future in the child and allows it to pass the different stages of affective development. What Dolto calls the "symboligenic castration" is a condition of accessing "me-ness": it is the responsibility of the caring adult to speak to the infant in order to awaken its sense of being a distinct subject from the other, of being "me."

Without castration, there is no possibility for the child to experience the permanence of itself and to relate all immediate experiences to a permanent instance called by a name. Call out to the child and leave it free to respond, enjoying the surprises of the relationship. This claim by Dolto is supported by the research of the last 30 years into infant development. One thinks of the highly influential works of Colwyn Trevarthen, who wrote that "Infant survival and development depends on communication with a caregiver to service the baby's need for an emotional *attachment*, but also to maintain and develop an intimate emotionally expressed *companionship* in changing purposes and conscious experiences" (Trevarthen and Aitken 2001, 7). What Dolto additionally brings to the debate is the specific effect of speech addressed to the infant, or the absence thereof.

Indeed, the name of the child is a crucial issue in order to build up the permanence of its me-ness and mine-ness, as she recounts in a clinical case of a 7-year-old boy who was abandoned by his parents and then lived in an infant care home until he was adopted at the age of 11 months (Dolto 1984: 46–49). His name is Frédéric; he seems retarded, shows psychotic autistic traits, and even after his state has improved, he still seems unable to write any other letter than "A." His mother then reveals that his birth name before he was adopted was Armand, but when the therapist tells him this in a session in her normal voice it produces no effect; the boy simply continues to draw as if nothing has happened. After a while, Dolto has another idea: she begins to scream his original name as if he were not there, as if Armand was someone both of them would have to search for. This strange process imitates the way his name was spoken out loud by the nurses at the care home when he was a baby, and only when he looks her way and their gazes cross each other, does a new intensity light up in the little boy. It is thus not only the name itself, but also the prosody and the way it is addressed to the child. Dolto makes the following comment:

> This enormous significance [*prégnance*] of the most archaic phonemes of which a given name is the typical example, shows that the body image is the structural trace of a human being's emotional history. It is the unconscious place [...] whence every expression of the subject is elaborated: the place where inter-human language-based feelings are received and given out. The durability of its cohesion is drawn from the attention and the style of love lavished on the child. (Dolto 2023, 35)

It is the form of the affective relations carrying the child through its own history, and from the phenomenological perspective, it is passively present, implicitly conditioning the possibility of an appropriation of the child's history. According to Dolto, the successive castrations already begin at birth with what she calls the umbilical castration. Birth is evidently a fundamental and traumatic event, but it is essentially the event when the human subject hears her name, or at least the words "it's a boy" or "it's a girl," with more or less joy. "Language symbolizes the castration of birth, which we call umbilical castration" (Dolto 2023, 65) she writes, meaning that the affective mode by which the new-born was welcomed by the speech of her parents remains as the first mode of being in the world in her subsequent life. To be called by one's name is the event which best represents the passage from the mere for-me-ness of experience to a sense of the continuity of the self. The proper name contains the potential of a future called for to be one's own, a promise of continuity and appropriation. However, in order to better understand the intertwining of speech and corporeality according to Dolto, we have to examine more closely the very notion of body image in its relation to somatic phenomena, and the role of speech in relation to other expressive features of subjective life. This remains to be dealt with in the next chapter.

The (at least) implicit presence of the other from the phase of primary narcissism, right from the symbolic separation represented by the event of birth itself, testifies to the fact that the unconscious is relational from the outset. Indeed, the umbilical castration is already invested with libidinal vibrations, with the "joy and anxiety that accompany the birth of the child" (ibid., 63). Moreover, as she writes, "Along with his respiration and the scream that he hears coming from himself, the coming into play of olfaction (the maternal smell) is unconsciously the first impact for the newborn of a specific marker of his relationship with his mother" (ibid.). This first event, necessary for the progressive constitution of an independent self, is both traumatic and non-verbal, and therefore belongs to the unconscious. It becomes pathological if it not accompanied with words, and thereby is allowed to escape the unconscious.

Transition

Both Schilder and Dolto claim that the affective attitudes of the others are essential to the unity and the continuity of the self. In Dolto, this amounts to the idea that the desire of the caring others allows the inchoative self of the infant to experience a real continuity in its own being. If this is so, it is a solid way to articulate the phenomenological approach affirming the essential reflexivity of subjective life as such and the psychoanalytical experience affirming the necessity of the presence of others in order to become a self (or one-self). It is also, and maybe foremost in the context of this book, a way of integrating the question of the unconscious into the argument, and show that the unconscious should be conceived as an intercorporeal phenomenon. But the continuity between the organic body and the symbolic space of the social world remains to be described and explained. How do the symbolic and the bodily act upon each other?

Notes

1. In the chapters about Dolto's conceptions, I chose to use the masculine pronoun to refer to the child or the infant, as does Dolto herself in her writings in French. The main reason is that it prevents any confusion with Dolto in the text.
2. As Emmanuel de Saint Aubert remarks, Shaun Gallagher "seems to have stopped at the first lines" of the introduction to Schilder's book (cf. Saint Aubert 2013, 55). He goes on to show that Merleau-Ponty's reception of Schilder is much more nuanced than Gallagher's dichotomy between implicit body schema and conscious body image.
3. An effective presentation of this notion of desire can be found in Barbaras 2005.
4. This reading of Freud's concept of narcissism is biased; Schilder does not quote any Freudian text; on this question, see Laplanche and Pontalis 1973.
5. Cf. Saint Aubert 2013: 59–75.
6. Dolto's conception thus contrasts with Schilder's reception of Freud. Of course, this capacity of the self is dependent upon others in terms of development, or impairment.
7. Cf. the relevant article in Laplanche and Pontalis' *Language of Psycho-Analysis* (1973), 337–8.
8. Here, the Freudian vocabulary that both Dolto and Schilder use can be misleading. The term "representation" suggests a conscious mental content, which is contradictory with its being unconscious. This is why I reformulate it in terms of "something in the world," a more vague and therefore rigorous way of expressing the matter.

References

Barbaras, Renaud. 2005. *Desire and Distance: Introduction to a Phenomenology of Perception* [1999]. Translated by P. B. Millan. Stanford: Stanford University Press.

Boukobza, Claude. 2018. The Unconscious Image of the Body. In *Theory and Practice in Child Psychoanalysis. An Introduction to the Work of Françoise Dolto.* Ed. by G. Hall, F. Hivernel and S. Morgan (2009). London, Routledge, 85–100.

de Saint Aubert, Emmanuel. 2013. *Être et chair. I. L'habilitation ontologique de la chair*. Paris: Vrin.

Dolto, Françoise. 1973. *Dominique: Analysis of an Adolescent*. Translated by I. Kats. New York: Outbridge & Lazard.

Dolto, Françoise. 1981. *Au jeu du désir. Essais cliniques*. Paris: Seuil.

Dolto, Françoise. 2023. *The Unconscious Body Image* [1984]. Translated by S. Bailly. London: Routledge.

Fuchs, Thomas. 2018. *Ecology of the Brain. The Phenomenology and Biology of the Embodied Mind*. Oxford: Oxford University Press.

Gallagher, Shaun. 2005. *How the Body Shapes the Mind*. Oxford: Oxford University Press.

Guillerault, Gérard. 1996. *Les Deux Corps du Moi. Schéma corporel et image du corps en psychanalyse*. Paris: Gallimard.

Guillot, Marie. 2017. *I, Me, Mine*: On a Confusion Concerning the Subjective Character of Experience. *Review of Philosophy and Psychology* 8:23–53.

Henry, Michel. 1973. The Essence of Manifestation. Translated by G. Etzkorn. The Hague, Martinus Nijhoff.

Laplanche, Jean, and Jean-Bertrand Pontalis. 1973. *The Language of Psycho-Analysis*. London: Karnac Books.

Maldiney, Henri. 1985. Art et existence. Paris, Klincksieck.

Merleau-Ponty Maurice. 2010. *Institution and Passivity: Course Notes From the Collège de France (1954–55)*. Translated by L. Lawlor and H. Massey. Evanston, IL: Northwestern University Press. Original edition, 2003.

Merleau-Ponty, Maurice. 2020. The Sensible World and the World of Expression. Course Notes from the Collège de France, 1953 [2011]. Trans. B. Smith. Evanston (IL): Northwestern University Press.

Nasio, J.-D. 2007. *Mon corps et ses images. Le corps est la voie royale qui mène à l'inconscient*. Paris: Payot.

Rochat, Philippe. 2001. *The Infant's World*. Cambridge MA/London: Harvard University Press.

Rogozinski, Jacob. 2006. Le Moi et la chair. Paris, Editions du Cerf.

Schilder, Paul. 1950. *The Image and Appearance of the Human Body. Studies in the Constructive Energies of the Psyche*. London: International Universities Press.

Trevarthen, C., and K. J. Aitken. 2001. Infant Intersubjectivity: Research, Theory, and Clinical Applications. *Journal of Child Psychology and Psychiatry* 42:3–48.

Weiss, Gail. 1999. *Body Images. Embodiment and Intercorporeality*. London: Routledge.

Zahavi, Dan. 2014. *Self and Other. Exploring Subjectivity, Empathy, and Shame*. Oxford: Oxford University Press.

Zahavi, Dan. 2020. *Consciousness and selfhood: Getting clearer on for-me-ness and mineness*." In U. Kriegel (ed.): The Oxford Handbook of the Philosophy of Consciousness. Oxford: Oxford University Press, 635–653.

CHAPTER 7

The Unconscious Body Image and the Symbolic

The unconscious = Freudian poetry, the premonition of the future in the present, the pre-formation of the present in the past: the echo of others in me, of me in others, of the wish in the reality. (Merleau-Ponty 2010, 204)

In the previous chapter, I supported the position of Dolto and Schilder that the other is always already present at the very core of minimal self-awareness, and that the unconscious therefore should be considered first and foremost a relational space. The question that follows is how this space is structured with regard to the relation between the organic and the symbolic. Is there an unconscious *of* the body, and how might this relate to the symbolic realm? Both Schilder and Dolto anchor their clinical reflections within the psychoanalytical tradition and refer to Freud's teachings, but neither of them had the project of interpreting the master's doctrine, as did for example Lacan. They both noticed that certain phenomena concerning the body could be explained by mechanisms described by Freud. The very meaning of the concept 'unconscious' therefore remains to be explained, particularly as a link between the organic and the symbolic.

The other highly influential psychoanalyst whose conception of the unconscious is based on language is indeed Lacan; he refers the unconscious to the symbolic, and considers it to belong to the signifying structures of interhuman relations. In *Seminar* 11, on the *Four Fundamental*

S. Kristensen, *The Intercorporeal Unconscious*,
https://doi.org/10.1007/978-3-032-22596-2_7

Concepts of Psychoanalysis, he starts with the concept of the unconscious and formulates the famous claim that the unconscious is "structured like a language," going on to affirm that linguistics and its model, a "combinatory operation, functioning spontaneously," "gives its status to the unconscious." (Lacan 1981, 20–1) He then remarks that this concept differs from the Freudian concept of the unconscious by making it "definable, accessible and objectifiable" (ibid.). But at the same time, he also emphasizes that the unconscious is always also a gap, impediment, failure, split, implying a dimension of loss (ibid., 25), and he defines it as "the unrealized" (ibid., 30). Since desire, contrary to the experience of need, is by definition the experience of a satisfaction simply igniting a new desire, of the very satisfaction opening up a gap within the subject, the subject of the unconscious is the subject of desire. The subject is thus called upon to bear this non-satisfaction and experience a state of tension characterizing his or her very life as a relational being. Dolto's notion of the subject of the unconscious is close to Lacan's conception, inasmuch as it is conceived as emerging from, and created by speech. From the outset, even when still in the womb, the human subject is a subject of language. However, Dolto's conception of language differs from Lacan's concerning her interpretation of the very notion of language, which will be the central topic of this chapter.

Schilder, for his part, was never close to Freud and didn't himself undergo analysis. His uses of Freudian concepts are based on his neurological and psychiatric experience and were never part of a collective project of founding a new discipline. And as Arzel-Nadal explains in her book about the concept of the body image, Dolto has nothing to do with the structural turn in the theory of psychoanalysis in the French context. It is not linked to the logical and signifying articulations, but rather it comes to represent the "relation of narcissism and language," (Arzel-Nadal 2006, 138) or in other words, the question of the emotions and their translation. My comment on their respective conceptions of the unconscious should therefore be read regardless of their being a part of the Freudian project, of a more or less orthodox psychoanalytical theory. The issue at stake here is the question of the relation between the body and the symbolic, between the organic and the interhuman relational domain. The hypothesis is that the unconscious should be defined as the interhuman space of desiring sensitivity; the reason why Dolto describes the body image as unconscious by definition is precisely that the unconscious is the medium of the affective relation. But she also uses the term 'bodily schema' for the exclusively organic, or physiological dimension of the body, suggesting a rather dualistic conception of the body and the unconscious. The purpose of the following pages is to explain how this holds up, and in what exact sense the body image can be dubbed 'unconscious'. Schilder again plays a central role in this chapter because his approach, as a neurologist, remains closely tied to the organic dimension of the body, to which he sought to apply Freudian concepts. But also because I suspect that Dolto's use of the term bodily schema comes from Schilder, although she never quotes him and uses it in contrast to the body image (whereas both expressions are rather synonymous in Schilder). Yet if we wish to make sense of a theory of the unconscious as "feeling or sensing itself," we have to maintain the link with the organic body. Let us therefore firstly examine how Schilder applies the Freudian notion of the unconscious to the body and how he places the organic and the symbolic in relation with one another.

Organic Repression and the Psychic Unconscious

In *The Image and Appearance of the Human Body*, Schilder proposes to apply Freudian concepts in order to speak of bodily phenomena such as cases of hemiplegia resulting from cortical lesions, cases similar to the Wernicke-Korsakoff syndrome where patients show a short-term amnesia and for example forget that they cannot feel anything on one side of their body. Such patients have not only lost sensitivity on one side, they also tend to ignore this very fact, or as Schilder puts it, "hemiplegics that behave as if they were not paralyzed" (Schilder 1950, 29), consistently forgetting about their impairment. Questioning what makes these patients neglect their paralyses, "What makes them disown one half of their bodies?" (ibid., 31), Schilder then mentions a "defense mechanism on an organic basis" (ibid., 32) after having rejected the Freudian notion of the unconscious wish because "we should be dealing with cases of superimposed hysteria" (ibid., 31). Phenomena of ignoring one body part or of forgetting on the short term that one is paralyzed are nevertheless "somewhat akin to (…) the unconscious wish" (ibid., 32), for which he proposes the notion of 'organic repression.' Schilder emphasizes that organic repression is located on the somatic level, but "repeats what is going on in other repressions in the so-called purely psychic level" (ibid.). In the article from 1925 about the psychology of brain injured persons, to which he refers in his book (in the footnote, 32), he already used the Freudian term '*Verdrängung*,' which is ordinarily translated as 'repression' in the psychoanalytic context. In this article, he formulates the hypothesis that in cases of brain injury, "amnesia maybe is a product of the tendencies to repression." (Schilder and Hartmann 1925, 293) There is a hesitation in the text about the distinction between the psychic and the corporeal, between the unconscious wish and the organic repression. But then Schilder goes on to point out not only an analogy, but also a "deep community" between the two aspects:

> This phenomenon is based on the deep community between the psychic life and the organic function. Every change in the organic function is liable to bring forth with it psychic mechanisms which are akin to this organic function. And this reflection into the psychic sphere will help us to understand the essence of the organic function. (Schilder 1950, 33)

This "deep community" involves not only an analogy between organic and psychic processes, but also an intertwining of the two. "The focal organic attitude carries with it unconscious wishes and even conscious ones," (ibid.) he writes, and a correspondence between the "unconscious wish" and the "primitive urge" is to be observed for example in patients with epilepsy since their "urges often carry a specific psychosexual coloring" (ibid.). Schilder points out four parallel "attitudes" or levels, from the point of view of the sentient subject: the focal (or localized) organic attitude, the general organic attitude (pertaining to the whole body), the unconscious psychosexual attitude, and the conscious wish. All four levels show similar dynamic structures, and are "closely interwoven with each other" (ibid., 34) Cases of non-perception of one part of the body are key to explore such situations of interweaving of psychic and somatic mechanisms of repression. "The conscious wish brings forth similar attitudes out of the unconscious" (ibid.). In short, Schilder doesn't separate organic processes from psychic processes; he notices similar defense mechanisms on both sides and also an intertwining of the different attitudes. The organic plays on the psychic, and vice-versa, in many cases, for example in cases of epileptic hypermotility. Schilder sums the issue up in the section which addresses the sociology of the body image, writing that the postural image of the body, "although it is primarily an experience of the senses, provokes attitudes of an emotional type" (ibid., 226).

Through this reading of Schilder's reflections about the different levels of the unconscious, from "organic repression" to the "unconscious wish," it appears that the organic level is not only analogous to the psychic level, but one side tends to influence the other. In the conclusion of *The Image and Appearance*, he even writes quite clearly about this intertwining:

> The physiological structure of the phantom and of the postural model of the body generally is itself very similar to the psychological structures which are concerned with the body as a whole and its integrity. Psychological factors determine the final shape of the phantom and also the final shape of the non-perception of parts of the body. (ibid., 293)

In sum, there is indeed, according to Schilder, a strong structural analogy between organic repression (when the person ignores one side of his/her body after a brain injury, also known as hemineglect) and the psychic unconscious (when the person lives as if an affective trauma never happened in his/her history, also known as neurosis). But Schilder admits that there is an intertwining between the two, and in both ways: for example, hemineglect often carries with it specific psychosexual attitudes, and conversely, certain unconscious wishes may carry with them specific organic repressions, as seems to be the case in allochiria or achiria (when the person ignores his/her hand or confuses the left with the right hand). This is where Schilder touches upon a meaningful structure of the sentient body, noting that the left side of the body, in particular the upper limbs, plays a special role in the subject's affective space.

Alternatively, as we saw in the last chapter, Dolto builds a sharp distinction between bodily schema [*schéma corporel*] and body image [*image du corps*], where the first is considered purely physiological, and the second essentially unconscious. Dolto does not apply the unconscious to the bodily schema, but only to the body image, that she describes as "eminently unconscious," whereas the bodily schema can be "partly unconscious, but also preconscious and conscious" (Dolto 2023, 18), as we saw in the previous chapter. But she also, like Schilder, concedes that there is an intertwining and a mutual influence between the two, albeit not with reference to the same clinical examples, since she draws on her own clinical experience with children. "The bodily schema cross-develops with the body image, which is attached to the erogenous excremental gift and to the pleasure of using his motor muscular strength." (Dolto 2023, 75) Dolto's dualism is neither philosophical nor ontological; rather, the bodily schema is the motor structure of the body removed from any affective dimension. Dolto explains that children with a disabled bodily schema can develop a perfectly healthy relation to their own body provided their parents have accepted their disability and have shown them enough love and confidence (ibid., 16f). If, on the contrary, the child's body has been neglected, the disability ignored or has provoked the parents' disgust, then the child's body image may also show signs of disability. This is why it is safe to state that Dolto's concept of the bodily schema simply refers to the purely conceptual idea of a body with no affective projection, a purely biological organism independent of any relation, whereas the body image is deemed unconscious precisely because it is the result of the affective relations within which the child is embedded.

Just as Schilder introduces the notion of organic repression only to note that it is structured analogously to the unconscious wish, Dolto points out that the bodily schema does not actually exist on its own; as the "place source of the drives", as the place of need, the bodily schema can only be experienced "when nobody is there, when there is a new sensory experience in the absence of any human witness" (ibid., 28). Dolto thus calls the experience "theoretical" and immediately in practice "covered by the memory of an already known symbolic relationship" (ibid.). Here, the otherwise excellent translation of Dolto's book contains an error: Dolto writes that the experience of the body schema is "covered" [*recouverte*] by a symbolic relationship, and not "recovered," in the sense of a recovery. It should be understood that there is no experience of the bodily schema as such, since it is immediately covered by the body image and its symbolic dimension, even in the earliest stages of the infant's development. In the subsequent example of a child constantly bumping himself against a table, Dolto aims to show that without the human witness superimposing words on the child's experience, with the bodily schema left on its own (so to speak), it would have "dramatic effects" (ibid., 29) on his health. It is indeed significant that Dolto only speaks about the bodily schema in order to distinguish it from the body image in the first chapter, and entirely stops talking about it in the rest of her book. The body according to Dolto is a desiring being, since desire is constantly renewing itself, embedded in relationships, and aims towards meaningful goals. The bodily schema is on the level of purely organic needs, defined as being entirely alien to any kind of human relationship. Yet any expression of need is aimed at some-one (present or absent in the moment) and is thus always already of the order of desire. The total absence of speech and relationships cannot be a real experience; rather, it is because every tangible experience is always already meaningful and thus calls upon language, or to use Lacan's famous phrase, because it is "structured like a language." In the following, I shall present Dolto's approach to this claim, thereby showing that her notion of language is by no means reduced to *verbal* language.

In the previous chapter, Dolto's concept of the unconscious body image was introduced in relation to the concept of the body schema; in the following, the issue is to situate it in relation to the symbolic realm, and from there to describe how it supports the corporeal dimension. The fundamental reason why Dolto chose the very term "body image" is convincingly explained by Gérard Guillerault in his book *Comprendre Dolto* (2008). Dolto indeed chose two terms quite alien to the dominant mood of her time, and in particular contrary to the teachings of her close friend Jacques Lacan, because she was convinced that the body was essential in understanding the constitution of the human psyche and because she needed an access to the realm in the human psychic life where the bodily and the symbolic are not yet separate, indeed the "archaic time of the infant," as Guillerault puts it (2008, 94s).

Speech and Desire

Dolto's argument emphasizes the power of the spoken word: Dolto is known for her emphasis on the power of speech; she repeated many times that the infant understands every word you say to him/her long before s/he starts to speak by him or herself. In a book with the title *Everything is Language*, a written version of a talk given to social workers, psychologists and physicians in 1984, she replies to a person asking how she undertakes psychoanalysis with children who have yet to acquire language: "They don't have verbal language to express themselves, but they have language." (Dolto 1994, 197) She then goes on to define language separately from its verbal dimension, as the space of interhuman communication, from one unconscious to another. Responding to another question, she says: "The way you look, is language. It's an exchange of interpsychic language, the gaze." (ibid., 198) I emphasize this aspect of Dolto's thinking because it is does explain the priority of the body image and the fragility of her notion of bodily schema.

In her talk at the French society of philosophy in 1972, she undertakes a profound and precise explanation of the symbolic dimension from the point of view of the fetus and the infant's experience. She starts with the claim that "the symbolic function is grounding the human being" because it is the condition of possibility of any interhuman relation. She goes on: "The symbolic function, linked to memory, which is not unique to the human species, means that any satisfaction or dissatisfaction for his flesh has language value for the baby human." (Dolto 1981, 270) I will come back in the last chapter to the little phrase in the middle, where Dolto affirms that it is not unique to the human species. At this moment, the important aspect in this passage is the link made by memory between the symbolic function and the satisfaction or dissatisfaction experienced by the baby for his "flesh." Dolto means any experience of contentment or frustration signified by bodily, clearly non-verbal, sensations. Such sensations, inasmuch as they are stabilized by the memory of certain behavioral patterns from the side of the caring persons, allow the infant to build a sense of self. In this sense, Dolto is able to claim that "language is present in fetal life, at least in hearing, with sensations of well-being and discomfort." (ibid.) She locates the origin of the symbolic in this nexus of sensations, memory of those sensations in relation to certain gestures or patterns from the side of the caring persons, and the presence of those caring persons. Since well-being and discomfort are correlated with the presence of caring persons, and with their particular ways of behaving, with their smell, the sound of their steps, the tone of their voice, etc., those very sensations acquire a "language value," and therefore constitute the core of the symbolic function.

At those locations of well-being or discomfort in the body, the infant experiences the distinction between need and desire, for example at the mucous-cutaneous borders of the body (in this case the mouth) when the mother ends the breastfeeding session, or when she refuses it because the infant has satisfied its needs, but wants to stay in touch and cuddle her. The mouth is one of the locations where the infant experiences the distinction between need and desire, that "has led to the psychoanalytic jargon that we know" (ibid., 271). The symbolic is rooted in the experience of desire correlated to a specific gesture by the caring person in relation with a specific area of the body of the infant. But indeed, the dimension of desire actually always already precedes and covers the experience of need: desire is "the call for interhuman communication" (ibid., 272), and it "precedes the need of a substantial assistance communication from the infant" (ibid., 273). The symbolic, in short, is rooted in the desire for communication supported by memory of the correlation between liminal zones of the body and the gestures and behavioral patterns of the caring persons. Memory provides the temporal and spatial continuity where the same behavior or gesture can reappear and be recognized by the infant. But obviously the memory here in question is a bodily memory, a memory tightly linked to specific liminal zones of the body, where the contact with the caring person plays out, or an olfactory memory, or the memory of certain noises or voices.

Even "the hearing of the maternal heart is already linguistic [*langagier*] for the human fetus, is a significant element for the symbolic function", she writes, emphasizing that it constitutes the "evidence of an interhuman relation" (ibid., 277). The heartbeat is one model of the alternating pattern of presence and absence that makes up the rhythm of desire. Indeed, the experience of desire entails an absence, and a frustration that comes to be appeased, before it is swiftly rekindled. This is where speech, in the sense of spoken verbal language, comes into play. The caring person's speech fills up the empty moments, when for example the infant has woken up and is still lying in bed without being too hungry, and there is space for the simple interhuman relation with no emergency involved. The continuity between the bodily sensations and the experience of the alternating presence and absence of the caring person is given by the recognizable patterns that are analogous with language in the verbal sense.

> It is this alternation in the desire to communicate, satisfied by the presence and not satisfied in the absence, but from then on expected and so to speak fabricated, followed sooner or later by the return of the satisfaction of seeing the mother found again, that is what organizes in the code of language the possibilities of what we have to call the *sublimation of the oral drives of desire*: because it is indeed desire as it is organized in orality that finds there the roots of humanization, that is to say that the symbolic function is placed at the service of the communication of desires between human beings. (Ibid., 283)

The roots of humanization are the acquisition and the use of the symbolic function, and the symbolic function is the capacity of coping with the absence of the caring persons. It is not primarily because of its signifying structure; it is not language in the sense of the web of meaning studied by the science of language. The alternating presence and absence, in tune with the expression of the desire for presence from both sides (the baby and the caring person) is the very root of the symbolic. It is only inasmuch as the desiring subject is shaped by the pulsating rhythm of the absence and presence of the caring persons, and inasmuch as the symbolic is the realm by which the subject is able to cope with the absence because it virtually fills it up and makes it bearable, that speech is central to the birth of self-awareness and to the development of a healthy body image. The spoken word, then, is the medium by which this absence maintains a relation to the presence that it is the absence of, thus allowing the infant to bridge the absence. If the infant experiences an absence, for example, in the form of a depressive mother not responding to its attempts at contact, it will develop traumatic symptoms. The spoken word is in direct relation with the bodily sensations tied to the presence of the caring person. Dolto does not use the notion of language as a system that carries meanings on a collective level; her focus is on the affective and relational functions of speech, as it is addressed by one subject to another being in the process of becoming a subject. Speech is the medium allowing the infant to go from "erotic satisfaction" to a genuine "love-relationship". She writes in *The Unconscious Body Image*:

> Speech, because of its symbolic function, causes a mutation of the level of desire: from partial erotic satisfaction to a love relationship that involves subject-to-subject communication, or rather from a pre-subject (the infant) to the subject that is the mother, total object for her baby, who only knows the world and himself through her. (Dolto 2023, 46)

The fact that Dolto uses the notion of language in the sense of a subject-building intimate communication, that the notion should not be mistaken with linguistic structures, and even less with the mastery of verbal language, has been noted by several commentators. Rather, Dolto uses the term "*langage*" as a synonym of communication, but where non-verbal and verbal communication are conceived and experienced as continuous. The British psychoanalyst Guy Hall puts it quite simply in his introductory article about Dolto's life and works:

> When she speaks of language, she means not only words and sounds, but also nonverbal communications, affects, turmoil, as well as internal and external perceptions that make up interpsychic life. (Hall 2009, 323)

And the French child-psychoanalyst Claude Boukobza, who can be considered one of Dolto's heirs, both theoretically and clinically, writes in an article about the unconscious body image:

> For Françoise Dolto, language—true language that conveys meaning for the subject—is always closely connected with the body. Understanding a word

> depends both on the body schema and on the unconscious image of the body linked to the real exchanges that accompanied the assimilation of the word. (Boukobza 2018, 88)

And a little further down in the same text:

> The subject's body is not mere meat; it is always humanized and invested in a relationship with the other. The image is always shaped in relation to the adult care-taker who speaks and gives meaning to the child's emotions and feelings. (Boukobza 2018, 90)

In sum, the issue is not to argue about whether or not the infant understands the verbal meaning of the words that the caring adults speak to it; Dolto argues that the infant makes a facial expression showing that it understands what the adults are talking about, if they are talking about the infant. But the real issue is to recognize that the addressed word fills the gap of the absence that correlates with the infant's desire.[1] Every word stands for a gap in the contiguous relationship between the infant and the caring person.

Dolto's phrase "everything is language" does echo the worry expressed by Merleau-Ponty at the 1960 conference in Bonneval, about seeing the category of language taking up all the space (see in Chap. 1 above). But as we have shown, her claim is not that the body image is intrinsically linguistic, or even "structured like a language," in the Lacanian sense[2]; her claim that the infant understands what the caring person says does not mean a semantic understanding of the verbal content. Her claim is that the caring persons' speech allows for the infant's desire to take (its) place, and the realm of meanings to take shape. She did not mean that verbal language is the only medium of interhuman communication, and even less that the body image is essentially a question of a signifier. Everything is dependent upon the intimate psychic communication of desire between the child and the caring persons, as she also explains in her 1972 lecture to the philosophers: "The structure of language as communication depends upon the human environment and the desire of the other towards the child in response to the child's desire" (1981, 286). The key is the pleasure of communication between psyches, and the role of language is to substitute the limited circuit of sensuous desire for a longer circuit of a pleasure yet to be discovered.

Dolto goes on in this lecture to further emphasize the libidinal dimension of language, and the libidinal roots of the symbolic. She defines language as "the coded communication of affects", "arousing the subject in the other through audible visual, tactile representatives, through emotions made of reciprocal attention and interest" (1981, 293). Such a definition is quite far from the idea of a system of signifiers where the meanings could be put into formulas; indeed, the emphasis is put on the dimension of desire in the sense of the pleasure of intimacy and complicity. Language is simply the way in which the libidinal structure of the little human develops, as she also states further on in her lecture (ibid., 295). The most fundamental aspect is the desire for togetherness, and language is but the medium of that. From the opposite point of view, it would be safe to claim that, for Dolto, verbal language operates as an unconscious for the infant before it is itself able to speak; the infant may not understand the specific meaning of the words used, but is supported by the affective vibration. Again, in the same text: "All the noises of the surroundings throughout the day only help the child to develop and become human in an intelligent way, i.e. in an unconsciously linguistic way." (Ibid., 290–1) The fact that the child is used to being in a social context, to hearing the other adults speak around it, to being surrounded by the noises of the city allows it to become a social human being.

Castration: The Institution of the Symbolic

The emergence of the symbolic for the infant in the affective desiring interaction with the caring persons happens in and through addressed and affectively loaded speech. The different stages in the child's development are dependent upon the correct affective communication by the caring others according to the symbolizing capacities of the child. Dolto proposes a whole original theory of the successive castrations the child has to go through on its journey to becoming an autonomous member of the human community. But although language is also a realm where meanings may float freely and carry abstract concepts, it also always retains the more primitive layers, those layers of meaning imbued with affectivity. The adult's language is never entirely free from any affective vibration; even the most abstract and rigorous mathematical equation may be invested with affective colors, not only because of the joy that one may feel when one finds the solutions, but also because of the conditions of its discovery, depending on a shift in the perception of the whole picture. The same structure applies to the body image itself: the human subject passes through the different stages, but the first stages are never completely abolished. They continue to reverberate throughout the subject's life.

In order to understand how Dolto accounts for the emergence of the symbolic in the subject's life, we must look at her descriptions of what she refers to as "symboligenic castrations." Indeed, the relative success of the castration process is key to the subject's capacity of handling symbolic meanings, and hence to experience his or her desire in community with other humans. Arzel-Nadal (2006) gives a good introduction to the evolution of Dolto's ideas and shows how the notions of the unconscious body image and the symboligenic castrations have developed in the course of her works, starting from the text about the flower-doll.[3] She emphasizes the importance of the opposition between mutilating and symboligenic castration (ibid., 139ss). A *mutilating* castration is a process that has the effect of cancelling the child's own desire or at least making it feel guilty, thereby leading to a regression to a previous stage of affective development and to the impossibility of symbolizing the absence of the caring person, whereas the *symboligenic* castration refers to the process of delaying, or blocking, the satisfaction of the child's wishes, all the while explaining the reasons for this. The most famous example in classic psychoanalysis is that of a 3 or 4-year-old girl wishing to marry her father, to whom the parents would say (both by their behavior and through their words) that they love each other and that the girl's wish is forbidden. If they manage to do that, the girl will be able to put a temporal distance between her wish (or desire) and its satisfaction, and in this way to experience her desire as such.

The last section of Dolto's lecture at the French society of philosophy is entirely devoted to introducing the issue of symboligenic castration, starting with the phrase "I must tell you about the term castration", then admitting that the word symboligenic is not to be found in the dictionary, "but should be." (Dolto 1981, 301). It is therefore safe to assume that this lecture includes one of the first mentions of the concept. In her main book however, *The Unconscious Body Image*, the second, and central, chapter entitled "The body images and their destiny: The castrations" is entirely devoted to the topic. The castrations are the very thresholds allowing the body image to evolve and eventually become a (potentially) healthy adult self-awareness. She identifies five such thresholds in the development of the child: the first is umbilical castration, that coincides with the birth and the cutting and ligature of the umbilical cord (Dolto

2023, 64–68). This first disruption in the bodily-affective life of the infant can be seen as a castration because it creates a distance between the infant's sensations and the satisfaction of its needs and desires. As a first separation on a primarily bodily level, it "can be considered as a prefiguration of all the trials" (ibid., 63) that the child will be facing later on in life. The second castration is oral castration (ibid., 68–74), also known as weaning: this establishes a new distance between baby and mother, leading to the expression of a "desire and to the possibility of talking" (ibid., 69). The third is anal castration (74–110), and refers to the stage when the toddler claims to be able to do things by itself. It implies a mastery of motor drives, and thus also of the anal sphincter, "it guides the child towards the mastery of its own motor functioning, and not only excremental" (ibid., 76). The fourth is "primary castration," (110–124) also referred to as "non-Oedipal genital castration," and involves "the discovery of the sexual difference between boy and girl" (ibid., 110). This is the stage corresponding to Freud's castration complex, when the little child notices the difference between those who have and those who don't have a willy. Finally, the fifth is the Oedipus complex, or "Oedipal genital castration," (124–139) which gives rise to the prohibition of incest. This is where the story of Oedipus plays out, for Dolto in both sexes, albeit more directly for the boy than for the girl.[4]

It is, in other words, a generalization of Freud's castration complex, that applies only to what Dolto refers to as "genital castration." In Freud's elaborations, starting with the 1908 "On the Sexual Theories of Children," there is a primacy of the phallus, and thus the term castration is taken literally, as the fantasy of cutting the genital organ of the boy, and only then used as a more general threshold to human society. As Laplanche and Pontalis sum it up in their *Language of Psychoanalysis*, the paradox of the Freudian theory of the castration complex might be put as follows (to restrict ourselves to the instance of the boy): the child cannot transcend the Oedipus complex and achieve identification with the father without first having overcome the castration crisis; in other words, he must have confronted the rejection of his demand to use his penis as an instrument of his desire for his mother." (Laplanche and Pontalis, 59) Dolto takes up the idea of cutting the source of immediate pleasure, but generalizes the process, making the genital castration but one of a series. She ultimately defines it as "the process that accomplishes itself in a human being when another human being signals to him that the gratification of desire in the form that he would like to give to it is forbidden by the Law. This signification is transmitted by language, be it gestural, in facial expressions or verbal." (Dolto 2023, 55)[5].

There is no privilege of verbal language although the ultimate issue of the successive castrations is to allow the child to "access sublimation and the symbolic order of human Law." (ibid., 57) a common feature of all the five stages is a greater opening each time of the space of desire. The fundamental assumption is that the human subject, from the fetal stage, is a desiring being, that is a being that seeks pleasure in relations with other humans. The presence of desire (not to be confused with need, as seen in the previous chapter) defines the very essence of the human subject with all its contradictory and troubling aspects. The corollary of this fundamental fact is that the world of the little human is, from the outset, a symbolic one. Desire and the symbolic are two aspects of the same reality: the modality of a pleasurable relation with another human. From the birth and the cutting of the umbilical cord to the acceptance of the prohibition of incest, the experience of desire is always also a quest for communication.

In other words, the symbolic is the realm of being with others. In order to be with others in a sustainable way, it is necessary to align one's desire with the desire of others. The successive castrations form the path leading to shaping the child's desire in accordance with the adult world. But this process does not imply a distancing from the body; each stage is an expansion of the possibilities of satisfaction by the prohibition of one particular source, followed by a widening of relational possibilities. The successive castrations build the human person, while the first stage is not overcome and obliterated. In other terms, the negativity of castration, the fact that it forbids the subject to obtain a certain satisfaction, is actually an opening towards greater possibilities of satisfaction. This is in line with Merleau-Ponty's reflections about the Freudian unconscious in his lecture on passivity in the spring of 1955; as noted in the first chapter above, he reads the Freudian unconscious also in the sense of a horizontal unconscious, of an "unconscious perception, i.e. a knowing prior to knowledge" (Merleau-Ponty 2010, 163). The philosopher explains this paradox of a "knowing prior to knowledge," of a "perception that is not knowledge" (ibid., 164) by the fact that perception can be the awareness of a lack, where we see that something is lacking without knowing what it is, and without even consciously *knowing* that something is actually lacking. And this awareness of a lack is precisely unconscious in the sense of an implicit perception of the content that does not become conscious, or if it does, only in the aftermath.

The notion of institution involves an event in the life of the subject (individual or collective, human or non-human) that opens up the possibility of other events that were not possible before this specific event. He studies different realms in which the event of institution occurs, such as the institution of an organism in the form of the development of the embryo; the institution of a new territory by a mammal or a bird; the institution of a feeling in the individual subject's history; the institution of a new meaning in the system of language (for example through the borrowing of a foreign word); the institution of a new piece of knowledge through scientific discovery. All these types of events share the common trait that they open up new possibilities: the institution of a territory is the possibility of dwelling in many different ways, the institution of a new meaning opens possibilities of speaking differently, etc. Merleau-Ponty speaks about "event-matrixes" opening "a historic field that has unity". It is a "symbolic matrix that results in the openness of a field, of a future according to certain dimensions" (ibid., 13). Moreover, such events show a paradoxical temporal structure: once it has happened, the system appears to have always already been like it has become, since the new meaning also applies to what existed in the past.

Significantly, the idea of a "matrix-event", an event that generates new meaning, is also used by Merleau-Ponty to describe the unconscious in a working note on "The Freudian Unconscious" linked to the second course of the same year 1954–55:

> The unconscious is the symbolic matrix left behind by the event. The return to the event, analysis, the *Deutung*, unravel this fabric, but these are only effective if that which generates the event is truly recovered such as it was lived, not abstractly formulated. The unconscious is existential eternity, the cohesion of a life, the fecundity of the event. (Merleau-Ponty 2010, 169).

And in an added note, some of the same phrases come again:

> The unconscious means fecundity of the event, a kind of existential eternity: whatever one does, it will be this relation between sense and what was lived, since the lived is generalized in dimensions, cohesion of a life. (Merleau-Ponty 2010, 242)

In both of these passages, Merleau-Ponty expresses his conception of the unconscious as the novelty in the system of meanings left by the event of an institution. This unconscious is not primarily the result of an active repression, it is a primary process in the classic Freudian sense, but not restricted to the psychic space of the individual. It is from the outset a shared space of meaning, but is unconscious in the sense that the individual is not cognitively conscious of it. It is also unconscious in the sense that it inaugurates new possibilities of meaning that were not conceivable from the point of view of the subject before it happened. With the phrases "existential eternity," "cohesion of a life," "fecundity of the event," Merleau-Ponty points to the broader environment in the context of which a change in the system of meanings may take place. No reference to the history of the subject means prevalence of the death drive. In other words, castration is the possibility of a history of the subject—therefore it means life, or as Merleau-Ponty puts it while talking about the event of birth, "institution of a future" (Merleau-Ponty 2010, 8).[6]

Similarly, the event of castration is not taken on by the subject, but imposed by the caring adults. In the first part of the institution course, Merleau-Ponty studies processes of imprinting in non-human and in human life, of how an animal establishes a new territory, how the attachment of an animal to a human appears, etc. In the first section of his course on "Institution and life," he devotes a few pages to the institution of the latency phase in the human child after the end of the Oedipal phase. Indeed, he comments on Freud's short article "The dissolution of the Oedipus complex" (1924) in which Freud reflects on how the Oedipus complex fades away. This is, by the way, the closest one gets to Dolto's successive castrations in Freud's writings. Merleau-Ponty quotes a passage at the beginning of the text where Freud writes that the Oedipus complex dissolves because of its "lack of success" and "its internal impossibility" (Freud 1975, 173; quoted by Merleau-Ponty 2010, 21), thereby refusing to choose between two reasons for its fading away—either maturation or experience:

> Human institution always resumes a prior institution, which has posed a question, i.e., a question which was its anticipation—and which has failed. It reactivates this problem and human institution reunites its givens in [a] totality that is centered otherwise. Instituted [means] segment of a history. (Merleau-Ponty 2010, 22f)

This conception of the institution of new meaning provides a relevant framework to Dolto's descriptions of the successive castrations in human life. Each stage in the process of becoming-adult is in this sense the institution of a new matrix by means of a prohibition given by a trustworthy caring person. The mere fact that it is a castration, i.e. a negative event, means that there is an essential unconscious dimension in the process. In short, each successful castration is the institution of a new structure of meanings through the suppression of a pre-existing possibility. The castration is symboligenic if it allows for the institution of new meanings that the subject could not expect beforehand. This unexpectedness is precisely the explanation why there is a need for the interdiction to come from outside. The violence of castration is correlated with the simple fact that the subject is in a system of meanings where the development promised to him or her is literally unconceivable, but then opens up thanks to the suppression of the immediate satisfaction that the subject has become used to.

Somatizations of the Unconscious Body Image

In her lecture at the *Société française de philosophie*, Dolto affirms the following: "It is the price of its symbolic function that the psychosomatic equilibrium of the human being is vulnerable." (1981, 324) The issue at stake in the development of the self, and the stability of the subject is literally its psychosomatic equilibrium; this entails that disbalances in the unconscious body image are very likely to have consequences on somatic health. The event of castration, successful or failed, has consequences in return on the organic body. In fact, Dolto's clinical cases often show rather psychotic symptoms of diminished bodily tonus, disorders of motility, among others, which is why she is known for her consideration of "child psychosis" or "autism".[7] Image *of* the body means the image acting on the body, unconscious body image is the way the symbolic acts upon the organic. In the long third chapter of her *Unconscious Body Image*, entitled "Pathology of body images and analytic practice," she shows how castrations (in particular the failed ones) have repercussions on the physiological body. A failed castration opens a dissociation between the three components of the body image, the functional, the erogenous and the dynamic image (see above), which in turn disconnects the subject from his own history, and therefore from the sense of self-awareness. For example, in relation to the case of Paul, a 3-year-old boy complaining about a headache, she writes: "There is a risk of organic pathology when the dissociation is such that there is no reference to the history of the subject; then, the death drive starts to prevail—something that maintains at least the vegetative life of the body." (Dolto 2023, 164)

While she surveys the pathological consequences of every particular castration stage, the anal stage is when the symbolic is the most clearly at stake, i.e. concerning children between two and 4 years old. With anxious parents who fail to consider their child as a subject of his own desire, but rather tend to use the child for the satisfaction of their own narcissistic image, the child can develop somatic disorders on top of his relational difficulties. Dolto writes in this respect:

> Such children, so raised, forbidden all desire, and introjecting the prohibition of desire, often fall into psychosomatic accidents and become ill, prey to other creatures, microbes, who are ready to take over the body of he who no longer assumes it, or certain bodily organs that lack vitality. If their bodies resist, they become dangerously ill-tempered children. (Dolto 2023, 183)

The cases treated by Dolto were likely to show psychosomatic symptoms as a consequence of a failed castration; the failure of one of those stages indeed means that the child loses the possibility of pursuing his desire, and even "introjects the prohibition" of his own desire. This leads to a prevalence of the death drive, which becomes visible in their behavior, or in their vulnerability towards infectious diseases, or in other bodily manifestations. Dolto gives an eminent example of this in her long introduction and commentary about the case of Léon, an 8-year-old boy "seeming unable to carry himself" but without "any neurological reason for his strange habits" (ibid., 189). Dolto describes a boy with a very weak tonus, while entering the consulting room, he "follows along the walls, pressing against them," and then "collapses into a chair," "a bit like a baby who is starting to stand upright and who cannot yet cross a space without auxiliary support. (*ibid.*) On top of this "inability to carry himself," Léon's IQ was tested and measured as very low, and he had a passive and expressionless attitude in general. His mother told the therapist that he was active as a baby, but that she stopped him from sucking his thumb by pinning shut his sleeves with safety pins, and that she would put him in a high chair as soon as he was able to sit, where he would quietly remain for several hours looking at his parents working in their clothing workshop. Dolto: "Thus, Léon had lived seated, tied, with nothing to do with his hands, watching his father, mother and their colleagues working, for three years." (ibid., 191)

This meant that he was simply cut off from any possibility of pursuing his desire, and that he therefore was unable to pass the stages of castration because they imply the possibility of transgressing the law. Moreover, his mother was sexually immature, with very tenuous consciousness of her sexual desires, and a very poor sex life with her husband, and also tendencies towards incestuous play and gestures with her son, leading him to confusions in his sexual identity and his relation with his father. Dolto describes in every detail the course of the therapy and reached a diagnosis in terms of the effects on the child's body:

> Here, we can very easily see how desire is damaged according to the constitution of the body image and its effects on the functioning of Leon's bodily schema, the damage of this loving upbringing of a child tied to his seat. The body image of the subject whose desire was forbidden to act upon the motor functioning of the bodily schema itself prohibited healthy neurological potentialities that nonetheless remained intact. Motor skills, the agility of distal parts of the body – hands, fingers, larynx, eyes and feet – were possible but not the cohesion of the images between these, and therefore the linking tonicity of the bodily schema. (ibid., 201–2)

The impairment on the bodily schema caused by the impossibility of carrying out one's desire is not directly physiological, but concerns the prohibition of "healthy neurological potentialities." In Léon's case, Dolto observes a resignation of the boy to his situation resulting in a delayed motor and intellectual development. This is explained by the fragmentation of the body into the different aspects (basic, functional-erogenous, dynamic) of the unconscious image, making it impossible to build and maintain the self-awareness that constitutes the unity of the person. The central aspect in this quotation is that Dolto emphasizes the consequences of this fragmentation of the aspects of the body image *on the bodily schema*, underscoring that the unity of the unconscious body image is key to the tonicity of the bodily schema, as she writes a few pages later noting that the "fragmentation of the body image" has "effects on the bodily schema" (ibid., 205). The "neurological potentialities" remain intact, retaining the possibility of a cure through the analytical therapy opening up again the possibility of experiencing desire as one's own desire. But the symptoms of this situation manifest themselves on the level of the bodily schema, on the tonus and the motor skills of the person.

Dolto thus admits that the symbolic may have a profound influence on the organic, since the organic is conceived as being open to the world of human interaction. The bodily schema, i.e. the body in its sensorimotor capabilities, manifests the state of the body image in the sense that motility disorders can be seen as signs of a lack of coherence in the body image due to a failed castration. There is an intertwining of both aspects: the distortions of the body image normally influence the very functioning of the body schema.

It is indeed important to talk to the child, but "on the condition of understanding what talking means at the age he is at" (Dolto 2023, 163). The body image is the link between the organic body and the medium of verbal language, a "pre-symbolization", as she writes in the same section.

> To say that *the body image is the symbolic incarnation of the subject* signifies that only symbolized emotions are inscribed in it, that is to say those that have the meaning of a language of interhuman communication, in any case those who have acquired this meaning for the subject. The symbolization in question here is in fact pre-symbolization. (Dolto 2023, 165)

The body image is unconscious insofar as the subject retains an implicit representation of his own body, a representation at odds with his actual needs and physiological development. It is a sensing intentionality, and it can give rise to pathological symptoms (autistic symptoms in many of Dolto's cases) if there is too wide a gap between the body image and the bodily schema at a given moment. But Dolto does not, unlike Schilder, use psychoanalytical concepts to look at somatic impairments. Her use of the notion of bodily schema is there to show how the unconscious in the psychic sense can have an effect upon the physiological body.

Transition

Dolto's conception of the unconscious shows three interrelated features: firstly, in the words of Gérard Guillerault, it is the site of an "expressive vitality," more or less hidden or hindered, it is a source of figuration. "it always seeks to present itself" (Guillerault 2008, 213). Secondly, it can be described as a "positive" unconscious in the sense that it is not only the result of repression, not only the "obscure point of oblivion," but rather a "source of desiring vitality" (ibid.). This is precisely because her notion of the unconscious inseparably refers to the body subject in both its carnal and symbolizing dimensions. Thirdly, it is a space of resonance between the subjects, as Dolto herself formulates it in some of her early works, for example in a text from 1957 where she describes the analyst as a "resonator of the spontaneous expressions of the subject in the experience of therapy". (Dolto 1999, 77)

A key aspect in Dolto's clinical thinking involves the respective definitions of body image as the symbolic dimension of the lived body, and the body schema as the organic dimension of the body. Her conception of the unconscious is based upon the negativity of castration, be it verbal or by another means of communication. Yet the relation between the gesture of castration and its effects on the body remain to a certain extent unclear. Castration happens to the body, or more precisely it occurs at locations at the limit of the body. Yet Dolto's account of the organic dimension of the body is trapped in a dualistic conception separating the symbolic relational dimension and the organic, although she does recognize and describe the intertwining of the two. But properly defining the unconscious as the field of relation between bodies requires a stronger notion of the intercorporeal interface. My task in the following chapters will be to get beyond Dolto's dualism between body image and bodily schema; this will be possible thanks to the notion of the skin-ego and the psychic envelope introduced by Didier Anzieu and René Kaës. This notion allows for a new definition of the unconscious as an inherently intersubjective realm, i.e. as the origin of the becoming subject.

Notes

1. The discussion in the field of developmental psychology about the infant's understanding of the semantic meaning of spoken language should be placed in relation to this philosophy of the infant's desire. In the works of Philippe Rochat, or Andrew Meltzoff, among many others, one sees the domination of a cognitive model, where the main goal is to explain how infants learn content by cognitive and neurological approaches, in particular through imitation. Cf. Rochat 2004, and Meltzoff's works.
2. Lacan refers at least twice in his *Seminars* to lectures given by Françoise Dolto, firstly in the second *Seminar* on *The Ego in Freud's Theory and the*

Technique of Psychoanalysis, during the 16th session in April 1955, and in the fourth *Seminar* on *The Object Relation* during the 3rd session in December 1956, each time stating that everything is dependent on the signifier. Cf. Lacan 1991, 191ss, and 2022, 33ss. In order to find out more about the relations between Dolto and Lacan, see Hivernel 2013, as well as Guillerault 2003 and 2008 (226–245).

3. Cf. Dolto 1981, 133–193. First published in the *Revue française de psychanalyse* in 1949.
4. This is not the place to discuss the extent of Dolto's heteronormative conceptions: it is indeed the case that she emphasizes more than once the dual nature of the parental couple, and she does mention a "homosexualizing effect of a "perverse symboligenic castration" (2023, 57) where the boy unconsciously understands the interdiction of his desire for his mother as the forbidding of any woman, and she mentions the deficiency of the father, either being absent or failing to deliver the Oedipal castration, as a possible cause of the "sensitization of the boy to homosexuality" (127). But she actually also put on the same level heterosexual and homosexual desire when she recalls the prohibition of incest (ibid., 121, 126, 133), and never diagnoses homosexuality as a perverse or pathological orientation of desire that should be cured. Dolto, then, may not be the best ally of contemporary queer psychoanalysis, but since her emphasis is mainly on the parental couple, and not on its binary identity, I would argue that her conceptions could quite easily be adapted.
5. Dolto capitalizes the *Law*, a detail missed by the translator. This is to emphasize that the issue in question here is not optional, but rather a condition of possibility of becoming human.
6. The expression in the French text is "*institution d'un à-venir*," i.e. institution of a *yet-to-come*. Merleau-Ponty makes a classic pun playing on the fact that 'avenir' in one word means future.
7. There is no good place to insert this comment. Since Dolto's time, since the second half of the twentieth Century, there has been much research and public debate about autism. Dolto's approach is psychoanalytical, in the sense that she always seeks to refer the child's behavior to its relationship with the caring others, in particular the mother. She clearly did not take into account the fact that autism could be innate. Another book would be required in order to sort out the Dolto cases of children with autistic symptoms due to failed castrations and cases of autism not due to any particular disbalance in their affective relations with their parents.

References

Arzel-Nadal, Laurence. 2006. *Françoise Dolto et l'image inconsciente du corps.* Louvain-la-Neuve: De Boeck Université.

Boukobza, Claude. 2018. *The Unconscious Image of the Body. In Theory and Practice in Child Psychoanalysis.* An Introduction to the Work of Françoise Dolto. Ed. by G. Hall, F. Hivernel and S. Morgan (2009). London, Routledge, 85–100.

Dolto, Françoise. 1981. *Au jeu du désir. Essais cliniques.* Paris: Seuil.

Dolto, Françoise. 1994. *Tout est langage.* Paris: Gallimard.

Dolto, Françoise. 1999. *Flower Dolls: Essays in Child Psychotherapy.* London: Marion Boyars.

Dolto, Françoise. 2023. *The Unconscious Body Image* [1984]. Translated by S. Bailly. London: Routledge.

Freud, Sigmund. 1975. "The dissolution of the Oedipus complex". In *The Standard Edition of the Complete Psychological Works of Sigmund Freud.* Vol. XIX, (1923–1925), translated by J. Strachey. London: The Hogarth press. 172-179.

Guillerault, Gérard. 2008. *Comprendre Dolto. Une éthique positive du désir.* Paris: Armand Colin.

Hall, Guy. 2009. *Le désir de vivre*: An Introduction to the Life and Work of Françoise Dolto. *British Journal of Psychotherapy* 25 (3): 312–330.

Hivernel, Françoise. 2013. "The Parental Couple": Françoise Dolto and Jacques Lacan: Contributions to the Mirror Stage. *British Journal of Psychotherapy* 29 (4): 505–518.

Lacan, Jacques. 1981. *The Seminar of Jacques Lacan. Book XI: The Four Fundamental Concepts of Psychoanalysis.* Translated by A. Sheridan. New York/London: W. W. Norton & Company.

Lacan, Jacques. 1991. *The Seminar of Jacques Lacan. Book II: The Ego in Freud's Theory and in the Technique of Psychoanalysis, 1954–1955.* Translated by S. Tomaselli. New York/London: W. W. Norton & Company.

Lacan, Jacques. 2022. *The Seminar of Jacques Lacan. Book IV: The Object Relation.* Translated by A. R. Price. New York/London: W. W. Norton & Company.

Merleau-Ponty, Maurice. 2010. *Institution and Passivity. Course Notes at the Collège de France (1954–1955).* Translated by L. Lawlor and H. Massey. Evanston: Northwestern University Press.

Rochat, Philippe. 2004. *The Infant's World.* Cambridge, MA/London: Harvard University Press.

Schilder, Paul. 1950. *The Image and Appearance of the Human Body.* New York: International Universities Press.

Schilder, Paul, and Heinz Hartmann. 1925. Zur Psychologie Schädelverletzter. *Archiv für Psychiatrie und Nervenkrankheiten* 75:287–300.

CHAPTER 8

The Skin-Deep Unconscious

Psychoanalysis presents itself—or is generally presented—as a theory of unconscious and preconscious psychical contents. The concept of psychoanalytic technique that follows from this aims to make those contents, respectively, preconscious and conscious. But there cannot be a content without it being related to a container.
Anzieu 2016, 12f

This chapter is an introduction and a discussion of Didier Anzieu's central notion of the skin-ego, and the psychic envelope, as an intercorporeal space of resonance. The aim is to show the structural necessity of the notion of the intercorporeal unconscious, from the perspective of the individual subject. We have seen in the previous chapters that the body should be conceived as being at the same time a bodily and a relational space, but both in Marty's psychosomatics and in Dolto's clinical thinking the connection between those two aspects remains unclear. Both Marty and Dolto point in that direction, but since Dolto's conception of the organic body itself remains undefined, and since Marty's puts an (otherwise rightful) emphasis on the mysterious character of the body and the domination of the death drive, the relational powers of the body itself remain in the shade. Schilder's notion of the body schema refers only to one (albeit crucial) aspect of the body, namely the coordination between perception,

S. Kristensen, *The Intercorporeal Unconscious*,
https://doi.org/10.1007/978-3-032-22596-2_8

motility, and desire in relation to another being; his approach does not apply to the body itself as a relational space.

Indeed, in my inquiry into the unconscious as an intercorporeal space, Anzieu's clinical thinking is key because it shapes the notion of skin as the space where the unconscious expresses its conflicts, since it is both the limit of the ego and the very realm of contact and relation. There is a wide reception of his works in the English-speaking world since many of his writings have been translated, and his main work *The Skin-Ego*, has been translated twice into English. Anzieu is also known for the practice of group psychoanalysis that he developed with his colleague René Kaës.[1] In this chapter and the following I will demonstrate that the two aspects are actually closely related. Anzieu's concept of the skin-ego is powerful because it allows us to bind together the organic, the psychic, the emotional, and the relational, in order to situate the unconscious not only in the history of the subject, but within the relationships of the subject, inasmuch as they shape his/her being. In other words, the notion of the skin allows the extension of the idea of the intercorporeal unconscious because the skin concerns the integrity of the subject in the first place. The skin-ego brings a theory of the container of conscious and unconscious content (Anzieu 2016, 11), a theory of the body-subject as the place where emotional events take place. Anzieu himself emphasizes that the body is "in the third quarter of the 20th Century, the thing that has been misunderstood, denied, or entirely absent" and notes that Schilder's notion of the body schema is absent in Laplanche and Pontalis' *Language of Psychoanalysis* (Anzieu 2016, 23). Thanks to Anzieu, we can begin to describe the integrity of the self *as* a relational being. In the following chapter then, the unconscious shall be described from the perspective of the collective.

The Skin as Boundary and as Interface

Maurice Merleau-Ponty's claim that the unconscious is sensing itself, implies that the sensing subject tends to disappear in the act of sensing. Indeed, when it comes to formulating this famous claim during the lecture at the Collège de France, Merleau-Ponty's notes show that he characterizes sensing as "dispossession," "nondifferentiated recognition of the touched and the touching," "the zero-degree of difference" (Merleau-Ponty 2003, 283), thereby suggesting that the unconscious in this sense implies a certain loss of the self, a certain degree of confusion with the sensed world. And yet, on the other side, in Merleau-Ponty's own descriptions of the relation of the sensing body with the world, the touch is central, since it is the body that perceives. As he writes in a famous passage of *The Visible and the Invisible*, vision is after all a "remarkable variant" of tactile palpation (Merleau-Ponty 1968, 133). Many other passages from his later writings can be quoted in support of the idea that vision is understood as touching from a distance. But what he does not mention is that the organ of touch is most certainly the skin, a term that hardly appears in his works. While Anzieu never explicitly refers to Merleau-Ponty, his elaboration of the skin-ego does answer this requirement.

When he introduces the concept of the skin-ego, Anzieu sketches a phenomenology of the infant's experience of its intimacy with the mother and the structure of its progressively becoming autonomous. He does so by using the relation of figure and ground, a relation that also constitutes the essential structure of Merleau-Ponty's thinking:

> Every figure presupposes a ground against which it appears (…). The baby's experience of its orifices as allowing things to pass either inwards (incorporation) or outwards (expulsion) is important, of course, but no orifice can be perceived without relating to a sensation of surface and volume, however vague. The *infans* begins to perceive its skin as a surface when it experiences contact between its body and that of its mother, in the framework of a secure relationship of attachment to her. Through these experiences it comes to develop not only the notion of a boundary between the inside and the outside but also the confidence it will need to control its orifices, for it can only feel confident of their functions if it also has a fundamental certainty of the integrity of its bodily wrapping. (Anzieu 2016, 41–2)

And a little further in the same paragraph:

> Moreover, the skin is the seat of proprioceptive sensations, whose important role in the development of character and thought has been emphasized by Henri Wallon: it is one of the organs that regulate muscle tone. If we think in economic terms—accumulation, displacement, and discharge of tension—we are presupposing a Skin-ego. (ibid., 42)

In these passages, Anzieu defines the skin-ego as the ground against which the infant human subject can experience particular sensations and perceptions, and the unity of the ground (the whole skin) and the figure (the particular sensations on a particular part of the body) make up the sense of self-awareness. The "framework of a secure relationship" with the mother is key to the development of the self, which means that the condition of possibility of self-awareness is the living active presence of the caring other, inasmuch as this presence offers a stable, secure and interactive framework. The interdependency of the sense of self and the active presence of the caring other constitutes the heart of the notion of the skin-ego. Thanks to the loving contact of the caring other, the infant may start to perceive its own skin as a surface and as the place of its own sensations, and develop not only a sense of the limits between self and other, but also a sense of its own capacity of control upon its own body. In other terms, the skin-ego is the key to both ownership and agency of the subject. Here's how Anzieu formulates it from the developmental perspective:

> From this epidermal, proprioceptive origin, the Ego inherits the double faculty of setting up barriers (which become psychical defense mechanisms) and filtering exchanges (with the Id, the superego and the outside world). (ibid., 44)

This "double faculty" is already at play in Freud's second attempt at a topology of the ego in his 1923 essay "The Ego and the Id"—a text that constitutes Anzieu's main reference among Freud's writings (alongside the "Project of a scientific psychology," of 1895, where Freud introduces the notion of the "contact barrier," a barrier that is both a separation and a link—cf. Anzieu 2016, 80–87). Anzieu's primary focus is on the ego and its structure; he claims in the introduction to *The Skin-Ego* that psychoanalysis presents itself as the theory of psychic *contents*, but that the theory of the *container* is "far more fragmentary, approximate and scattered" (ibid., 12). Therefore, it is not surprising that he speaks very little about the unconscious as such; he refers to Freud's second topic with the three instances of the Ego in a container, the Id, the Ego, and the Superego. The id is the undetermined and partly impersonal region of the ego where the drives and the affects originate, according to Freud.

Showing this "double faculty," performing the double function of being both a barrier and an interface, the ego in Anzieu's sense, as psychodermatological skin, is the key to the distinction between conscious and unconscious. His focus is primarily on the structure of the ego rather than on the description of the dynamic processes of repression; therefore, the question that was at the center of the first chapter above, i.e. whether we should consider equally the "latent unconscious" and the "repressed unconscious," is not relevant in the context of Anzieu's thinking. The unconscious from Anzieu's perspective seems to arise from defects or disorders in the functions of the skin-ego. He distinguishes eight functions of the skin-ego, established by analogy with the functions of the skin in the dermatological sense: (1) the skin-ego "maintains the psyche" in Winnicott's sense of the mother holding the baby's body; this function develops through "interiorizing the mother's holding" (Anzieu 2016, 106). The disorder when this function fails is the horror of the inner void due to the lack of support by the mother's gestures. The unconscious is in the relation. (2) The skin-ego "contains the psyche," a function carried out by the mother's handling; in particular, what the skin is supposed to contain are the drives directed towards others, and they can only be felt if the skin contains them. This grounds "the sense of a continuous Self" (ibid, 110), and the disorder related to a failure in this aspect is a diffuse, unlocalized, and unappeasable anxiety that translates as a psyche that is like "a kernel without a shell" (ibid.), again related to the presence of others. (3) The third function of the skin-ego is the shield against stimuli, and if this function fails, we encounter autistic symptoms: with an excessively rigid shield we have a container rejecting all otherness, and with a deficient shield we may have a vulnerable subject. Here again, it is in relation with what comes from outside and the issue at stake is the capacity of the subject to regulate stimuli. (4) The fourth function is to enable the self to become an individuum and involves "making it feel unique" (ibid, 111); the failure of this function corresponds with schizophrenic symptoms characteristic of subjects who have trouble distinguishing between their own perception of themselves and others' perception of them. (5) The fifth function is the intersensorial perception that leads to the sensation of the unity of the senses. The deficiency of this function is the "terror of the body falling apart, or of being dismantled" (ibid, 112). (6) The skin-ego is also the surface supporting sexual arousal, and if this function is deficient, the adult will "not feel safe enough to engage in complete sexual relations leading to mutual genital satisfaction" (ibid, 113). This function, as with all the others, is intimately related to the desiring relation with others. (7) The seventh function of the skin is the "libidinal recharging" of the psyche; failure in this function can lead to the explosion of the psychical apparatus "under the pressure of too much excitation" or, conversely, to the fear of what would happen if there were no more tension. (8) The last function listed by Anzieu is that the skin registers sensory traces; it is the memorial and cognitive function of the skin-ego. It concerns the way the skin registers reality for the subject as well as his/her belonging to a group through visible inscriptions on the surface of his/her body.

In all these functions (maybe except the intersensorial one—but even that function can be considered as the condition of a reciprocal relation with the other), the skin-ego is, so to speak, *the* organ of relations. Failure in one or the other function leads to a disorder in the desiring relation with others or with the world. Therefore, for Anzieu, psychotherapy consists in repairing the deficient functions of the skin-ego, and making the unconscious become conscious, letting the ego become, where the it played alone, as for example in the case of the second function of the skin-ego. In this sense, the unconscious concerns the subject's capacity to establish and develop relations with others, and must therefore be considered a relational space.

Yet, is the unconscious in this conception simply the result of troubles in the functions of the skin-ego? How does it appear to the subject itself? A psychic content is unconscious *from the perspective of* the subject—the skin, or envelope, carries the task of self-awareness (and its failures). In what sense is it an image?

The Skin-Ego as Intersensorial Figuration

The resemblance of Anzieu's presentation of the skin-ego and Dolto's unconscious body image is striking: they both take as the point of departure the situation of the infant and the origin of self-awareness and they both describe the skin-ego and the body image respectively as a mental image, or figuration, conditioning self-awareness. They never quote each other—probably because Dolto remained close to Lacan while Anzieu was very much against Lacan and faithful to the French society of psychoanalysis[2]—but their common interest in the body and their conception of the interdependence of the individual subject on the presence of the other are certainly aspects that they share. Anzieu's definition of the skin-ego as a "figuration" is very much analogous to Dolto's concept of the unconscious body image, as can be seen in the following passage:

> By "Skin-ego" I am referring to a mental image [*figuration*] used by the child's Ego during its early stages of development to represent itself as an Ego containing psychical contents, based on its experience of the surface of the body. This corresponds to the moment when the psychical Ego

> differentiates itself from the bodily Ego in operative terms but remains mixed up with it in figurative terms. (Anzieu 2016, 43)

The French term for "mental image" in the translation is "*figuration*"; indeed it refers to a kind of psychic representation of the body, an image in that sense. Anzieu points out that the double nature of the skin-ego is there: as an image *and* as a container of psychical contents. The child needs the connection of both those aspects since the security of self-awareness must be grounded in the bodily sensations of the subject, and that those bodily sensations must be represented in a stable image for the child. The sensations here in question are those of hunger, pain, pleasure, all resulting from drives that the subject experiences only inasmuch as they appear to him/her against the background of his/her skin. More precisely, the skin-ego is a representation of the self that emerges for the child on the basis of her experiences of her body's surface. This passage from Anzieu echoes what Dolto writes about the origins of primary narcissism (or basic self-awareness) in the umbilical castration, the very first moment of separation of the infant from the mother, the first moment in life of becoming a self:

> From the umbilical severance and in separating from the placenta and the membranes that he leaves behind in the uterus to which they belong, the bodily schema comes into being within the limits of the skin envelope. The body image, which in part originates in rhythms, warmth, sounds, fetal perceptions, becomes modified by the sudden change of these perceptions. (Dolto 2023, 63)

Dolto specifies the act of severing the umbilical cord as the decisive moment when the human subject becomes aware of his sensorimotor nature thanks to the "skin envelope" [*l'enveloppe qui est la peau*]. Dolto does not elaborate on the role of the skin in the process, but she does suggest that it plays a central role in the emergence of the bodily schema as well as the body schema. The body image is supported by the bodily schema—as we have seen above, the different castrations are made possible by the maturation of the bodily schema (no anal castration if the child doesn't master its sphincter). It is thus safe to claim that Dolto, in other words, also considers the skin envelope as a condition of possibility of the emergence of self-awareness.

In *The Skin-Ego*, Anzieu devotes a whole chapter to the "taboo on touching," presenting the prohibition of touching as the process allowing the subject to develop a sense of self as a whole, that is an intersensorial sense of self. He writes: "The primary taboo on touching transposes the effects of biological birth onto the psychical plane. It imposes a separate existence on the living person who is becoming an individual" (Anzieu 2016, 162). The "taboo of touching" is signified with a gesture addressed to the little child, based on the conviction that "communication by language [*parole*] is spiritually superior to communication between bodies" (ibid., 158). This last sentence could very well have been found in Dolto's writings; Dolto remarks in her speech at the *Société française de philosophie* that the infant experiences the difference between desire and need at the "border of the skin and the mucous" when the baby is separated from the breast at the end of the feed (Dolto 1981, 271). The skin plays an essential role in the fundamental distinction that grounds the very possibility of self-awareness through the successive experiences of the productive castrations, all relying on the experience of a cut and a loss.

Anzieu indeed implicitly echoes Dolto's successive castrations when he writes that "the taboo of touching [*interdit du toucher*] prepares the ground for the oedipal taboo [*interdit oedipien*] by providing it with a presexual foundation" (Anzieu 2016, 159). But the point here is not primarily to pursue a comparison between the two psychoanalysts; it is rather to explain the way in which the ego constitutes itself as a whole through the experience of its skin-envelope. The prohibition of touching for Anzieu is crucial because it reveals how psychic life is based on sensorial experience, how the capacity of thinking (the "thinking Ego") is based on the "skin-ego." Anzieu describes four dual features of the prohibition of touching: it relates to both the sexual and the aggressive drives, and guards "against an excess of excitation and its consequence, the surging of the drive" (ibid., 159); it has a double face, one turned outwards, the other inwards and allows the subject to distinguish what is familiar and what is not; it is constructed in two phases, the first being the prohibition of fusion with the mother, the other the prohibition of appropriating everything; finally, it applies to the person issuing it as much as to the one it is addressed to. Each of these features involves the subject as much as its affective environment. It defines the conditions under which the subject is able to become a thinking ego on the basis of the skin-ego, that is, it allows for the constitution of a social envelope whose stability is sufficient to maintain the subject's existence in society. The function, then, of the taboo of touching is to break with the primacy of tactile experience in the narrow sense, and open up all the other sensorial dimensions of the subjective envelope, olfactory, auditory, gustatory, proprioceptive: the ego, he writes, "can only acquire a new structure by breaking off the primacy of tactile experience and constituting itself as a space of intersensory inscription, as a *sensorium commune*" (ibid., 168). Indeed, the third part of *The Skin-Ego* proposes the descriptions of the various envelopes and their clinical importance (wrapping of sound, thermal wrapping, olfactory wrapping, qualities of taste, the muscular skin, the wrapping of suffering, etc.). In fact, already in his description of fetal life, Anzieu notes that the skin-image is not only tactile in the strict sense, but also "probably olfactory," and this intersensoriality goes together with the fundamental resonance of the affective relation:

> In the language of archaic thought, the symbiotic union with the mother appears in the form of a tactile (and probably olfactory) image of the two bodies of mother and child sharing a common interface. Separation from the mother is represented by the tearing of this common skin. (Anzieu 2016, 46)

But this first community is only unconsciously multiple for the child; it has to discover progressively its autonomy through the interactions with the affective environment and constitute the structure of its wrapping across the different sensorial modalities and relational configurations.

The Ego and the Group

As Anzieu explains in the second edition of *Le groupe et l'inconscient*, "The group is a bringing together of internal images and anxieties of the participants" (Anzieu 1984, 27). The group is the place where images are not only expressed and transformed, but according to Anzieu actually created or, as he puts it, *fomented*. In the first edition, he states:

> The group is a place where images are transformed in interaction. When human beings are together to work, to play, to defend themselves, to steal, to kill, to believe, to change the world, to be taught or cared for, feelings, desires, fears and anxieties excite or paralyze them. They may experience a common emotion, which may give them an impression of unity: conflicting emotions may tear the group apart; several members may withdraw and defend themselves against group emotions that they feel threatening,

> whereas the others, frantically, joyfully, let themselves go; or most members may withdraw when faced with invasive emotions, in which case the group is dull, apathetic and wordy. (Anzieu 2015, 105–6)

In 1975 Anzieu introduced the role of emotions in group dynamics by writing that they "are transformed in interaction," the key term being *interaction*. The interplay between the subjects composing the group does affect the emotions felt by them individually; in the second edition, he goes on to claim that the group actually creates the images. The first sentence in the passage just quoted was modified in the following way: "The group is a place where images are fomented" (Anzieu 1984, 27). He refers to the English school of psychoanalysis on this central question, in particular Winfried Bion,[3] who found that the level of conscious cooperation in groups with a common task "requires a free circulation of feelings and unconscious phantasies" (ibid., 110), and this deeper level may either paralyze or stimulate the conscious level. Those affective states organize groups unconsciously according to three alternative "basic assumptions": dependence on the leader, fight of flight, or pairing, where one is usually predominant and masks the others (ibid., 111–2).

The unconscious dimension is particularly relevant for the people inside the group, just as it is on the individual level for the subject of whose unconscious it is:

> The violence of emotions – the power of images that triggers off or sustains those emotions – are group phenomena at once patently obvious and masked: but those who are most obvious to an observer are the most masked for the people, especially for those in charge. (ibid., 108)

From the point of view of the individual subject, the affects and phantasies that underpin the group are mostly unconscious; the reason why they are unconscious is not only that there is a correspondence between weaknesses of the individual and weaknesses of the group, but also that this correspondence triggers a degree of violence of the emotions, a violence that is responsible for their repression, and therefore their being unconscious. Anzieu refers to the main source of such emotions as "narcissistic cathexis," in other words a tendency of the human subject to "fix, protect and even idolize" a wound or a sick part of oneself.[4] Just as the individual subject tends to invest a weak part of their emotional economy in order to protect a sick zone, there is a tendency for groups to create a fixation on a weak point that no one is ready to recognize. But this mechanism goes beyond a mere structural analogy between the individual psyche and the dynamics of the group: the very cohesion and functioning of the group depends on the emotional investments and phantasmatic defenses of the individuals composing the group. What is unconscious in this case is simply the resistance towards the recognition of the singular weakness of the group.

This resistance unfolds in the space between subjects. Its dynamic, its strength, and the fact that it may be shared by other members of the group, constitute the interstitial tissue that ensures the cohesion of the group. This tissue, this skin, that forms *both* the boundary of the individual subject *and* the link with others, may be called a mental image or a figuration in the sense that it is experienced by the subject as a decisive part of the process of becoming aware of oneself, of one's subjectivation process. As I have tried to show in the first chapter about Merleau-Ponty's interpretation of the dynamics of the unconscious, there is no essential difference between the psychic content, whether conscious or unconscious; the mental image of the skin may have different "weak spots" or "wounds" (ibid.), that may be imaginary as well as physiological (the physiological can also often symbolize the imaginary), mental as well as psychic. The double aspect of the skin mirrors the Freudian phrase from *The Ego and the It* that the Ego is "first and foremost a bodily ego, not merely a surface entity, but is itself the projection of a surface." And Freud added a footnote in the Standard Edition saying that the ego is "derived from bodily sensations, chiefly those springing from the surface of the body," and may be considered as a "mental projection of the surface of the body" (Freud 1961, 26; quoted by Anzieu 2016, 91). The Freudian formulations, endorsed by Anzieu, are spectacularly and deliberately ambiguous: the Ego is *at the same time* the body and a projection of the body. Only the skin can retain both natures.

In the next chapter, I shall discuss the claim that the group is not simply the extension of an ego, but rather becomes a *sui generis* collective subjectivity due to subjective projections on to the group. Such collective subjectivity, however, does not obliterate individual subjectivity, but constitutes its condition of possibility. Its paradigm and developmental origin is the mother-infant dyad, as Anzieu explains in *The Skin-Ego*:

> We can consider the mother–infant dyad as a single system made up of interdependent elements communicating information to each other, going in

both directions, from mother to baby and from baby to mother. (Anzieu 2016, 60)

The back and forth of feedback between the infant and its parents within a "single system" of "interdependent elements" is crucial to the development of the infant's sense of self. Anzieu writes primarily about the "mother-infant dyad," but he also notes that the "double feedback" is between the infant and the parents, not only the mother. The essential point is that the infant's individual sense of self spring from a dyadic system where its expressions must encounter a feedback from the caring others in order to become aware of oneself. Precisely for this very reason, it is a collective subjective unity. Anzieu expressed this same idea already in the first version of *The Group and the Unconscious*:

> Human groups are the consequence of topographical subjective projections; if the individual did not project on to the group, the result would be a mere aggregate of individuals, not a group. (Anzieu 1984, 100)

The point here is that Anzieu does not simply state that the group is the result of individual projections; he also clearly affirms that the group is more that the aggregate of individuals. His notion of the subjective envelope offers a convincing solution for the question of the interdependence of the individual and the collective. His claim is that the projection by the individual onto the group is the reason why the group is more than an aggregate. If we take into account the importance of the double Freudian thesis about the ego as body and projection, this duplicity also applies to the relation between the individual and the group. It is the very dynamic of individual projection that accounts for the fact that a group is more than an aggregate of individuals. This would seem paradoxical at first glance, but is grounded in the fact that the projection of phantasies by individuals occurs in the relational space between the other members, and that these contents start to circulate in this space. In the whole chapter about "Group phantasies," Anzieu explains how individual phantasies ground the very existence of a group once they circulate between its members:

> In fact, group phantasies are produced by a circulation of individual phantasies among group members; for the group is the result of economic and topographical organizations, which it represents and disguises. But in turn

> it produces particular effects on the thoughts, affects and behavior of group members. (ibid., 101)

Didier Anzieu introduced, with René Kaës, the practice of diagnostic groups in the 1960s: groups where the members had never met, yet called one another by their first names, leading to the hypothesis that "the group is felt by each of its members as a multi-faceted mirror in which he sees an infinite number of distorted and infinitely repeated reflections of himself" (ibid., 118). Indeed, for the individual subject, the situation of being present without any filter or social mask, without knowing who "they" are, and they not knowing who "I" am, generates anxiety and raises the question "Who am I?" (ibid.). The individual generally feels threatened in such an indeterminate group setting because the subject needs coherent and stable identifications in order to feel safe. The absence of such clear positions in the group leads the individual subject to fear fragmentation: when faced with more than one or two wishes of what the others expect from the subject, he runs "the risk of no longer existing for himself, of losing meaning by being torn by so many different demands" (ibid., 122). This is why the first image, the first phantasy produced by the individuals in the group is the image of the dismembered body, and the group really starts to exist once that image is overcome and replaced by other unconscious phantasies. The different scenarios are summed up by Anzieu in the following passage:

> Because unconscious can communicate directly with unconscious, the disparity between these phantasies produces a group disunity; the anxiety aroused by predominant phantasies produces the paralysis of the group; the convergence of phantasies may produce an ideology, even a mythology [...], or it may provide the group with the energy for its work. (ibid., 142)

Anzieu describes cases of such diagnostic group processes in the chapter on "Group illusion," the first case based on the account by René Kaës (cf. Anzieu 1984, 145–152). This group was composed of 13 participants, six women and seven men, all psychologists, psychiatrists, social workers or teachers. It would take too long to retell the entire course of the sessions; the essential process is the unconscious extension of the image of Léonore, one of the women in the group, who declares at the end of the first session that, before working as a physician, she was a social worker engaged in family planning. On top of the fact that this woman seemed to attract the attention of the male members of the group, this admission made her the center of the group, and therefore a rival to the monitor. She came to be perceived by the other group members as "the one who knew the secrets of life, birth, and sex, and had mastered them" (ibid., 146). The whole process was then dominated by the question of whether the monitor or Léonore was the dominant figure in the eyes of the members of the group. Léonore was the one in the first session to (unintentionally) introduce, through her self-presentation as a family planning specialist and her appearance to the male members as an attractive woman, the phantasy of the primal scene, which the group resisted during the whole process. The primal scene, as interpreted by Anzieu and Kaës, is in this case that the human beings originate "from the sexual union of a man and a woman," and not from a "self-fertilizing parthenogenic mother" (ibid., 151). The whole dynamic of the group during the course of the 12 sessions had turned around and avoided the confrontation with this representation. The meaning of this, when transferred onto the group, is that the group can be founded out of nothing and preserve the free will of its members, and not be dependent on an exterior power (the couple represented by the matriarch and the monitor, for example).

It is necessary for the structuring phantasy brought into the group by one of its members to be unconscious in order to acquire and to retain its power among the other members. It is also necessary for this phantasy to belong to one of the participants of the group, and then be the object of the projections of the others. In this case, Anzieu actually describes how a phantasy expressed involuntarily by one of the participants extends into the group and becomes the very motor of the group's interactions, and the very reason why the group maintains itself. It was an essential part of Léonore's self-image, of her representation of herself, that she, as a former family planning worker, was in a position of (so to speak) mastering life and death, since she spoke about it in the very first session. This figuration of herself, this skin-as-interface, encountered such resonance among the other participant's phantasies that it became the unconscious representation structuring the group's dynamic.

But it remains to be explained why the individual phantasy potentially resonates so powerfully in the realm of a group; this is explained by the fact that the individual phantasies in groups mostly have an "internal group organization": the subject identifies with "one or several real persons of importance to him and one or several representations of internal psychic processes" (ibid., 230), as Anzieu writes in the last chapter of *The*

Group and the Unconscious. He and René Kaës have a common strong reference to Freud's early writings as well as the second topic, where the subject is represented as a group composed of three instances, the super-ego, the ego, and the it. René Kaës in turn points out that Freud's very first representation, in 1895, of the unconscious is actually a "split psychic group" (Kaës 2007, 98). On this basis, he formulates the claim that the unconscious is "structured as a group":

> It is probable that living matter is a group – that is, a movement of grouping and ungrouping, under the effect of Narcissus, Eros, and Thanatos. To restrict myself to the domain of psychic life, I retain the notion of *primal psychic group* to account for the primal binding of objects in a structure and in forms that constitute the unconscious. The unconscious, structured as a group, is constantly recombining itself in its figures, its energy, its formations, and its effects. (ibid., 99)

The unconscious is thus always already collective in its essence: which explains its dynamic already on the individual level. It is precisely because the ego, the superego, and the it (or any other configuration) have a power relation within the subject that the subject may actually feel alive and act, for example when the it desires something that the superego is not strong enough to prevent. An extension of the skin-ego means that the envelopes where the relation with the other subjects takes place is made up of phantasies that hold the group together, and that those phantasies themselves involve several persons that the subject partly identifies with.

A Skin-Deep Unconscious

In the first chapter, I discussed in certain detail the interpretations of Merleau-Ponty's phrase that "the unconscious is sensing itself." The notion of the skin-ego allows a better understanding of its implications. Anzieu sets the skin-ego as a mediating concept between two antagonistic tendencies in psychoanalysis in the second half of the twentieth century: the "empiricist, pragmatic, psychogenetic tendency, most common among the British and Americans," and "a structuralist tendency, predominant in France in the last few decades," rejecting the claim that the structure of the unconscious may emerge from experience, but rather that "any experience must itself have been organized by preexisting structures" (Anzieu 2016, 4f). Anzieu did not write a text explicitly about the notion of the unconscious; he indeed presupposes the Freudian approach whereby the unconscious is the depository of repressed content, as well as the source of the affects and drives. His focus, as we have seen, was more on the ego as a *container* of—both conscious and unconscious—*contents*, than on the unconscious quality of those contents. There is nevertheless a passage in his book about creativity, *The Body of the Work*, where he thematizes the unconscious from his perspective:

> The unconscious I'm dealing with is a living, individual reality. It's alive because it's linked to the body, both real and imaginary, to its drives and functions, and to the representations, first sensory-motor and secondarily verbal, that certain parts of the psychic apparatus make of it. Individual, because throughout a psychoanalysis, it's a question of a particular person, with his or her singular unconscious, with the multiplicity of his or her identifications and the subsystems that make up his or her psychic apparatus as an internal group. (Anzieu 1981, 11)

The unconscious is "linked to the body" of this singular individual person with this singular irreplaceable history. At the same time, the individual unconscious is essentially conditioned and shaped by the relations that have formed it. The notion of the skin-ego is from the outset a relational notion. The skin is, both in the dermatological and in the metaphorical sense, a place of encounter. If we feel concerned by an action or by the presence of someone, we commonly say that we are touched, or that it was touching.

The claim that the unconscious is between the subjects, and that it is at play for an individual as well as for a group, since the individual is also himself a group of at least three characters (the ego, the superego, and the it), implies that the power of the unconscious is not its depth inside the subject, but rather how it permeates the skin of the subject. Indeed, the skin, as sensitive envelope, is the organ of sensing; to say that we are "touched" by an event, or something that appears and affects us, is not a metaphor, it refers to the fact that our skin-envelope has been affected in some way.

The dimension of depth should nevertheless be maintained: firstly, the skin, even if only in the dermatological sense, does have several layers and depths; secondly, the depth of the unconscious in the skin can be assessed according to the power of the impact experienced by the subject, as the root cause of its disorder. This leads to the third meaning, that is that depth can be understood as temporal depth, and not only as spatial depth. In order to articulate together the vertical and the horizontal dimensions of the unconscious, the personal and the relational, it is reasonable to consider the vertical as temporally deep, linked to the subject's personal (more or less traumatic) history, and the horizontal as the space of relations, as we have seen in all the authors that we have examined so far. My argument here is that the depth of the unconscious is not spatial: there is nothing to look for beyond the surfaces and the envelopes inside the mind of a subject. All that matters lies between subjects, in the depths of their relations. The unconscious is skin-deep because its depth is in the sensitive membrane by which the subject is in the presence of others, and without which the subject could not become what it is meant to be. It is skin-deep because it consists of movements, affects and thoughts that all stand for the subject's relations with others. This is what Kaës also claims when he writes that the subject of the unconscious is "formed conjointly in intersubjectivity" (Kaës 2007, 231), and this will be the topic of the next chapter.

Notes

1. Anzieu's book *The Skin-Ego* was first published in 1985, and in a revised version in 1995; the idea was first published in an article in *Nouvelle Revue de Psychanalyse* in 1974. In English, there are already two translations: the first by Chris Turner, in 1989, based on the first edition, was published by Yale University Press; the second, from which I shall be quoting in the following chapters, is based on the 1995 revised edition, by Naomi Segal, and published in 2016 by Karnac books, and then in 2018 by Routledge. Anzieu's book *The Group and the Unconscious* was published originally in 1975, and in English by Benjamin Kilborne in 1984 as the first volume of a series on group therapy; a second French edition was also published in 1984. I will quote from the English, but also from the second French edition when the latter elaborates more.
2. Anzieu was analyzed by Lacan during his early years until he discovered the clinical case cited in Lacan's thesis was actually Anzieu's mother. But apart from this ethical question, Anzieu claims that Lacan's mistake is to pretend to reconstruct the entire psychoanalysis from a single form of data, i.e. language. But "The unconscious is not language; language can be used by the unconscious to express itself, but also by the ego to mask it" (Anzieu 2009, 152).
3. Anzieu refers in particular to Bion's book, *Experiences in Groups* (1961).

4. Cathexis is a technical term in psychoanalysis designating the economics of emotional investment, or projection, by the individual in something or someone else. Laplanche and Pontalis define it as "the fact that a certain amount of psychical energy is attached to an idea or to a group of ideas, to a part of the body, to an object, etc." (Laplanche and Pontalis 1973, 62ff).

References

Anzieu, Didier. 1981. *Le corps de l'œuvre. Essais psychanalytiques sur le travail créateur*. Paris: Gallimard.

Anzieu, Didier. 1984. *Le groupe et l'inconscient. L'imaginaire groupal.* 2nd ed. Paris: Dunod.

Anzieu, Didier. 2009. *Le Travail de l'inconscient. Textes choisis, présentés et annotés par René Kaës.* Paris: Dunod.

Anzieu, Didier. 2015. *The Group and the Unconscious.* Translated by B. Kilborne [1984]. London/New York: Routledge. Translation of the first French edition of 1975.

Anzieu, Didier. 2016. *The Skin-Ego.* Translated by N. Segal. [1985]. London: Karnac Books.

Bion, Winfried. 1961. *Experiences in Groups.* London: Tavistock.

Dolto, Françoise. 1981. *Au jeu du désir. Essais cliniques.* Paris: Seuil.

Dolto, Françoise. 2023. *The Unconscious Body Image [1984].* Trans. S. Bailly. London: Routledge.

Freud, Sigmund. 1923. *The Ego and the Id.* [Das Ich und das Es]. *Standard Edition, 19,* vol XIX, 1923–1925. London: Hogarth, 1961; Vintage 2001, pp. 3–66.

Freud, Sigmund. 1961. The Standard Edition of the Complete Psychological Works of Sigmund Freud, ed. J. Strachey. Vol. XIX.

Kaës, René. 2007. *Linking, Alliances, and Shared Space. Groups and the Psychoanalyst.* Translated by A. Weller. London: The International Psychoanalytical Association.

Laplanche, Jean and Pontalis, Jean-Bertrand. 1973. *The Language of Psycho-Analysis.* London, Karnac Books.

Merleau-Ponty, Maurice. 1968. The Visible and the Invisible [1964]. Trans A. Lingis. Evanston (IL), Northwestern University Press.

Merleau-Ponty, Maurice. 2003. *Nature. Course Notes from the Collège de France* [1995]. Translated by R. Vallier. Evanston, Northwestern University Press.

Rogozinski, Jacob. 2006. *Le moi et la chair. Introduction à l'ego-analyse.* Paris: Cerf.

CHAPTER 9

Extended Minds and Unconscious Alliances

A first version of this chapter was presented at the Nordic Society of Phenomenology in 2018.

The subject of the unconscious is formed in the division between the fulfillment of its own end and its embedding into intersubjective bonds. (…) This double status of the subject, the requirements of psychic work associated with it, as a result of his connection with the intersubjective groups, divide him from inside, and square with the constitutive division of the unconscious.
Kaës 2013, 222

Didier Anzieu and René Kaës are not the only ones to have defined the individual unconscious in relation to the group. In order to further explore the interaction between collective and individual subjectivities, this time from the perspective of the collective, I propose in this chapter to examine the approach found in contemporary phenomenology. A few years ago, there was intensive phenomenological production concerning the ways in which we might "extend" the individual mind to understand collective intentionality. What is the foundation of a "socially extended mind," as Shaun Gallagher dubbed it? What is it that holds together a multiplicity of individual minds in a collective whole? What are the origins of the phenomenon of "togetherness"? How might we take affectivity into account, and argue for the claim that the extension of the individual mind is

S. Kristensen, *The Intercorporeal Unconscious*,
https://doi.org/10.1007/978-3-032-22596-2_9

produced through the "integration of shared emotions" as do Dan Zahavi and his colleagues? Similarly to the psychoanalysts, we shall find that mimicry and emotional contagion is neither necessary nor equivalent to emotional sharing, and that some kind of identification is required.

A common reference for contemporary phenomenologists and group psychoanalysts is Paul Schilder and his notion of the body schema: Gallagher's conception of the body relies on Schilder's work, and Schilder is very much considered by Anzieu as being as important as Paul Federn. It is striking to observe that the reference to Schilder is central to the phenomenology of Shaun Gallagher and Dan Zahavi, even though there is no consideration of psychoanalysis in their works. But, as Merleau-Ponty himself said in his lectures on child psychology at the Sorbonne, it is indeed "antiscientific" to disregard the contributions of psychoanalysis to this topic (Merleau-Ponty 2010, 261). Schilder is important because he is the main source of Merleau-Ponty's conception of the body, and Anzieu and Kaës are important because they can be regarded as the continuators of Merleau-Ponty's reception of psychoanalysis. Since the extended mind debate is essentially rooted in the phenomenological tradition, my aim here is to reconnect contemporary conceptions with the articulations already sketched out by Merleau-Ponty in his later works from the 1950s, and psychoanalysis. The central issue is to account for boundaries of the ego and group membership at the same time, or as Leon, Szanto, and Zahavi put it, when a self-other difference is required, it must allow for a "feeling of togetherness." From this feeling of togetherness to the psychoanalysis of intersubjectivity and the subject of the unconscious link, my aim here is to articulate the notion of the envelope with the concept of the body schema and thereby provide an account of the group as a sui generis phenomenon without surrendering the singularity of each subject composing the group. This should help to build a new interface between phenomenological and psychodynamic thinking.

The Contemporary Phenomenology of Togetherness

There have been significant developments in the field of collective intentionality, following Andy Clark's and David Chalmers' idea of the extended mind, where the philosophers argue in favor of an "active externalism," that is the claim that the environment plays an active role in "driving cognitive processes" (Clark and Chalmers 1998, 7). Gallagher, in a paper from 2013 on the "socially extended mind," and Krueger on joint attention (Krueger 2014) among others, have contributed to a debate where the stakes are to sketch out a phenomenology of a collective intentionality. What does such a collective, superindividual mind consist in? Does it consist in a simple extension of individual minds, or does it imply a logic of its own, irreducible to the aggregation of individual subjectivities? And perhaps more importantly, how does it hold together, what is it that holds a collective intentionality together?

Gallagher introduces the notion of institution in an attempt to describe the substance of the extension. He criticizes Clark and Chalmers for sticking to a conception of the mind committed to the Cartesian view of the "mental process as something that would normally happen in the head" (2013, 5). He proposes instead a view where the institutions in which a mental process takes place are also part of this very process. Let us take the example of a judgment in a court case: in such an example, judgments are not happening simply inside the individual mind of the judge, but they are the result of collective processes shaped by the institution within which they are made: "The practice of law", Gallagher writes, "[…] is carried out via the cooperation of many people relying on external (and conventional) cognitive schemas and rules of evidence provided by the legal institution itself" (2013, 7). This "social extension" of the mind doesn't explain however how different individual subjects might share an experience and a relation with the world. Certainly, "technologies and institutions shape our cognitive processes, make our brains work in certain ways" (ibid.), as Gallagher notes, meaning that those institutions enable the individual subject to accomplish the cognitive tasks it is supposed to. But the horizontal dimension of sharing that is at the root of group belonging, and group cohesion, remains untouched by this idea; it is a relevant description of the situation seen from the outside, but it doesn't explain how this institution emerges in the first place, and what keeps it alive. In order to go further in that direction, we need to explore the dynamics of identification, as Zahavi, Szanto, and Leon do in a paper published in 2017 on "Emotional sharing and the extended mind," since they raise the question of affectivity at the core of collective intentionality. Their paper rests on the claim of the extension of individual minds and their integration into a higher unity, which is the basis of a phenomenological approach, and their "socially extended emotion thesis" amounts to the claim that there is a type of process consisting in the "constitutive integration of individual experiences" into a higher unit that they call "togetherness." There are individually delimited minds, and the task then of a phenomenology of group belonging is to describe such togetherness without an outright "phenomenal fusion" or "breakdown of individual boundaries." They hold that among the conditions to call an emotion "shared" is the experiencing subject's awareness of "the presence and participation of others and vice-versa." Their claim at the end of the paper is that "the Socially Extended Emotion Thesis should primarily be construed in terms of a constitutive integration of the experiences of different individuals," which means that the individuality of experience is preserved but that there is nevertheless a possibility of sharing the experience, and thus of "extending" the individual's experience. The important contribution here is that this extending happens through a precise phenomenology of affectivity, of shared emotions, and this opens up the space for a dialogue with certain psychoanalytic contributions, in particular around the mechanisms of identification.

There have been quite a few developments in the field since 2017, but Zahavi's very recent book *Being We* only contains one (very questionable) allusion to psychoanalysis, claiming that psychoanalysis "occasionally" suggests that "the psychological life of infants is characterized by some kind of undifferentiated fusional we-ness" (Zahavi 2025, 37). As seen in the previous chapter about Anzieu, and more particularly concerning Dolto's insistence on the personhood of the infant being from the outset a subject of desire, this claim is simply absurd. There are no undifferentiated fusions in psychoanalysis, instead there are complex projections and introjections that play a decisive role in the progressive process of development of the child's self.

The Other in Me: Body Schema and Identification

In order to account for the autonomy of a collective subjectivity in the first person plural, the path followed by the contemporary phenomenologists is to explore the structure of identification, a notion that is also found in psychoanalysis. Identification supposes the existence of two distinct individual subjectivities, and yet a certain degree of indistinctness between the two. Leon, Szanto, and Zahavi formulate the problem in the following terms, where the contradiction clearly appears:

> To feel an emotion not simply as one's own but as ours requires that one *identifies* with the other(s) in order to experience oneself as one of us, where the latter expression is understood in non-distributive terms. (…) A self-

other difference is indeed required, but if it is too salient, it will impede the feeling of togetherness.

Further they claim that shared emotions should be understood in "transactional terms," meaning that the emotion itself is fully explained as a result of intersubjective processes. But they do not explain what makes such a transaction possible, how the "breakdown of individual boundaries" actually happens. One solution that they critically discuss would be to accept the idea of an originary undifferentiation of the infant and the caregiver, like the thesis of "joint ownership" that Krueger attributes to Merleau-Ponty in his lecture on "The child's relation with others" given at the Sorbonne in 1951: "The core feature of Merleau-Ponty's view here is the claim that certain early experiences are jointly owned, in that they are numerically single experiences that are nevertheless given to more than one subject (e.g., the infant and caregiver). Call this the 'joint ownership thesis'" (Krueger 2014). Identification is understandable from the point of view of a supposed original state of undifferentiated awareness, where the self and the (caregiving) other are not yet distinguished as two separate egos. If identification is possible, it is indeed plausible to admit that there is a phase in the development of the human subject where experiences can indeed be shared, in particular between the infant and the caregiving person. However, Merleau-Ponty's Sorbonne lecture doesn't really present a clear theory of such a fusion, and the passages Kruger quotes are actually rather more critical of the presupposition of "classical psychology" claiming that each subjectivity is separated from the others, than they are affirmative about the reality of a fusion of the subjective flow of experiences. In other passages, there is more than this criticism, there is also a description and comment on the psychoanalytic conceptions of child development, and he deems it "antiscientific to lose interest in this material" (Merleau-Ponty 2010, 261), as already evoked above. He thereby mainly discusses Freud's and Melanie Klein's conceptions, and this aspect of the lecture is strangely ignored by Krueger in his article. Merleau-Ponty also explains that psychoanalysis "puts the comprehension of the image and the child's identification with the other in relation to one another" (ibid., 254s), and emphasizes in particular the importance of transference, i.e. the relationship with the analyst that allows the subject to "take up the totality of his attitudes toward people and objects that make him what he is" (ibid., 262). In his interpretation of psychoanalysis, the philosopher points to what we have repeatedly called the horizontal dimension of the clinical practice, as a space for experiencing the affects and emotions belonging to one relationship (e.g. the relation of a daughter with her father) in another (e.g. with the analyst). Throughout his lectures at the Sorbonne's psychology department and at the Collège de France, Merleau-Ponty's approach was to provide a conceptual explanation of the practice itself, to measure the relevance of the concepts against their ability to explain how clinical practice works in real life.

The relevant concept that Merleau-Ponty discusses in this lecture is the concept of "transitivism." He defines it as "aptitude to find in the other what appears in himself" (Merleau-Ponty 2010, 258). The concept captures the general movements of projection and introjection, by which the subject tends to see him or herself in the other, or to adopt as his or hers what s/he sees in the other. Merleau-Ponty also uses the term "mimesis" in reference to the teachings of Henri Wallon. There are "striking examples of transitivism in children," he writes on the same page, and presents a case described by Wallon of a little girl who unexpectedly slaps her friend sitting next to her, saying that it was him who was nasty and slapped her. The transfer here consists in a displacement of the origin of her anxiety outside of herself. This phenomenon is at the core of psychoanalytic teachings, and it is generally explained by the fact that the child's sense of self-awareness is dependent upon the stability of the relationships in which the dynamics of projection and introjection take place. The child's sense of self is dependent upon its affective environment, its autonomy upon the predictability and safety of its caregivers' attitudes.

Identification from this point of view is a sort of regression into, or recalling of the primitive stages of becoming-self. In other terms, it necessarily involves an affective and at times unconscious component. Indeed, when Merleau-Ponty started to teach at the Collège de France in the spring of 1953, and took up the question of perception yet again in his first lecture about "The Sensible World and the World of Expression," he devoted nearly half of his lecture to Schilder's *Image and Appearance of the Human Body*, and was in particular interested in the intersubjective (or rather intercorporeal) dimension of the body schema. In order to understand what Merleau-Ponty meant by the notion of identification, a closer look at this lecture is relevant. He was particularly interested in Schilder's ideas about the interrelations of two or more subjects' body images, and cases in which there is a disorder in the perception of the other's body. In the 14th lecture of the 1953 course, he comments on a passage in which Schilder states the following:

> Whenever there are disturbances in the postural model of the body, the patients also have difficulty in recognizing the different parts of the bodies of others. They cannot distinguish between their fingers; they cannot recognize the left and right side of the bodies of others. We arrive at the general formulation that the postural models of human beings are connected with each other and that where we are not able to come to a true perception of our own body, we are also unable to perceive the bodies of others. (Schilder 1950, 43s)

Merleau-Ponty refers in his commentary to "affective emphasizing [*accentuation*]," a "libidinal structure" that opens up to the "social structure of the body schema." The body is "the bearer of a whole symbolic system which shapes it in return" (Merleau-Ponty 2020, 118). This means that some areas of the body are more valued and desirable than others according to the perception of others, for example the right side can be favored over the left. This entails that the symbolic libidinal structure of the body is, on the one hand, dependent upon the perception of others, but on the other hand, that there already *is* a body-subject able to receive and embody such accentuations. The body is defined as a "medium of intercorporeal significations that take hold of it" (ibid., 119) but this does not mean that the individual subject is indistinct from the others; it means that the individual subject is autonomous *as* a part of the social structures in which it develops.

Since Merleau-Ponty's focus in the 1953 course was on the first part of Schilder's book about the individual body subject, he didn't comment on the two other parts, on the libidinal structure and the social structure of the body schema. Yet Schilder offers an important definition of identification in the third part of his book, a definition that Merleau-Ponty could not have missed:

> In identification, the individual identifies himself with persons in his actual or imagined surroundings, and expresses his identification in symptoms, either actions of phantasies. He plays a role, enriches himself by the experiences of others [...]. In the development of infantile sexuality, the little boy admires the father and wants to take his place. We may be dealing with a conscious wish. But often this wish will never come to a clear inner conception. He will only betray it by taking over gestures, habits, and trends of the father, which then become symptoms of identification. (...) The fact that identification is in the unconscious makes it possible to identify oneself with several persons at the same time. (Schilder 1950, 251)

Schilder outlines the condition under which there can be identification: the existence of two distinct subjects, where the identifying subject is able to develop symptoms, in the form of actions or phantasies. There can be no symptoms if there is no subject whose symptoms it is. But if an identification takes place, it must be unconsciously, since it derives from a desire to become someone else. The bodily self incorporates parts of the body schema of the other, and the other incorporates parts of the body of the self, but this does not mean that there is no boundary between the self and the other. Merleau-Ponty navigated this quite subtle dialectic until the end of his life; in the summary of his 1960 lecture on "Nature and logos, the human body," he affirms that corporeality should be understood as a "global power of incorporation" (Merleau-Ponty 1968, 178), and a few lines before on the previous page: "The schema of the body proper, since I am able to see myself, can be shared by all other bodies, which I can also see. The body schema is a lexicon of corporeality in general, a system of equivalences between the inside and the outside" (ibid.). The body schema, as we have seen also in the chapter about Schilder and Dolto, is the schema of my own body as much as it is also the schema of other bodies, indeed the principle of translation of one bodily structure into the other.

The self-other relation is a complex and changing chiasmus where there is as much of me in the other as in myself. I agree with Leon, Szanto, and Zahavi when they criticize the thesis of joint ownership, and search to account for both a delimitation between self and other and the possibility of shared emotions. My proposal in the following pages will that the key to this issue of describing the articulation of the collective and the individual without opposing them lies in the psychoanalytic definition of intersubjectivity by Anzieu and Kaës, around the notions of collective envelopes and unconscious alliances. Instead of going outwards from the individual Ego and from there extending the mind onto the collective, it is worth trying to take the fact of intersubjectivity as a starting point.

Collective Boundaries: Group Phantasies

The body schema does not account for the boundaries of the self—in fact it is the contrary: my sentient body extends onto the stars, when I perceive I am *at* the perceived object. As a perceiving sensitive subject, I am constantly extending into the world, and my unity and integrity is constantly problematic. The risk is indeed, as Leon, Szanto and Zahavi have pointed out, to end up with a conception of identification that leads to a confusion of self and other, since no concept able to account for the articulation of self and other is provided. As we have seen, Anzieu's concept of the skin-ego refers to skin both in the dermatological sense and in the sense of an intersensorial envelope between the ego and the others. It is both an organic and a psychical fact that fulfills several functions in the life of the human subject: it maintains the psyche through the experience of being held by the caregiver; it contains the body of the subject and keeps the body united; it protects the subject from aggressive stimuli and acts like a shield; it allows the process of individuation of the subject; it also allows for intersensoriality since touch is the basic reference for all the senses; it is the surface supporting sexual excitation; finally, it fulfills the function of registering sensorial tactile traces, and thus functions as a mirror for the image of reality (2016, Chap. 7). Across all such functions of the skin-ego, the core idea is that it is at the same time a container, a warrant of the unity and continuity of the Ego, and a condition for relation with others, in particular in virtue of its libidinal dimensions. In the list of functions, Anzieu describes the skin as a surface for libidinal investments (in the psychoanalytic language), for sexual excitation, in other terms as the place where the real, affective, relation with the other takes place. The eight functions of the skin-ego can actually be summarized in terms of three essential features: it is a container, an interface and a site and surface for communication. By combining these three features, we can account for the origin of the self-other distinction in the infant, precisely in the sensations of the skin, of being touched by the caregiver and the experience of reversibility into the sensation of actively touching.

Anzieu writes about the caregiver-infant dyad and what keeps it together both bodily and affectively. In the following passage, he draws on Brazelton's approach and offers a beautiful description of the dynamics of resonance between the two, introducing the notion of the skin as interface:

> The double feedback observed by Brazelton results, in my opinion, in an interface, represented as a skin common to the mother and the child, with the mother on one side and the child on the other. This common skin keeps them attached to each other but has a certain symmetry that prefigures their later separation. "Plugged in" to each other through the common skin, the two partners communicate directly, with reciprocal empathy and an adhesive identification: it is a single screen that resonates with the sensations, affects, mental images, and vital rhythms of both. (Anzieu 2016, 67)

(Here, the term "mental images" is the same in French.) The common skin is the primary phenomenon that serves as a model for thinking and figuring the collective envelopes. Indeed, Anzieu and Kaës have developed a practice and a theory of group analysis, based on, and in dialogue with, practices and theories of English psychoanalysts such as W. Bion. When Anzieu describes the essential features of the "group apparatus" in his book *The Group and the Unconscious*, he doesn't simply make do with the principle of "containing," of delimitation of the group towards other groups. This would amount to simply extending the idea of the skin to collective identities. He also mentions two other important features: the undifferentiation of individual and group, as well as the principle of self-sufficiency of the group. In the chapter summing up "Psychoanalytic group theory," Anzieu makes clear that an individual phantasy in a group, despite being individual, in itself has an "internal group organization" (Anzieu 1984, 229). As we have already seen in the previous chapter, a particular phantasy "derives from the subject's identification with one or several persons" (ibid., 230).

The metaphor of the skin is not enough to account for group belonging, a clear account of interactions within the group is also required; but it is useful when put in articulation with the specific affective schema that characterizes its internal structure. Anzieu explains his central claim that relations between humans persist thanks to an interhuman unconscious bond resulting from the circulation of phantasies [*circulation fantasmatique*], uniting persons around ways of being and feeling rather than ways of acting: it "seeks to provoke the common sharing the imaginary accomplishment of the individual unconscious threats and desires" (Anzieu 1984, 180). In the second edition of the *Group and Unconscious*, he then presents five unconscious psychic organizers of this circulation within the group: the individual fantasy; the imago, the originary fantasies, the Oedipus complex, and the group envelope. There are thus organizing principles specific to groups composed of several subjects, different from "internal" groups such as individual subjects, and these principles operate according to the way in which an individual phantasy starts to circulate unconsciously among the others in the group.

> The supposed imago of a group body is in fact a pseudo organizing principle; it corresponds to a nostalgic dream of symbiosis between group members. [...] However, the psychic apparatus, whether of individuals or groups, constitutes a containing envelope; it is delimited and protected by what I

have called an skin-ego. (Anzieu 2016, 242; the corresponding passage in the second edition is p. 200)

The second edition adds after the "symbiosis between group members": "In a primitive maternal matrix," referring to the phantasy of Léonore who involuntarily shares her phantasy of being the woman who masters life and death, as I mentioned in the previous chapter. But the crucial part of this quotation is when Anzieu affirms that groups, and not only individuals, also have a "psychic apparatus" and a "containing envelope." The phantasy originates in an individual, but as soon as it is appropriated (unconsciously) by the members of the group, as soon as it starts to spread and circulate, it becomes the envelope that confers its singularity to the group. As Anzieu explains, this envelope can be the leader, the representation of the group as a horde or matrix, or any idea that fulfills the function of containing the processes happening within the group, maintaining the group through time and also creating a sense of belonging among members.

As I mentioned in passing, according to Anzieu, the Oedipus complex is but one of the possible organizing principles of a group, and not the founding myth of every culture, as Freud and the orthodox Freudians would have it. In the same chapter, Anzieu presents a series of arguments against the universality of the Oedipus complex (Anzieu 2015, 237–40), just 3 years after Deleuze and Guattari's *Anti-Oedipus* (the first edition of *The Group and the Unconscious* was published in 1975). The organizing principles of groups are much larger than the binary family that the Oedipus phantasy is supposed to symbolize; Oedipus only applies in a traditional family because the affective power that maintains the group can take so many different forms according to what resonates among the members and enables the orientation of their libido.

A Psychoanalytical Conception of Intersubjectivity

So, if the infant-caregiver dyad is the first social institution, where the socially extended mind is first instituted, if an individual phantasy can become the unconscious organizing principle of groups, then groups also have a skin-envelope that functions both as an interface and as a boundary. But, as we just saw, the description of how a phantasy circulates among the members of a group is not precise enough; an account of the internal structure of the group is also needed. This is where René Kaës' concept of unconscious alliances comes into play. He introduced this concept in his 2007 book *Linking, Alliances, and Shared Space* (the first version of his *Un Singulier Pluriel*), in order to designate the collective envelopes defining the boundaries between the inside and outside of the group, as well as the interfaces between the singular individual and the rest of the group (similar to the "common skin" of caregiver and infant). The unconscious alliances characterize specifically the implicit structure of the group, the web of affective dynamics and relations that give the group the form and atmosphere it has. Kaës defines it as follows:

> I have used the term 'unconscious alliance' to refer to an intersubjective psychic formation constructed by the subjects of a link in order to strengthen in each of them, and to establish as the basis of their link, the narcissistic and object-investments that they need, and the processes, functions, and psychic structures that are necessary for them, which derive from repression, or from denial, rejection, and disavowal. The alliance is formed in such a way that that the link acquires a decisive psychic value for each of its subjects. (Kaës 2007, 206)

The alliances are effective because their being unconscious endows them with a power that "requires from the subjects involved in them obligations and subjections; they distribute benefits to them and promise them pleasures" (ibid.). They are crucial to the very structure and balance of the individuals' unconsciouses, and Kaës goes so far as to claim that they "produce a part of the unconscious and psychic reality of each subject" (ibid., 206–7). In other words, the unconscious alliance refers to the very moment, or act, by which the members of a group take up and make theirs a phantasy or an imago, and where this phantasy becomes the organizing principle. This is founded on a specific notion of intersubjectivity defined by Kaës in the following way:

> By intersubjectivity I mean not a system of behavioral interactions between individuals communicating their feelings through empathy, but the experience and space of psychic reality that is specified by their relations as subjects inasmuch as they are subjects of the unconscious. Intersubjectivity is what is shared by these subjects, who are formed and bound to each other by their reciprocal subjections – structuring or alienating –to the constitutive mechanisms of the unconscious: common repressions and denials, shared phantasies and signifiers, unconscious wishes and the fundamental taboos that organize them. (Kaës 2007, 6)

These two definitions by Kaës, of the unconscious alliance and of intersubjectivity, attempt to capture the real intertwining and common originarity of the individual and the collective. Differently from the phenomenological conception that goes out schematically from the ego, and then constitutes the common realm by virtue of empathy, i.e. of the perception of the other as another ego in his or her own right, the psychoanalytic conception implies a codependency of the individual and the common. The phenomenological conception also tends to favor the cognitive dimension of the encounter with the other, whereas the psychoanalytic approach favors the affective dimension of attraction and repulsion, projection and introjection, where the subject is not only the subject having experiences, but also the subject in the sense of being *subjected to* affective movements. The primacy of the affective dimension is decisive in describing the subject as divided, not only within himself, but also "divided in his relations with the other, and with more than one other" (ibid., 233).

The human subject as such is a "subject of the unconscious" and where the whole experienced social reality is made up by affective relations. Being "subjects of the unconscious" means that the subjects are essentially constituted by dynamics of the unconscious such as repressions or denials, phantasies, desires or taboos, and since such dynamics circulate both inside and outside the subject, it entails the subject being essentially divided. More fundamentally, being a subject of the unconscious implies the experience of an unbridgeable alterity within the subject, an irreducible division of the subject within itself. Kaës emphasizes the "paradox of the subject: subjected and structured in this subjection" (ibid., 233).

Kaës distinguishes three different categories of alliances according to their structure and effects: the first contributes to the structuring of the psyche, such as for example the Oedipean pact between the brothers and the father that Freud introduces in *Totem and Taboo*; the second type are defensive alliances such as the community of denial; the third category is the offensive pact, that fuels the attack or the domination of one group upon another.[1] Kaës' example of the negative pact [*pacte dénégatif*] is a good example of strong group belonging based on the exclusion of some specific other. For example, the cohesion of the modern Turkish nation is largely based on the denial of the destruction of its Christian minorities, while the group belonging of members of neo-Nazi groups is based on the denial of the destruction of the Jews during the Second World War. In such cases, it is difficult to discern the interface dimension of the unconscious alliance. An alliance relying essentially on denial or repression seems to be more exclusive of other groups than it is open to exchanges and cooperation. Inside the group, the alliance articulates the singularity of each subject and his or her belonging, functioning, rather like the skin-ego, as a container and an interface at the same time.

But Kaës doesn't just point out a paradox; he describes a dialectic. The paradox of the subject is also the condition of possibility for the subject to become itself. "It is because he has been subjected that the process of subjectivation is possible" (ibid.), he writes in a striking formulation. This means that the subject must encounter a power (a phantasy, a drive, etc.) that s/he perceives as sufficiently threatening or desirable that it triggers a movement of repression or denial in him/her, i.e. that s/he is subjected to this power. This in turn allows this phantasy to play its role and to exercise its power. Kaës then immediately answers the implicit objection that this would reduce the subject to an alienated subject, a subject essentially trapped in the desire of another; he explains that alienation is "but one of the vicissitudes of subjection" (ibid., 242), albeit a very common one. Subjection in the sense of the condition of possibility of becoming a subject is not necessarily alienating, but the encounter with an alien desire is considered necessary in order to become aware of oneself as a subject bearer of links with others, as the *subject of linking*. Unconscious alliances, Kaës writes are "the base and the cement that links us to one another"; they even form "the material of the psychic reality that is characteristic of intersubjective links," such as a couple, a family, a group, or an institution. This is precisely the reason why they "fabricate a part of the unconscious of each subject," and are "constitutive of the psychic reality of each subject" (ibid., 237).

In his 2015 book on the *Metapsychology of the third type*, Kaës defines psychoanalytical intersubjectivity as an "articulation of two psychic spaces":

> The question of intersubjectivity raises the question of the recognition and the articulation of two psychic spaces partially heterogenous, each endowed with their own contents, processes and logics. It explicitly contains the notion of a gap between self and self in the core of the subject as well as in the heart of the link. This conception of alterity, that implies the vicissitudes of internal alterity, defines intersubjectivity as a central problematic in psychoanalysis [...]. I understand by intersubjectivity [...] the experience and space of psychic reality that is specified by subjective relations of the individuals inasmuch as they are subjects of the unconscious. One can also say

> that intersubjectivity is the dynamic structure of psychic space between two or more subjects. (Kaës 2015, 248)

In a third type metapsychology, the central question is that of the unconscious, writes René Kaës in 2015: the unconscious is "not only of a psychosexual origin, but also and jointly grounded in intersubjectivity" (Kaës 2015, 21).

> Our knowledge of the unconscious is not exhausted by the experience that individual psychoanalytical treatment makes possible. The metapsychology that has been developed needs to be revised when the practice of psychoanalysis is modified and when our knowledge of psychic apparatus is transformed. The hypothesis of a psyche shared in intersubjectivity leads us to build models of intelligibility for this reality, its consistency, its structures, and its laws of transformation. (Kaës 2007, 239)

Kaës identifies three fundamental concepts that describe this third space: unconscious alliances, phoric functions, and polyphonic dream space, all of which "have a double metapsychological status": not only can they be described equally from the individual and the collective perspective, but they also show an interdependence of the individual in relation to the collective. Kaës writes that they are "dialogically related to each other." Any change in the alliances "calls into question the unconscious structure of each subject" whereas reciprocally, any change in the dynamic of the subject is hindered by the force of the alliances (ibid.). As a result, the unconscious "is not entirely contained within the limits of individual psychic space" (ibid., 240; the same sentence can be found in Kaës 2015, 249).

Consequently, the unconscious spreads out in three spaces at the same time: it is *in the subject* [*dans le sujet*] in the sense that it belongs to his particular history; it is *between the subjects* [*entre les sujets*] in the sense of a phantasy circulating in a group; but it is also *outside the subject* [*hors sujet*], in the sense that it belongs to the very link that keeps a group together. The purpose of the third type metapsychology is indeed to propose a "logic of [such] subjectivity correlations" (Kaës 2015, 249) that constitute the coherence of those three spaces, the *intra*psychic space of the subject itself, the *inter*psychic space of the links, and the *trans*psychic space of the group itself. Kaës describes a structure of codependence of the ego and the relations that make him/her who s/he is: "The path of 'becoming me' [*devenir Je*], of the Freudian *Ich werden*, [...] is partly mapped out in the intersubjective relation with the other" (ibid.), making a part of the unconscious inaccessible to individual cure on the couch. The repressions, denials and narcissistic pacts that produce the unconscious in all three spaces are essential components in the constitution of the subject. Intersubjectivity is a "work" both within the group, between the subjects and within the individual psyche because the links with the others, made up by desires, phantasies and emotions, define who the subject is. Based on his clinical experience, Kaës claims that the links and alliances are constitutive of the individual subject's unconscious, that is the psychic contents that have been repressed, the modalities of the return of the repressed. All those processes indeed occur in relation to the others; desire is always necessarily for someone or something alien; a phantasy has always to do with something or someone outside the subject; feeling or sensing is necessarily directed towards something that appears and attracts or repels the subject; etc. Thus, the ego is at the same time within itself and outside itself, and between itself and others:

> It is in this setting [*appareillage*] between ensembles organized by processes and mental formations common to several subjects, and to each subject individually, that the ego can occur. (ibid., 251)

Transition

I have tried to describe how the dynamics of identification, which are the core condition of group belonging, work in practice between real desiring human subjects. The condition to be satisfied was that it should at the same time respect the singularity of each subject (even the infant with its weak sense of self) and allow for the emergence of collective intentionalities, of shared affective experiences. I started with the discussion in contemporary phenomenology and philosophy of mind, and argued that while this discussion takes the emotions into account, it does not have a conception of the desiring subject. Merleau-Ponty did have such a conception that he elaborated in dialogue with Sigmund Freud, Paul Schilder, and Melanie Klein, three more or less known figures from the psychoanalytic tradition. But as he focused on the Schilderian notion of the body image, Merleau-Ponty did not allow himself to account for the delimitation of the self and the other and tended to exaggerate the possibility of fusion with the other, or the indistinction between the self of the infant and the self of the caregiver. In order to safeguard this possibility, I propose to take seriously the notion of the skin-ego introduced by Didier Anzieu, and its role as interface between subjects, and as a common skin of a dyad and possibly also larger groups. The body image and the skin-ego must be combined to form the structure of the human corporeal subject; the extension of the skin-ego to a collective envelope is at the center of Anzieu's and his colleague René Kaës' work from the 1970s. Kaës in particular developed the concept of unconscious alliance as a way of accounting for collective envelopes, movements of identification. The reason why those alliances are unconscious is because they rely on affective bonds that are to a large extent unconscious to the subjects composing the group, but nevertheless active and effective. And he defines the subject of the unconscious as the subject of the bond. The phenomenon of togetherness can be explained by using such concepts, precisely because the bonds between the individual subjects in a group, the "constitutive integration of experiences," are not entirely conscious in order to be efficient. Just as the motor subject cannot think about all his/her movements while doing them, the subject of the bond cannot be conscious of all the reasons why s/he feels s/he belongs to the group.

Note

1. We should add a fourth to this rather masculine and violent list, the pact of sisterhood, that Maniglier and Lippi argue for in their recent book, *Sœurs* (2023b). But this would be the topic of another work.

References

Anzieu, Didier. 1984. *Le Groupe et l'Inconscient. L'imaginaire groupal.* 2nd ed. Paris: Dunod.

Anzieu, Didier. 2015. *The Group and the Unconscious.* Translated by B. Kilborne [1984], from the first edition. London/New York, Routledge.

Anzieu, Didier. 2016. *The Skin-Ego. Trans. N. Segal. [1985].* London, Karnac Books.

Clark, Andy, and David Chalmers. 1998. The extended mind. *Analysis* 58 (1): 7–19.

Gallagher, Shaun. 2013. The Socially Extended Mind. *Cognitive Systems Research*, 25–26: 4–12.

Kaës, René. 2007. *Linking, Alliances, and Shared Space. Groups and the Psychoanalyst.* Translated by A. Weller. London: The International Psychoanalytical Association.

Kaës, René. 2013. *Être singulier pluriel [2007]*. Paris: Dunod.
Kaës, René. 2015. *L'extension de la psychanalyse. Pour une métapsychologie de troisième type*. Paris: Dunod.
Krueger, Joel. 2013. Ontogenesis of the Socially Extended Mind. *Cognitive Systems Research* 25–26:40–46.
Krueger, Joel. 2014. Merleau-Ponty on Shared Emotions and the Joint Ownership Thesis. *Continental Philosophy Review* 46:509–531.
León, Felipe, Thomas Szanto, and Dan Zahavi. 2017. Emotional Sharing and the Extended Mind. *Synthese* 196 (12): 4847–4867.
Merleau-Ponty, Maurice. 1968. *The Visible and the Invisible [1964]*. Trans A. Lingis. Evanston (IL): Northwestern University Press.
Merleau-Ponty, Maurice. 2010. *Child Psychology and Pedagogy. The Sorbonne Lectures 1949–1952.* Translated by T. Welsh. Evanston: Northwestern University Press.
Merleau-Ponty, Maurice. 2020. *The Sensible World and the World of Expression. Course Notes from the Collège de France, 1953* [2011]. Translated by B. Smith. Evanston: Northwestern University Press.
Schilder, Paul. 1950. *The Image and Appearance of the Human Body*. New York: International Universities Press.
Zahavi, Dan. 2015. You, Me, and We: The Sharing of Emotional Experiences. *Journal of Consciousness Studies* 22 (1–2): 84–101.
Zahavi, Dan. 2025. *Being We: Phenomenological Contributions to Social Ontology*. Oxford: Oxford University Press.

CHAPTER 10

The Unconscious and the More-than-Human

Thus it is that the relationship of every human being with his mother – the source of his existence – appears enrooted in what for lack of other words we may call the sacred. This is about the evidence felt by every human being of an aesthetic and ethical experience of contact with nature and its beauty.
Dolto 2023, 147

In the previous chapters, I have discussed in various ways the idea that the unconscious is between human bodies as much as it is within the subject's psyche. I hope it has become plausible to admit that the unconscious is not a radically separated realm, but it is precisely the space where our most intimate and at the same time our most shared emotions and phantasies play out, and that it unfolds powerfully between subjects, effecting oftentimes decisive parts of their lives. Yet, from the psychosomatic unconscious where the disease appears as an expression of a relational trauma to the unconscious as interface between humans, as envelope and as relational space in Anzieu and Kaës, the unconscious in the psychoanalytical tradition is widely considered as an exclusively human realm. One of the reasons for this is, firstly, that psychoanalysis belongs to twentieth century European traditions, and that twentieth century European thought is generally anthropocentric and colonialist. Freud's conceptions were anchored in Western rationalist traditions and considered "primitive" peoples from

S. Kristensen, *The Intercorporeal Unconscious*,
https://doi.org/10.1007/978-3-032-22596-2_10

a colonial perspective; as appears in his *Civilization and its Discontents*, the "progress" of civilization is paid for by a heavy price in terms of social violence, but the representation that human history goes from a situation of raw instincts to a regime of tightly tamed customs is pervasive. However, there is a path out of this exclusively human conception of the unconscious, a path all the more necessary given that the significant presences for a human subject can also be nonhuman entities. A mountain, a house, a pet, a river, a rock at the bottom of the garden, or any other entity may play a crucial role in the psychological development of a human subject. And more deeply, if the unconscious is "sensing itself," it appears obvious that the activity of sensing also aims at nonhumans, that more-than-human entities do actively solicit our attention, and that we tend to repress the experience of such expression.

The human mind in psychoanalysis in general is considered as being in relation essentially with other humans; relations with nonhumans, or more-than-human entities are generally not seen as affectively significant. But indeed, humans are not the only subjects that humans have desiring relationships with. In her recent book *The Imaginary of Animals*, Annabelle Dufourcq makes the case of a transcendental inter*animality*, that should replace the traditional intersubjectivity that the phenomenological tradition has so extensively discussed. To consider intersubjectivity as transcendental means that the encounter of other subjects is a condition of possibility of perceiving the world, as Husserl famously states in his *Cartesian Meditations.* Dufourcq's idea is that "Taking the subjectivity of non-human animals seriously proves crucial in the investigation of the true nature of things" (Dufourcq 2022, 81). Empathy extends to other than human subjectivities, and "we belong to a unique and yet manifold and dynamic transcendental interanimality" (ibid., 82).

While Dufourcq places her discussion at the service of an extension of Husserl's idea of a transcendental intersubjectivity, and thus an epistemological perspective, the suggestion here is that the relation with what David Abram calls the "more-than-human world" is crucial to the understanding of what makes us human. A tree, a river, a rock formation, or an animal, can play a central role in the development of the individual human subject because they can be the object of a strong affective attachment. In other words, if the unconscious is feeling, or sensing, itself, as we have mentioned several times, then nonhuman entities are thoroughly present as objects of this sensing. Moreover, as it is safe to claim that the presence of the more-than-human world has largely been repressed or ignored, particularly in the Western world, its very presence should be considered part of our shared unconscious. This is what Theodore Roszak probably meant when he wrote that "our estrangement from Gaia" is a neurosis (Roszak 1992, 304).

Ecological Approaches in Dolto, Marty, Anzieu, and Kaës

Our three psychoanalysts do make some allusions to the importance of more-than-human actors. They did not, of course, have at the core of their project the idea of extending psychoanalysis to the nonhuman, but they do open up to the possibility of an ecological approach to the unconscious. In the following pages, I shall pick up on a few hints that point in such a direction.

In fact, Freud himself did make reference to animals throughout his work, as Jean-Pierre Kamieniak explains in an article about Freud and dogs. As a faithful Darwinian, Freud emphasizes the proximity of animals with humans, and recognizes the human itself as an animal, as well as the role of animals in the human psyche (Kamieniak 2013, 96). In his own life however, it was only after 1925, that he established a personal relation with one animal, the German shepherd Wolf that he gave his daughter for her birthday. Kamieniak follows Freud's relationship with this dog in his correspondence, and underlines his identification with it, as well as with the other dogs that his daughter would have after the death of Wolf, and even more deeply with his own dog Jofie, between 1930 and 1937. He named her Jofie with a 'J' to hint at his Jewish identity, in yet another sign of identification with the dog. On the one hand, the dogs were in a sense a substitute for Freud's grandchildren who died, but he clearly saw them as personalities in their own right, and during her lifetime, Jofie would for example actively collaborate with Freud in his clinical practice by barking at the end of the sessions and guiding the patients to the exit (ibid., 101). When she died in 1937, Freud wrote in a letter to Stefan Zweig that "Jofie was a child who came from far away, who was devoted to you like a true child, with a heart wiser than most of our children" (ibid., 103). One of the main reasons of Freud's love for dogs was their absence of ambivalence, their capacity for the sincerest attachment, making it possible to have a relationship of intimate kinship, an unquestionable affinity. This feature of Freud's relationship with his dog is analogous to the relationship between mother and son, when it is not troubled by rivalry or sexual attraction. Kamieniak suggests that Freud's relationship with Jofie was "an equivalent of the primal relationship between mother and child" where Freud played the role of the good mother, thereby remembering the presence of his own mother. He suggests, in other words, that Freud's relationships with his dogs were a transfer from his relationship with his mother, but beyond the particular case of Sigmund Freud, the very possibility of a defining relationship with a dog clearly opens the possibility of attachments with nonhumans defining the human subject.

But it is not enough to spot the mere possibility of a relationship with an animal as a substitution for the mother-child relation, as suggested by the inquiry into Freud's relationship with his dogs. Since human children actually do not operate with the distinction between animate subjects and inanimate objects, there is no reason to think that groups would be composed of human only. Dolto's lifelong involvement with children led her to understand their tendency to a kind of spontaneous animism, and since she often refers to human children as "man-cub" [*petit d'homme*], she considered them on the same level as other animals. In her 1972 lecture at the French society of philosophy, in a passage where she emphasizes the crucial importance of groups and social bonds outside the nuclear family for the development of the child, she goes on to extend this to the nonhuman environment (although she remained in the urban Parisian space):

> All the contacts and perceptions that children have with people, animals, and things prompt them to make observations and notice differences in perception. If their mother talks to them about these differences, they will assimilate them into their sense of existential security and form a code for understanding the language of things, animals, and humans. I don't want to forget trees—we know how much toddlers love to enjoy the sight of foliage, and how older children adorn themselves with it [...]. How sad it is that, in our cities, public parks have lawns that are off-limits to young children, who are so in need of greenery; that picking flowers and giving them as gifts is so often accompanied by the horrified cries of mothers who call it vandalism, when in fact it is a gesture that comes from the heart. (Dolto 1981, 291–2)

Dolto encourages the mothers to make their children respect all that is living because everything in the environment is potentially significant for the child. She writes in passing about the "language of things, animals and humans," (ibid.) implying that there is a desiring relationship between children and all the things, human and nonhuman, and that they are able to perceive the way that nonhuman entities also express themselves. The quoted passage shows that Dolto did not limit the space of desire to the sole interhuman space, but recognized the role played by nonhuman entities in the constitution of the human desiring subject. She did not, to my knowledge write specifically on this question, so I take her suggestion as an encouragement to pursue the idea.

Marty's psychosomatics, in his turn, is eminently open to an ecological interpretation since it explores the somatic consequences of the subject's emotional and relational life. Although Marty does not, to my knowledge develop any explicitly ecological approach, psychosomatics is evidently the field where the interaction between the psychic and the biological are taken seriously. But, as I noted in the third chapter above, Marty takes a philosophical stance in his book about *Individual Movements of Life and Death*, when he writes that his approach "overtly abandons the principle of the psyche-soma dualism" (Marty 1976, 16). Ecological philosophy also tends to reject dualistic thinking, and move towards a philosophy that considers all matter as meaningful, if not living. Psychosomatics invites us to consider the body as an expressive being, and the psyche as one of the paths through which the body finds its expressions. The expressions of the suffering subject must be received by the therapist who resonates with them in his or her posture, attitude, and words.

If we turn to Anzieu and Kaës, and their notions of skin, envelope and intersubjectivity, it does not seem difficult to further "extend" the psychic space from interhuman relations to relations with nonhumans, as I already suggested above in Chap. 8. A few passages from the ecological philosopher David Abram's *Becoming Animal* may help to do this; Abram is not unfamiliar with psychological questions, and it is no wonder that we encounter the image of the envelope or entanglement, to describe the secure situation of the human subject held by the sensorial surroundings. Describing the atmosphere on the shore of a mountain lake in the afternoon, he writes that the air "thick with light is an enveloping spell, a trance into which the whole place has now fallen, a viscous state of mind shared by you and the spruces and the bees in this honeyed moment" (Abram 2010, 14); he describes the consequences of being no longer "enveloped by a many-voiced world at least as alive and mysterious as my own sentient self" once he started to study biology, that his "animal senses began to shut down" (ibid., 67f); concerning our body's relation with the air and the wind, he writes that "we can feel the air envelop and settle around us as it takes a mold of our shifting shape" (ibid., 61), and that "We feel enveloped by a rushing crowd of unseen essences—sighing, whooshing lives that reveal themselves to us only as fleeting smells" (ibid., 148). Among many other passages, this one also describes our relation with the Earth as an enveloping: "We are carnally enfolded by the round expanse of the terrain and the curving vault of the sky" (ibid., 270). These passages are all suggestions that being enveloped is essential to the subject's belonging to the world. Abram's entire book is a description of the extreme importance of the affective relationships we can, and should, have with what he calls the more-than-human world: the shadow of that mountain, this rock outside the house, these trees behind which a deer is hiding, etc. The envelope necessary for the human subject to become "fully human" (ibid., 3), as he writes at the beginning of the introduction. This very short dive into Abram's ecological phenomenology suggests that the notion of the skin-ego, when extended to the sphere of the social and the environmental, is a promising path to find an articulation between psychoanalysis and ecological thinking.

Theodor Roszak's Ecological Unconscious

But the precursor of ecological psychology is Theodor Roszak. In his founding book of ecopsychology, *The Voice of the Earth*, he wrote a chapter about the "Ecological Ego." In this chapter, a passage is devoted to "the ecological unconscious" referring for that matter to Jungian psychoanalysis. While he recognizes that Jung's conceptions were rather "suffused with a certain Platonic-Gnostic aversion to the physical" (Roszak 1992, 303), he admits that Jungian spiritualism must be repatriated on Earth and the ecological unconscious be considered as "the repository of an evolutionary record that ties the psyche to the full sweep of cosmic history" (ibid.); he writes similarly about the id, this notion of "a repository of unruly energy that resides at the instinctual core of our nature," that Freud took to replace the concept of the unconscious in his second topic. The id is "that very protohuman psychic core that our evolution has spent millions of years molding to fit the planetary environment" (ibid., 289). His claim is that the id, or the unconscious, must have appeared and developed in relation to the environment—and that "what the id conserves from its long maturing process is our treasury of ecological intelligence" (ibid., 290). In this claim, he refers to Groddeck's description of the id, as "the enduring reservoir of intuitive environmental knowledge" (ibid.,

291) and he significatively affirms the environmental dimension of the id and criticizes its reduction to a "minimal social content" (ibid., 301). But in the short section about "The ecological unconscious," Roszak refers, as mentioned, to C. G. Jung's idea of the "collective unconscious," as a "massive cultural storehouse especially suited to housing the great religious symbols of the human race" (ibid., 302), but then goes on to criticize Jung for neglecting the body. He very rapidly and schematically sums up the main schools of psychoanalysis, leaving French psychoanalysis completely out of sight, and affirms that the Gestalt school is the only one using the concept of ecology in its theories. But he doesn't depart from the Jungian notion of an evolutionary collective unconscious. It is a shame he failed to dig a bit deeper into the psychoanalytical tradition in search of an ecological concept of the unconscious that would also work clinically. I hope to have shown that there are resources in French psychoanalysis to think about the unconscious as a relational space in real life, and not hypostasizing it as an archetype mysteriously delivered by evolution. This, I would suggest, implies a shift towards an animist cosmology, as David Abram proposes.

Psychoanalysis of the Occult: Merleau-Ponty's Animist Approach

In fact, it is plausible to claim that Merleau-Ponty's interpretation of psychoanalysis is animist. Since David Abram's writings of the late 1980s and his book *The Spell of the Sensuous*, the animist, or panpsychist, reading of his late ontology has taken hold. Jennifer McWeeny gives a good overview of the issue and adds a few strong arguments in favor of the claim that Merleau-Ponty's late philosophy actually implies the thesis of the world itself being animated. Here is not the place to dive deeply into this disputed issue and weigh all the arguments; my point here is to contribute in moving his thought further. As McWeeny beautifully formulates it:

> The panpsychism question brings us to this as yet unthought of terrain whose trails lead horizontally and down, out of modernity and humanism, out of epistemology and classical phenomenology, toward wild-flowering meadows of sentient-sensible beings. (McWeeny 2019, 140)

My point here is to show that Merleau-Ponty's take on psychoanalysis in his late work is indeed infused by an animist approach, and that it is necessary to take this into account in order to develop an ecological conception of the unconscious. The philosopher does not use psychoanalysis to rationalize animist or "occult" phenomena; rather, he interprets such phenomena as reasons to sketch out his ontology of the flesh. In a working note for *The Visible and the Invisible* dated May 2, 1959, he writes about "the impression of telepathy and the occult":

> perception is unconsciousness. What is the unconscious? What functions as a pivot, an existential, and in this sense, is and is not perceived. For one perceives only figures upon levels – And one perceives them only by relation to the level, which therefore is unperceived. – The perception of the level: always between the objects, it is that about which... The occult in psychoanalysis (the unconscious) is of this sort (cf. a woman in the street feeling that they are looking at her breasts, and checking her clothing. Her corporeal schema is for itself — for the other – It is the hinge of the for itself and the for the other – To have a body is to be looked at (it is not only that), it is to be visible – Here the impression of telepathy, of the occult = vivacity in reading the look of the other in a flash. (Merleau-Ponty 1968, 189–90)

This working note passage deserves a feminist reading focusing on the power relations through the gaze in public space, but my concern here is in the reciprocity of visibility ("to have a body is to be looked at") and the idea that the unconscious is the perception of this very visibility. There is an "impression" of telepathy manifested by the gesture of the woman checking her clothing: she senses that she's being looked at and her body moves accordingly. "The occult in psychoanalysis (the unconscious) is of this sort," he writes, like a woman in the street feeling that she is looked upon, and checking her clothing in order to protect herself from the dominant male gaze, without knowing it, giving an "impression of telepathy," of action from a distance. Her gesture is rooted in her body schema, but her body schema does not entirely belong to her, it is, Merleau-Ponty writes, "the hinge of the for itself and the for the other." This characterization of the body schema is very significant: to claim that the body schema itself is the hinge between one's own body and the gaze of the other is an apparent paradox. Normally, one would expect that the subject of perception and motility, i.e. the body schema, belong to one person, and that this one person may experience different levels of awareness and consciousness. But what Merleau-Ponty hints at is that the very level of perceptual awareness actually occurs in between subjects, and not within the perceiving subject. To phrase it paradoxically, the body schema is not limited to the very person of which it is the body schema; it does in fact belong to the person whose body schema it is, and at the same time it spreads out in between that person and others. It is indeed an intercorporeal unconscious, whose function is to be the field of the relation.

If we follow this thread, the unconscious figures as the relational space in which there is an action upon the bodies, and not only upon the psyche. In the example of the woman in the working note, the unconscious produces a gesture (of checking the clothing), and not literally a bodily state. But inasmuch as the distortions and tensions of the body schema are not limited to the "mental" sphere, but are likely to influence the somatic side as well, one may claim that the fact of being gazed at in public space may also induce bodily symptoms, such as symptoms arising from anxiety, stress or the reawakening of past traumas. Clinical examples in this direction can be found in Schilder's *Image and Appearance of the Human Body*, that Merleau-Ponty extensively refers to throughout the 1950s, or in the very extensive psychosomatic literature, such as the writings of Pierre Marty and his colleagues.

One last remark about the term "occult" is in order: The term "occult" is taken from Georges Devereux, the founder of ethnopsychiatry, who published a volume with the title *Psychoanalysis and the Occult* in 1953. Merleau-Ponty may have had the volume in his hands, but we don't find any in-depth commentary on such contributions in his working notes, only a reference in another working note, dated April 1960 about Telepathy (Merleau-Ponty 1968, 245). This completely forgotten volume contains the translations of Freud's writings about telepathy and the occult meaning of dreams, and a range of studies on how to handle such inexplicable phenomena in psychoanalytic practice. The main example is telepathy, i.e. action from a distance, without a direct visible contact between subjects. This kind of phenomena, if taken seriously, would lead to the idea that the flesh of the world is a medium in which different beings can act upon each other.

The Unconscious of the Body-Territory

In a recent article with the title "The Unconscious in the Eye of the Shaman," Silvia Lippi and Patrice Maniglier draw on the anthropologist Eduardo Viveiros de Castro and show that the subject in the Freudian sense "is placed, with respect to the forces in the midst of which it negotiates its own precarious reality, in a relationship very similar to that of the beings with whom the Amazonian shaman attempts to come to terms" (Lippi & Maniglier 2023, 539). The libidinal forces at play for the human subject do not come only from inside, but also, and maybe foremost from the more-than-human world, which is the reason why the cure is more about negotiating relations between human and nonhuman agents, than it is to tame the private demons of the patient. "Putting psychoanalysis back on the cosmological level of animist therapies allows us to put it back quite simply where it has an effect: outside" (ibid., 541).

This approach resonates with the recent developments in Latin-American indigenous thinking around the notion of body-territory. In a recent article, the Colombian philosopher Lina Alvarez-Villareal describes the main features of what she calls the "Rooted-South feminisms" of Latin-American philosophers and activists, such as Lorena Cabnal, Raquel Gutierrez-Aguilar, Moira Millan, and Rita Segato. She presents the central critical thesis of Rooted-South feminism: that "the exploitation of women and feminized bodies (such as nature, infants, and persons of non-heteronormative genders) is not just one form of domination among others," but that it is "upon the bodies of women and feminized bodies (including the Earth) that humanity has learned and continues to learn the inferiorization of the other, its domination, and (…) its objectification" (Alvarez-Villareal 2023, 12). In front of this fundamental observation, she brings up the notion of the "territory-body-Earth" (*territorio cuerpo-tierra*) introduced by Lorena Cabnal, designating the "relational and interdependent character of the human body with the place it inhabits" (ibid.). Colonial patriarchal power is understood as the active repression of this interdependence by the reduction of the Earth to a depository of disposable resources and the mastery of women's bodies. In this critical eco-feminist perspective, interdependence becomes unconscious because repressed; but before it is actively repressed by capitalist extractivism, there is a possibility of experiencing it. The interdependence of body and Earth-territory is an affective bond that can only be felt, or sensed, and therefore leaves many aspects unconscious, in the precise sense that we have explored throughout this book.

In David Abram's cosmology, which is very much inspired by and in dialogue with indigenous conceptions, the relation of the body and the Earth is first and foremost an erotic relation, of mutual attraction experienced by me through gravity. He writes in *Becoming Animal*: "This gravitational draw that holds us to the ground was once known as Eros – as Desire! – the lovelorn yearning of our body for the larger body of Earth, and of the earth for us" (Abram 2010, 27). Our belonging to the perceptible world is indeed foundational for the way we are being subjects, but European "civilization" has succeeded in pushing most of this dependence into the limbo of the unconscious.

The attraction between our bodies and the Earth is overwhelming, which is why we tend to repress it so massively; the level of our dependence on the more-than-human world is so strong that it is no wonder that we tend to deny it; the climatic, geological, biological, and biochemical forces that our life is based on are so powerful, that we act as if we could control them. My proposal at this point is to extend the circle of intersubjectivity to more-than-human actors; to sharpen our capacity to communicate and to listen to their expressions as well; to understand psychosomatic diseases as a consequence of the repressed polluted environment.

References

Abram, David. 2010. *Becoming Animal. An Earthly Cosmology*. New York: Pantheon Books.

Alvarez Villareal, Lina. 2023. Rooted-South Feminisms. Disobedient Epistemologies and Transformative Politics. *Capitalism Nature Socialism* 35 (2): 116–137.

Devereux, George, ed. 1953. *Psycnoanalysis and the Occult*. International Universities Press.

Dolto, Françoise. 2023. *The Unconscious Body Image [1984]*. Trans. Sharmini Bailly. London, Routledge.

Dufourcq, Annabelle. 2022. *The Imaginary of Animals*. London/New York: Routledge.

Kamieniak, Jean-Pierre. 2013. Citizen Canis. Freud et les chiens. *Le Coq-héron* 215:96–107.

Lippi, Silvia, and Patrice Maniglier. 2023. L'inconscient dans l'œil du chamane. Le tournant ontologique en psychanalyse. In *Psychanalyse du reste du monde. Géo-histoire d'une subversion*, ed. L. Boni and S. Mendelsohn, 525–545. Paris: La Découverte.

McWeeny, Jennifer. 2019. The Panpsychism Question in Merleau-Ponty's Ontology. In *Merleau-Ponty and Contemporary Philosophy*, ed. E. Alloa,

F. Chouraqui, and R. Kaushik, 121–144. Albany: State University of New York Press.
Merleau-Ponty, Maurice. 1968. *The Visible and the Invisible* [1964]. Translated by A. Lingis. Evanston: Northwestern University Press.
Roszak, Theodor. 1992. *The Voice of the Earth. An Exploration of Ecopsychology*. New York: Touchstone.

CHAPTER 11

In Lieu of a Conclusion: A Conversation In-Between

There should be no conclusion to such a book; its purpose is to encourage the reading of lesser-known psychoanalysts and to show the fecundity of a philosophical phenomenological reading of those authors, and thereby make the Merleau-Pontian claim that the unconscious is feeling itself plausible. Instead of a real conclusion, I shall try to stage a conversation as if all my protagonists were gathered in Maurice Merleau-Ponty's apartment, not long before his death, and were having a conversation.

Actually, two of them did meet in real life: Françoise Dolto and her husband were invited by the Merleau-Pontys for an "after dinner" gathering on March 31st, 1960, a few months after a first encounter at the famous Café de Flore. In Dolto's published correspondence, we find the invitation letter signed by Maurice Merleau-Ponty, and dated March 16, 1960:

> Dear Madam,
>
> You would give us a great pleasure, Mr. Dolto and you, if you would agree to come to our place on Monday March 31st after dinner together with a few friends that we will be gathering. I keep the best memory of our encounter at the Flore, already months ago, and I would be very pleased if you would be free on the 31st. I hope to say see you soon, dear Madam. Please do pass on my greeting to your husband, and accept the tribute of my respect. (Dolto 2005, 313)

S. Kristensen, *The Intercorporeal Unconscious*,
https://doi.org/10.1007/978-3-032-22596-2_11

A few months later, we find a short card by Suzanne Merleau-Ponty, dated January 4, 1961, thanking the Doltos' for their gift of sweets for the New Year, and expressing her hope that they will be able to meet soon with other friends (Dolto 2005, 333). Apart from the fact that Dolto and Merleau-Ponty were both born in 1908, they lived in the same city and were acquainted with many of the same people. Dolto was a pioneer in psychoanalytical child psychotherapy and Merleau-Ponty was keenly interested in both experimental and clinical psychology—and was a professor of child psychology at the Sorbonne between 1949 and 1952, before being elected to the Collège de France. During that period at the latest, he got acquainted with Dolto, who was at that time starting her practice and publishing her first clinical studies. He commented in particular on her study of jealousy at the birth of a younger child and its consequences on language learning (Dolto 1981, first published in 1948) in his 1954 lecture at the Collège de France about the problem of speech, in order to emphasize the affective condition of acquiring the sense of verbal tenses.[1]

Who those other "few friends" were is unknown, but let's imagine it was our protagonists: Pierre Marty, Didier Anzieu, and René Kaës, and also Paul Schilder (had he not died in a car accident in 1940), as well as the young Bernhard Waldenfels, but not Lacan (although he was a friend of both Dolto and Merleau-Ponty). Lacan would attract all the attention and tend to monopolize the conversation. Of course, only Dolto and Merleau-Ponty really met each other; Anzieu and Kaës never quote the philosopher, so that an acquaintance in real life is unlikely; the same applies to Marty. Around the table, sharing a bottle or two of Loire wine, are Anzieu and Kaës, respectively 36 and 24 years old; Marty, 42; Dolto and her husband Boris, respectively 52 and 60 years old; the young Waldenfels, 26, who just arrived from Munich and the Merleau-Pontys, Maurice and his wife Suzanne, who was 46. And the ghost of Paul Schilder (born in 1886) is also present and makes itself heard.

The tone is respectful and friendly, the conversation goes back and forth, while there sometimes arise quite long speeches. Merleau-Ponty is curious as to how to better understand how to think about the clinical experience, particularly when interaction with patients is nonverbal, in the case of children. Dolto's wish is to have a conversation with a philosopher, a person whose job it is to conceptualize experiences across different realms, but this is also, she thinks, a limitation of philosophy, since human reality is so diverse and unforeseeable that any rigid concepts might only succeed in distorting it. Marty is mostly listening and trying to concentrate on the rhythms of the others' ways of speaking, of interrupting each other, etc. Anzieu was a professor of psychology at the University of Strasbourg at that time, and he was already thinking actively about the role of the skin, after having worked as a psychologist in a dermatology department, and practicing psychodrama. Kaës is student, the youngest at the table, and he is already acquainted with Anzieu's research on psychodrama.

Merleau-Ponty	Dear friends, now that everyone has his or her glass charged, I'd like to say welcome to all of you and how glad I am to have you all here tonight. The idea of this invitation came from my recent discussion with Françoise, when we talked about children, about the acquisition of language and various other questions. Actually, Françoise and I already met a few years ago, in January 1955, when I was invited to give a speech at the Psychoanalytic society[2] – maybe Didier and Pierre were there too, but we didn't get to talk. Before that I had read one of her articles about the jealousy of her second child and its consequences for the acquisition of language. Whatever it was, years passed, and we met again recently and thought it might be a good idea to catch up. I've always been very curious about her practice, and in general about the role of the body in psychoanalytic practice. In the project I've been working on for the last few years, I've been trying to figure out what kind of being the human body is, both subject for the world and part of the world itself.
Dolto	Thank you for the invitation, dear Maurice (may I use you first name?). When I recall your lecture at the Psychoanalytical Society, I also recall what Lacan said about it in his seminar the very next day. He said something like "Merleau-Ponty is focused on understanding, and just considers that some matters are harder to swallow and some less." He used you to show that his take on the unconscious as a completely separated realm is the only one faithful to Freud.
Merleau-Ponty	I did send an invitation to Jacques for tonight but he didn't answer. We'll have other opportunities to talk,

certainly this fall in Bonneval at Henri Ey's conference about the unconscious.[3] Do you see it as he does?

Dolto I wasn't sure back then, I'm still not really sure. What I would say is that Lacan is right about the claim that the unconscious is ultimately related to language, but then what is language? The infant, even if it can't speak, understands what you say when you really relate to it as a real person, and not as a toy or an animal. How is that possible? But I'm not sure I want to follow him all the way and consider the unconscious as actually being the very system of language. There's also a language of feelings, of touching, of smiling.

Anzieu I'm sorry, but I'd rather not talk about Lacan too much. He never told me that his great clinical case, Aimée, about whom he wrote his thesis, was actually my mother; that wasn't right. In any case, I completely agree with Ms. Dolto – the little child is certainly meant for language, but in order to become a speaking subject, many things must happen in the first stages of life, and it's not just communication in the sense of an exchange of information. The issue is first and foremost about developing a sense of safety with the mother (and the father, why not!). And, in order enable that, the mother must not only speak to the child, but also communicate warmth, touch, wrapping the baby in an envelope of safety with her body. And I don't think that the father has a very different role, that he should be outside waiting to intervene with the Law… (sorry I can't help talk about Lacan, I promise – it's the last time!)

Marty Indeed, language is a complex phenomenon. I'm quite certain that it's not only verbal. I've already seen quite a few cases at the hospital who were physically sick with no infectious cause; it's like their body was expressing a problem. Communication is not always voluntary and about using language in the sense of French or English. We practitioners should train to be in resonance with the people we receive in therapy.

Boris Dolto	If I may, Françoise, Marty and Anzieu are right as far as I can see - I don't know about Lacan, he's your friend - but about the body, and about the way the body speaks. There's something about language – maybe we should conceive of language as a way of being together, of communion, and not primarily of conveying information.
Dolto	*rolling her eyes at her husband* – yes but Boris, I've never said that language is just to convey information, never. What I did say, again and again, is that everything speaks, the body speaks, the intestine speaks, the skin speaks, and so on, and that the parents have to tune in to that, treat their child like a whole person. The origin of language lies in gesture; to begin with, a communication desired by the child, then the reactions of the adults, get associated by the child with some audible words. Therefore, the origin of language is in gesture, facial expression, posture, even vomiting, urination and defecation.
Merleau-Ponty	I like that; it seems we may be able to agree on something. Of course, if we look closer into the issue, we have to think about the relation of language to the body, as the place where we have feelings, emotions, and so on. I'm trying to talk about that in my lecture at the Collège de France – it's the third year about the concept of nature, this time the human body. I'm reading Schilder again, as I did back in the first year, 1953. His clinical cases are fascinating, he always presents cases where the body and the emotions are intertwined and mixed up.
Schilder's ghost	dear philosopher, dear colleagues. Indeed, I saw that my book about the body image was republished ten years ago. You didn't have it, Merleau, during the war when you were writing your *Phenomenology of Perception*, did you? I enjoy very much hearing you speak, and seeing that French psychoanalysis is developing. As you know, I wasn't in Freud's circle, but I was very much inspired by his ideas – I have simply always retained the link to the sciences, to neurology,

physiology, and even sociology. As for this question about language, I'm not sure, it seems to me that the body does express its history in different ways, and that it often acts as a subject in its own right. For example, I've been fascinated by the phantom limb, you know, and I think it shows that the body itself is mourning the loss of a limb. Pain in this case is an expression, does that correspond to what you were saying?

Merleau-Ponty yes indeed Dr. Schilder. I'm honored that you were able to join us. I'm quite certain that the concepts that come from psychoanalytical practice are very useful to us. Particularly when we philosophers somehow discover that cognition is not the only sort of relation we have with the world. In my lecture this year, I'm quoting you, and also Melanie Klein, and you help me see that you cannot think about the body and its relation to the world without the notion of desire, of the libido. There is this force that draws me towards things, or repels me. Your concept of body schema helps me think about that.

Schilder this is probably Freud's main contribution to human culture. The idea that libido, attraction, is governing the world. This is what makes it unpredictable, don't you think? But Freud didn't really think about it as something the body has, it's like a stream pouring through the body and making it move. It's like in Freud, you have the organic body on one side, and the mind on the other, and then the power of the drives somehow creating a unity. It doesn't seem to work out…

Anzieu well, Mr. Schilder, if I may, if you read Freud's *Ego and the Id* closely, the second attempt at a theory of the ego, it seems to me that he clearly defines the ego as the body. We all remember the drawing of the ego as an open bag, where the repressed is in a corner of the id, and the ego occupies the upper zone, and so on. He says something like "the ego is the body," and he focuses on the surface of the body. We should try to follow that path, don't you think?

Schilder oh, I'm not so sure. The body is as much a being in motion as it is a container of ideas and emotions. But we certainly would agree about the libido, that the body is a desiring being. The whole body, and – by the way – I was interested in what you said earlier: did you talk about the skin and the envelope? We do need a theory about how the body is in contact with the other… and obviously, the skin is where we touch each other, isn't it? I made some observations about the skin in my book.

Waldenfels I just arrived from Germany to follow professor Merleau-Ponty's courses, and I'm also very grateful to you, Professor, for the invitation. Professor Schilder, you spoke about the other, and how we perceive the other – and I'm asking myself: how do we know it's another than me, since his being other means that he escapes our grasp? Maybe that's where the desire sets in; I can only desire that which I don't know… there's something unconscious there, that corresponds to me being in a sense invaded, having to withdraw.

Merleau-Ponty indeed the concept of desire is essential. If you want to do phenomenology, I mean describe the experience, its structure and its contents, you also have to focus on the intensity, and not only on *what* appears, I agree. From Professor Schilder, I understand that the body itself desires, and not an immaterial soul hidden behind some organ… As for what you just said, Bernhard, I'd encourage you to develop this idea of the subject withdrawing from oneself once it feels desire. Maybe it's the fundamental reason why we live surrounded by unconsciousness.

Dolto desire is a big deal. Gentlemen, you just talked about the experience of desire, and what it implies for the subject. From a psychoanalyst's perspective, and also from a woman's perspective, I'd like us not to neglect the experience of *being* desired. You cannot develop properly if you don't feel desired. By the way, that's terrible for the kids born from rape – but even in those terrible cases, it is necessary for the child to be convinced that it is desired. If it's just by God it may be enough. But then it's love. Sorry, I'm turning theological, let's leave that for next time…

Kaës — this is a conversation I'll remember. Being together presupposes reciprocal desire of being, but also the consequences of being overwhelmed by it. As you said, when you desire someone or something, it's like an alien power running through you, and then you push some of it aside. Ms. Dolto, it's no different when you face the other's desire, that can also be felt as a threat…

Dolto — indeed, that's why I insist so much on communication! The pathological then is when the bodily dimension of existence is left on its own, not animated by anything relational. To be normal you need love.

Kaës — of course! But what I was wondering while listening to you all, is what keeps groups, couples, families together. What is it in our feelings toward one another that works as the glue, that maintains our groups through time?

Suzanne Merleau-Ponty — it's fascinating listening to all of you, and I'm grateful for this quite fraternal discussion, different from others we're used to in the psychoanalytic community, which is already so divided. I was wondering if the divisions within that community (like so many other communities) are linked to the fact that they are just human. I mean, if our colleagues let more animals into their lives – that's real otherness – not just the familiar otherness of our neighbor who we can easily project ourselves onto. Animals remain something of a mystery, we are never sure we understand what they are expressing, even if there are clues. Don't you agree, Maurice?

Maurice Merleau-Ponty *smiling awkwardly* — – oh, that's a huge topic, Suzanne. Do we need other living beings to become really human? I'd say we need to recognize the other in ourselves, the fact that our bodies are made of the same stuff as the rest of the world. But you're right – if our bodies are subjects of desire, and if they are of the same stuff as the world, then desire is probably also in the rest of the world. Each time quite differently according to which kind of subject… but you know that's what I'm working on right now. If we all agree that desire is at the heart of our sensory interactions with the world, it means that many of those interactions are actually unconscious. Your experience and practice in the psychoanalytic clinic are very precious – thank you!

Notes

1. Cf. Merleau-Ponty 2020, 97; Dolto's article that he comments on in the course notes was first published in 1947 in the journal *Psyché*, and reprinted in *Au jeu du désir* (Dolto 1981, 96–131).
2. The only trace of this lecture is in Lacan's seminar about the Ego in Freud's theory, at the session on January 19, 1955. Lacan starts with the "extraordinary lecture of yesterday evening," and then presents his own conception of the unconscious as "the discourse of the other" in contrast to Merleau-Ponty's conception. According to Emmanuel de Saint Aubert, the notes for this lecture have certainly been lost—I thank him for the information.
3. See above in Chap. 2.

References

Dolto, Françoise. 1981. *Au jeu du désir. Essais cliniques.* Paris: Seuil.

Dolto, Françoise. 2005. In *Une vie de correspondances (1938–1988)*, ed. Muriel Djéribi-Valentin. Paris: Gallimard.

Merleau-Ponty, Maurice. 2020. *Le problème de la parole. Cours au Collège de France. Notes, 1953-1954.* Geneva: MetisPresses.

Index[1]

[1] Note: Page numbers followed by 'n' refer to notes.

S. Kristensen, *The Intercorporeal Unconscious*,
https://doi.org/10.1007/978-3-032-22596-2

Kolibri 360 GmbH
Ferdinand-Jühlke-Straße 7
99095 Erfurt, Deutschland
produktsicherheit@kolibri360.de